PROJECT PHASES

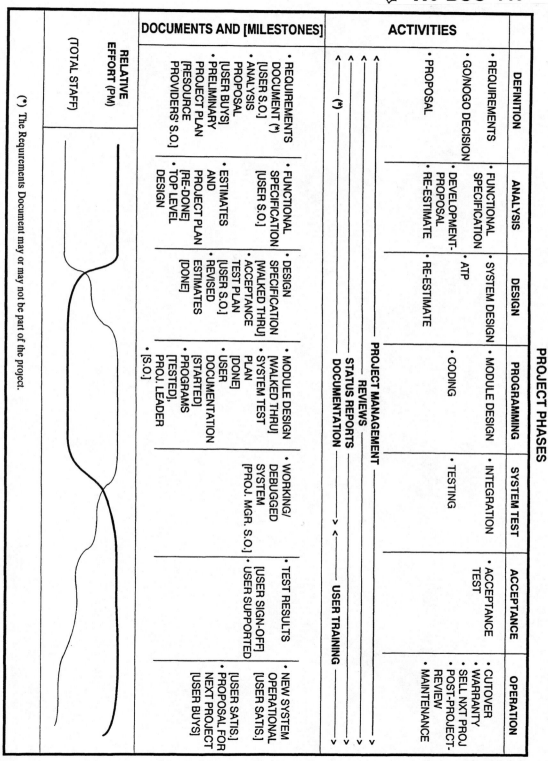

	DEFINITION	ANALYSIS	DESIGN	PROGRAMMING	SYSTEM TEST	ACCEPTANCE	OPERATION
ACTIVITIES	• REQUIREMENTS • GO/NOGO DECISION • PROPOSAL	• FUNCTIONAL SPECIFICATION • DEVELOPMENT-PROPOSAL • RE-ESTIMATE	• SYSTEM DESIGN • ATP • RE-ESTIMATE	• MODULE DESIGN • CODING	• INTEGRATION • TESTING	• ACCEPTANCE TEST	• CUTOVER • WARRANTY • SELL NXT PROJ • POST-PROJECT-REVIEW • MAINTENANCE
	^ ^ ^ ^ (*)	PROJECT MANAGEMENT —————— REVIEWS —————— STATUS REPORTS —————— DOCUMENTATION ——————			v < —————— USER TRAINING ——————		v v v v
DOCUMENTS AND [MILESTONES]	• REQUIREMENTS DOCUMENT (*) [USER S.O.] • ANALYSIS PROPOSAL [USER BUYS] • PRELIMINARY PROJECT PLAN [RESOURCE PROVIDERS' S.O.]	• FUNCTIONAL SPECIFICATION [USER S.O.] • ESTIMATES AND PROJECT PLAN [RE-DONE] • TOP LEVEL DESIGN	• DESIGN SPECIFICATION [WALKED THRU] • ACCEPTANCE TEST PLAN [DONE] • REVISED ESTIMATES [DONE]	• MODULE DESIGN [WALKED THRU] • SYSTEM TEST PLAN [DONE] • USER DOCUMENTATION [STARTED] • PROGRAMS [TESTED], PROJ. LEADER [S.O.]	• WORKING/DEBUGGED SYSTEM [PROJ. MGR. S.O.]	• TEST RESULTS [USER SIGN-OFF] [USER SUPPORTED]	• NEW SYSTEM OPERATIONAL [USER SATIS.] • PROPOSAL FOR NEXT PROJECT [USER BUYS]

RELATIVE EFFORT (PM)

(TOTAL STAFF)

(*) The Requirements Document may or may not be part of the project.

Figure 1.1   PROJECT PHASE DIAGRAM

Software Project Management

For Small to Medium Sized Projects

John J. Rakos

John J. Rakos & Associates Consultants Ltd.

PRENTICE HALL
Upper Saddle River, New Jersey 07458

Library of Congress Cataloging-in-Publication Data
RAKOS, JOHN J.

      Software project management for small to medium sized projects /
John J. Rakos.

        p.   cm.

Includes bibliographical references.

ISBN 0-13-826173-3 :

      1. Computer software—Development—Management.   I. Title.

QA76.76.D47R35   1990   90-6745

005.1'068—dc20   CIP

Editorial/production supervision: *MAI Publishing*
Cover design: *Wanda Lubelska*
Manufacturing buyer: *Margaret Rizzi/Lori Bulwin*

The author and publisher of this book have used their best efforts in preparing this book. These efforts include the development, research and testing of the theories and programs to determine their effectiveness. The author and publisher make no warranty of any kind, expressed or implied, with regard to these programs or the documentation contained in this book. The author and publisher shall not be liable in any event for incidental or consequential damages in connection with, or arising out of, the furnishing, performance, or use of these programs.

Printed in the United States of America

13

ISBN 0-13-826173-3

Prentice-Hall International (UK) Limited,London
Prentice-Hall of Australia Pty. Limited, Sydney
Prentice-Hall Canada Inc., Toronto
Prentice-Hall Hispanoamericana, S.A., Mexico
Prentice-Hall of India Private Limited, New Delhi
Prentice-Hall of Japan, Inc., Tokyo
Pearson Education Asia Pte. Ltd., Singapore
Editora Prentice-Hall do Brasil, Ltda., Rio de Janeiro

Trademark Information

DEC, CMS, MMS, SCA, PCA, DTM, DECSPM, LSE, and *DECDESIGN* are registered trademarks of Digital Equipment Corporation. *ORACLE* is a registered trademark of Oracle Corporation. *IBM, MVS,* and *VM* are registered trademarks of International Business Machines Corporation. *Cognos, PowerHouse, QUIZ, QDESIGN,* and *PowerPlay* are registered trademarks of Cognos Incorporated. *Excelerator* is a registered trademark of Index Technologies Incorporated. *SUPERPROJECT* is a registered trademark of Computer Associates International Incorporated. *Harvard Project Manager* is a registered trademark of Software Publishing Incorporated. *MICROSOFT PROJECT* is a registered trademark of Microsoft Corporation. *TIMELINE* is a registered trademark of Symantec Corporation. *ARTEMIS* is a registered trademark of Metier Management Systems Incorporated. *Project/2* is a registered trademark of Project Software and Development Incorporated. *Primavera* is a registered trademark of Primavera Systems Incorporated. *PAC I, PAC II, PAC III* and *WINGS* are registered trademarks of AGS Management Systems Incorporated. *FOCUS* is a registered trademark of Information Builders Incorporated.

Contents

Preface

PURPOSE OF THIS BOOK

Many methods for Software Project Management have been invented and written about. These methods were developed for large projects on mainframe computers requiring at least one hundred person-years or more. With the advent of very powerful mini and microcomputers, the average software project has become much smaller. But when older methods are applied to small projects, they prove to be so cumbersome that the cost of the management can exceed the cost of the development! The approach presented in this book is best used on small to medium sized projects—ones that take no longer than 15 person-years. This method has worked in Digital Equipment Corporation and elsewhere to produce some of the world's most successful mini and microcomputer software. Those who have projects longer than 15 person-years will also find the book useful since we will see how to break larger projects into small, manageable pieces.

The development method that I will describe in this book uses the time-phased approach, but the phases and especially the documentation are greatly simplified. The approach focuses on planning and control. The book also emphasizes risk management—knowing what can go wrong in a project and tempering estimates accordingly.

ORGANIZATION OF THE BOOK

This text is divided into three parts:

Part 1 The Methodology of Project Management covers the phases and activities involved in building a project. Whether you are a project manager, programmer, or user, it is essential that you read this section, because the subsequent sections are based on Part 1.

Part 2 Practical Methods covers the skills and tools required for project management, especially for estimating and scheduling. Project management software products that run on mini and micro computers will be described in Chapter 17. One tool, which is becoming more and more popular for application design, prototyping and development is Fourth Generation Languages. Chapter 16 gives an example of how to develop a project using a Fourth Generation Language.

Part 3 People describes the responsibilities of the individuals involved, how to organize the project team, and how to keep your people motivated. Chapters 20 and 21 show how to control a project with effective reports and meetings. We will also see how to detect and solve problems as they arise.

Appendix A at the end of the book contains an example of all the documents that have to be produced in the project. This example is used throughout the book as a case study.

WAR STORIES

I have introduced some chapters with 'War Stories.' The stories provide you with real life examples of common problems that can occur. The stories are based on real events in my experience, but the details have been changed so that no individual organization can be recognized.

WHO ARE YOU?

The book is intended mainly for the Project Manager—the person responsible for planning and controlling a project. Analysts, programmers and even users of software will enjoy reading it as well, because they will see their role in the process. The book is generally nontechnical, although we go into some depth on certain topics such as Design and Programming. You can skip these chapters if you wish (the Introduction will tell you if the chapter is technical) because I attempted to make every chapter as stand-alone as possible.

TO THE TEACHER

This book is intended as a management text as well as a teaching text. It will prove to be a valuable training tool for use in formal schools as well as for training internal to a company.

There is an Instructor's Guide available to help teach this book. The guide provides the answers to the end of chapter questions, and explains how to run the group exercises, most of which are related to producing the documents in the project. To order the Instructor's Guide, please write or call. John J. Rakos & Assoc. Ltd., 14 Palsen St., Ottawa, ON, Canada K2G 2V8, Tel: (613) 727-1626.

ACKNOWLEDGEMENTS

I would like to acknowledge the helpful comments of David Reed, *Digital Equipment Corporation;* Perry Kelly, *Cognos Inc.;* Ruth Ravenel, *University of Colorado;* Charles Shubra, *Indiana University of Pennsylvania.*

Introduction

Your Project Can Succeed

WHAT IS A PROJECT?

A project is any activity that results in a deliverable or a product. Those of us in the computer field tend to think of a project as a full application system comprised of many program modules. But software projects vary in scope from the development of large systems to the programming of a single module. Even a document resulting from a feasibility study or analysis is a project. Conversions, benchmarks, or training courses are projects.

Projects always begin with a problem. The user approaches the project team with a request to provide the solution to his or her problem. When a project is completed it must be evaluated to determine whether four essential elements exist:

First, does the finished product actually solve the user's problem?

Second, was the user satisfied with the development process? The product as delivered may be perfect, but if the user is unhappy with the process of development or method of delivery, he or she may reject the results. The user must therefore be involved with the process.

Third, was the project team's upper management satisfied with the product as well as the process? They need to be informed about project progress, profit, and user and team satisfaction.

Fourth, (and often overlooked), is the project team satisfied? If it was an external project (formally contracted), the project team must get paid. If the project was for an internal department, the project team members must get other forms of payment: they may get a raise, a promotion or other type of reward. The team must feel that they have learned from the experience.

PROJECT SIZE

Why the title 'Small to Medium Sized' Projects? There are many publications (References 2, 3) on projects that are over 100 person-years. This size is typical for large, mainframe oriented applications. Our focus will be on projects developed for minicomputers or microcomputers. My experience has been on projects averaging approximately 5 man-years. However, the method shown works for tiny projects (one man-month or less), as well as for much larger projects, with only minor modifications.

It has been proven (Reference 4) that the most effective project teams consist of 5 to 7 people, working on a single problem until it is completed. In Chapter 18 on ORGANIZATION we will discuss the advantages of breaking larger projects into many 'small to medium sized' ones. In other words, there should not be projects that are over 25 person-years. Small is beautiful in the project business.

WHY PROJECTS FAIL

Let us take a look at some of the problems that cause projects to fail. These problems will all be dealt with in this book.

Failure at the Start

Most projects that fail go astray because they do not 'get off the ground' properly. People suddenly find themselves programming, without a clear description of why the project was started and what exactly it is to accomplish; in other words, without a plan. If you do not estimate what the extent of the effort will be, you will have no idea of the required staffing, which is the major cost factor in a project.

If no one bothers to clearly outline and get agreement with the user as to what the project will accomplish, it will not be accepted by the user. There is a saying in the business:

> Projects very quickly reach 90% completion, and stay there forever. (Reference 1)

It is very common in the industry to deliver a project, only to have the user refuse to pay until some changes and additions are made. He feels that these functions were promised (explicitly or implied). If there is no written agreement up front, who can argue that they were not promised?

Unrealistic deadlines and budgets are often foisted on a project team by 'authorities' who are unaware of the importance of an accurate estimate, and the project team is locked into an impossible committment. (I call this estimates by edict.)

Planning is knowing ahead of time where you are going, how you are going to get there, and how you will be able to prove that you are there.

Failure in the Development Stages

After you plan your project, you will analyze the problem and draw up a design (see Chapters 2 and 3). Then the actual building, or development stages, can begin. Projects can fail in these stages as well. If the analysis and design results are not documented properly, misinterpretation in the development stages will occur.

The responsibilities for project management must be clearly assigned to specific individuals, or everyone will think it is some other person's responsibility. Nothing will get done!

The project team must have a thorough understanding of the development tools available. Structured design, testing, and implementation methods are invaluable. Software tools such as Fourth Generation Languages, computer terminal screen handlers and form generators, data base management systems and report generators reduce development time. Your personal computer can be immensely helpful in managing your project. Spreadsheets help in decision making, graphics in making presentations, word processors in documentation. PERT (Network Analysis) and Gantt (Scheduling) charting systems are essential for project planning and control. Without knowledge of these tools the project may take a lot longer than necessary, or not be completed at all.

You will not be able to approach your word processing secretary on a Friday afternoon and request that he/she devote one month to typing your 250 page user Documentation starting next Monday. One must plan the required resources and schedule them ahead of time. Otherwise they will not be available when needed. Think not only of the obvious resources such as computer time and programming staff, but the less obvious such as clerical help, programs for conversions or simulation, software manuals, and outside experts for reviews and approval.

Premature coding can be the cause of inferior code or design. It is tempting to get down to coding—it is what most of us do best. Usually you are reluctant to begin difficult tasks such as analysis or design, so you begin with programming. You feel that after coding a few programs you will know more. Management may find that the programmers have nothing to do except play Adventure, so they are told to 'code something'. If you start coding before the System Design is done, you will either have to design around the existing code (which may not be the best design), or subsequently alter the programs to fit the design (which may take extensive effort).

Lack of walk-through's and reviews will cause major problems to go unnoticed during and after development. Walk-through's and reviews give us the opportunity to have experts outside of the project team walk through (go over each and every detail) of the results of our activities. Walkthroughs are technically oriented: designs, programs or documentation can be walked through. Reviews are management oriented: proposals, budgets, schedules may have to be discussed. These meetings make up for lack of full time expertise on the project team. For example, if your company has an expert designer (Mr. or Ms. Designer) on staff, you will be very fortunate if he can devote full time to your project for several months to do the design. Usually this expert's time is in such demand that all you can get is a few hours per week. But that is enough! Mr. Designer can walk through your design efforts weekly to point out faults and discrepancies that you have overlooked.

Many project failures are blamed on turnover. You must plan on key personnel leaving the team. It is dangerous to place all your eggs in one basket, which is the case when you depend completely upon a 'Guru' Programmer. Any project that I have ever worked on has experienced turnover if it lasted for six calendar months or more. Plan for it.

Lack of development standards can cause failure to some degree. The seven phased development method shown in this book is one standard. But standards must be drawn up and strictly enforced in the individual phases as well. For example, in the design phase you should develop standards of structured design, intermodule communication, structured programming and even documentation.

And lastly, as Brooks showed so well in The Mythical Man-Month (Reference 3), when a project is behind, brute force techniques such as 'add more manpower' do not work. It may slow the project down, instead of speeding it up. This is due to the additional training, orientation, and extra communication (which creates the opportunity for miscommunication) needed.

Failure at the End

When the due date arrives (or the budget has been exhausted) and everything is not completed, the requirements are usually compromised. Some feel that three fourths of a project is better than none. Most users have a total problem to solve, and three fourths solutions rarely work.

Applications are sometimes delivered without thorough debugging. These systems will cause so much frustration and intimidation at startup that they will rarely be used, even if the problems are solved later on.

Some systems do not deliver the promised performance. It is not lack of computer power that causes poor performance; it is usually caused by 'gold plating'. The user asks for a Volkswagen, and the project team delivers a Cadillac that must fit in the VW garage. (Or a VW with every power option, 1000 watt stereo, etc.)

Sometimes a project seems successful until someone tries to apply a minor change, either because a bug needs to be corrected or the user requests an enhancement. If the cost of making a change, called the 'maintenance cost', is too high the system will be scrapped. Since the user is usually unable to give the project team all of his or her requirements ahead of time, very few systems remain unchanged. Maintainability is an absolute must.

Some projects are cancelled outright at some point in the development. This may be due to many reasons. The user or the project team may have run out of funds. Major personnel or business changes on the user side make the project no longer necessary. Maybe the only person on the project team that understands the programs quits, and the remainder of the team is unable to (or does not want to) continue. This is usually the result of inadequate documentation standards. Or the development thus far is such a disaster that it is unwise to continue. This may be the case where you are 'thrown into' a project partially completed by someone else who has mysteriously left the company.

Be aware that cancelling the project or starting over is sometimes the best alternative. There are many cases where, after significant development effort has been spent, someone really knowledgeable gets around to calculating the real cost/benefit of the project. He or she may conclude that it is not worth going on. If you can prove that cancelling or restarting is less costly than continuing, by all means bite the bullet and do so. It is unwise to throw good money after bad, but be prepared to defend your decision.

In conclusion, cursory treatment of software development can cause overrun in expense and schedule, unhappy users, damaged reputations and also waste expensive talent—yours. Some failed products simply fade into oblivion, others are 'flaming disasters': everyone knows about them and uses them as examples for the 'how not to do it' portions of Project Management courses. Do not let it happen to you.

WHY PROJECTS SUCCEED

Planning and Control

Successful projects have a clean beginning—a written plan that defines what will be delivered, and how it will be accomplished. Measurable acceptance criteria are written down and are used to prove that the promises have been met.

During development there is close monitoring to ensure that the project stays on plan. The staff is adequately experienced to produce the product. The right documents for the right people are produced even in a tight situation, because the management realizes that documentation is one of the most important aspects of the project. Frequent reviews are held to measure progress against the schedule. When a problem occurs, it is noticed at once, and solved if possible, otherwise estimates and schedules are redrawn, and expectations are reset as necessary.

At the end, the user is satisfied because the team has delivered the product as promised. The cost is 'reasonably close' to the quoted estimates. There is no hassle about acceptance. The user agreed ahead of time to a precise and detailed method of demonstrating that the product functions as required. Payment is made where applicable.

A PROFESSIONAL APPROACH

All of these reasons indicate that a project cannot be approached in a haphazard manner. Project management requires a professional approach. A professional person approaches her project armed with management tools that help her plan and control. She has the discipline to stay with the tools, because she is committed to deliver the product. The methods presented in SECTION I are part of the tool kit required to produce quality and success.

QUESTIONS

1. What is the traditional definition of a successful project? Would you add any other criteria?

PART 1
The Methodology of Project Management

1

The Seven Phases of Project Management

A Clean, Ordered Approach

1.1 INTRODUCTION

To plan and control anything, you must break it up into small, manageable pieces. Projects in general are broken down by the component pieces or by the jobs the individuals working on the project will perform. A high-tech project, a research and development project or a software project is broken up by time phases. Time phases are a 'first we do this, afterward we do that' approach. The phases should be chosen so that they are reasonably distinct, and produce one or more milestones — clear events that prove that the phase is successfully completed.

1.2 THE PHASES TABLE

Figure 1.1 (on inside front cover!) shows the seven phases of a project. The horizontal scale is time. Appearing left to right, chronologically, are the project phases: DEFINITION, ANALYSIS, DESIGN, PROGRAMMING, SYSTEM TEST, ACCEPTANCE and OPERATION.

Reading downwards, the following divisions are made:

ACTIVITIES

What we must do in each phase. Certain on-going activities such as PROJECT MANAGEMENT, REVIEWS, STATUS REPORTS, DOCUMENTATION and user TRAINING are indicated with horizontal time lines across the applicable phases.

OUTPUT
DOCUMENTS
[AND
MILESTONES]

The documents that must be produced during the particular phase. Milestones, enclosed in [ ], that must be completed.

RELATIVE
EFFORT (PM)

The relative manpower that must be expended. The heavy line (PM) is the effort expended by the Project Manager. Note that his or her effort is heavy in the beginning, light in the middle, and becomes heavy again toward the end.

(TOTAL
STAFF)

The light line is the total relative manpower expended by everyone on the project. Note that it is light up front, since only the management is involved, gets heavy in the middle where many designers and programmers are working, and is light at the end when again only management is involved.

Time scale or relative duration of the phases is not shown in the diagram.

1.3   THE 'BUILDING A HOUSE' ANALOGY
FOR SOFTWARE PROJECTS

To have an overall understanding of the project development life cycle, let us compare building a project to building a house. If you have ever worked on a house, whether building a complete house, finishing a basement or perhaps just building a privy, you were probably not aware that there were seven phases involved. Whenever the terminology used is the same as that in Figure 1.1 (the Phases), the words are **bold** to help you reference that diagram.

The DEFINITION phase of building a house. Let us start with a little scenario. The prospective user of a house comes to you (the Project Manager of a house building company) stating his or her problems:

I am living in a tent on an empty lot in the north eastern part of the country.

You may ask, "What is the problem with this arrangement?" The user would answer:

It is wintertime and it is cold in my tent; in the summer it is too hot. I need *temperature control.*

It is too bright inside in the day time, and too dark at night. I need *lighting control.*

When I need to perform my necessities, I have to go out and shovel a hole in the snow. If I need to wash, I must heat the water on an open fire. I need *plumbing.*

My spouse and two children are living with me in this tent. We need privacy and sound isolation.

And so forth until all of the user's problems are listed. If the user's problems are not written you may have to help write them down to produce the **Requirements Document.** At this point you may have to estimate how much it will cost to build a house to suit the user. You present this cost, as well as the date for completion, in a **Proposal.** The cost and schedule at this point may be very inaccurate. It would be much more accurate if you could convince the user to wait for the estimate until the end of the Analysis Phase. In this case you could present here only the cost of the **Analysis Phase** in an **Analysis Proposal.**

The ANALYSIS phase of building a house. The Analyst now produces the **Functional Specification** for the house. The Functional Specification contains such promises as:

Mr./Ms. User, we will build a house for you. This house will have rooms with opaque and soundproof walls, to provide you with *privacy* and *sound isolation.*

We will put a 'gizmo' on the wall called a thermostat, (include a diagram of a thermostat), which will provide you with *temperature control.* If you turn the thermostat to the right, the house will get warmer. If you turn it to the left, the house will become colder.

In each room there will be a 'gizmo' called a light switch (provide a diagram) to provide you with *light control.* If you push the switch upward, the room will be bright, if downward, the room will be dark.

Plumbing will be provided in a room called the 'bathroom' with utilities to do the necessities and for washing. There will be a lever on one utility, which, when pushed downward, will flush (provide a diagram?). There will be utilities with 'taps'. When you turn the left tap clockwise hot water will come out. When you turn the right tap clockwise cold water will come out (provide a diagram).

And so forth.

Note that the Functional Specification lists what the house does for the user: the inputs, outputs and interfaces between the house and the user. There is no mention of how it will be built. The Functional Specification lists the promises (deliverables) that are made in order to solve the user's problems as stated in the Requirements Document.

The DESIGN phase of building a house. The Designer of the house is the Architect. The goal of design is to divide the system into functional components, and then interconnect the components efficiently. The design of the house goes on the blueprint. The Architect may divide the house into a living area, an eating area, and a sleeping area. Each of these areas may comprise one or more rooms.

The blueprint contains not only the divisions, but also how the pieces are interconnected. The Architect will design the placement of each room, as well as the doors and halls for the most efficient interconnection (traffic) between the rooms.

He must design places for the furnace and ductwork so that the promise of temperature control can be met. He must also design wiring locations so that the light switches promised will all work. The placement of all the plumbing is detailed so the facilities promised will work. In other words, all of the connections are detailed.

The Design shows how the system works. The blueprint is the **Top Level Design**. Some sections of the blueprint, such as details of the individual rooms or schematics are lower levels of the design. All of this goes into the **Design Specification** document.

The PROGRAMMING phase of building a house. The equivalent of programming is the actual construction of the house: the work of the contractor, carpenters, plumbers, electricians and so forth. They all work according to the dictates of the blueprint, or Design Specification.

The SYSTEM TEST phase of building a house. System test involves putting the pieces together, and ensuring that everything works together (Integration). In the house we may begin with the basement: we will first put together all the components comprising the basement and ensure that they all work together. We may then go on to the first floor, ensuring that all of those components work, and that the first floor is correctly connected to the basement. We can then go on to the second floor, and so forth, and fix any problems that occur. At the end, the Architect and all the trade contractors must systematically test each component: all the lights, thermostats, plumbing, and so on to ensure that they all work together according to specs.

The ACCEPTANCE phase of building a house. The user (or her manager) now sees the complete house, perhaps for the first time. At a prearranged time, she systematically tests each light switch, faucet, thermostat, and so forth to ensure that they work according to the promises made to her in the Functional Specification. If any problems occur, the project team must fix them. Most problems should be easy to fix, since the project team has already gone through the same tests during System Test. Some problems, such as major requirements problems, may be difficult to fix. Imagine if the user said, "I thought you promised to build me a four bedroom house, not a three bedroom one!"

This kind of problem is not uncommon in the software industry. If the user is satisfied she pays for the house; this was previously agreed to in an acceptance agreement.

The OPERATION phase of building a house. At operation the real end user—in our case the user's family—moves in and lives in the house. The key to operation is that the Architect and Contractors do not leave town yet. A period of warranty (six months to one year is common) must be provided, because problems may still be found that need to be fixed. Furthermore, most systems are outdated at, or soon after, implementation. If the project manager is a good salesperson, he will suggest the building of a bigger and better house (Version 2!) at this point.

Note that this phase does not include maintenance, wherein changes and enhancements are added. The problem with including maintenance as a phase is that the project will never end! Since you get promotions and raises based upon accomplishments, cutting the project off six months after delivery gives you a clean, measurable end point for the project. Major enhancement(s) is a new project.

Comments on the 'House Analogy'

The analogy is valuable because the science of building a house is so close to the science of building a project. We will be referring to this analogy throughout the book. But the analogy is inaccurate for two reasons:

First, we know too much about house building. You can ask almost anyone to describe their dream house. They will be able to describe it down to the color of the last brick used. How many software users can describe their requirements accurately?

Second, the house building industry is old enough to have standards. In the software industry we have not even invented the equivalent of a two-by-four. We have not yet been able to define a foundation, a floor or a room. So until our industry matures further and standard building blocks and conventions are established, we may have to re-invent and build everything down to the last component.

The chapters that follow detail each phase in the life of a project.

QUESTIONS

1. List the seven phases of a software project, along with activities and milestones associated with each phase.
2. List the seven phases of a building a house, and compare the milestones in each phase to those of a software project.
3. Why is building a house not analogous to building a computer project?

2

The Definition Phase

Understanding the User's Problem

2.1 INTRODUCTION

The goal of the definition phase is to gain sufficient understanding of the user's problem in order to estimate cost and time. There are three major activities that you must do in the Definition Phase (see Figure 1.1): First, you must gain an excellent understanding of the user's problem and what is required to solve it (REQUIREMENTS). Second, you must decide whether or not to do the project. You must ensure that the project is technically feasible and has a good chance of success before you undertake it (GO/NOGO DECISION). If the decision is to go ahead, you must analyze all the possible risk items that may beset your project. This analysis will help in writing the PROPOSAL which details what will be delivered, when and at what cost. (Including the cost of the risk items!)

Note that the ongoing activities of PROJECT MANAGEMENT, REVIEWS, STATUS REPORTING and DOCUMENTATION start here and go on until the end of the project (Figure 1.1).

You will have to write several documents and reach several milestones by the end of this phase. First of all a Requirements Document (RD) must be written. The RD must be so clear and complete that the project team (PT) can grasp the full extent of the user's problem and estimate the cost of the solution. Your first milestone will be the approval or *signing off* of the RD by the user and the Project Team (PT).

Next, a Preliminary Project Plan (PPP) will have to be written. The PPP is a 'first crack' at planning the steps that will have to be taken to develop the product, and the resources that will be required for each step. The plan outlines how long the resources will be needed and how much they will cost. This gives you the first 'ballpark' estimate and schedule.

And last, you will have to give the user this estimate in a PROPOSAL. How reliable is this estimate? We in the data processing industry have a terrible reputation for under-estimating our projects. There are a couple of good reasons for this. One is that we do not know how to estimate. The other is that we make our estimate at definition time, when we have little knowledge of the extent of the problem. Referring to the 'house analogy' (Section 1.3) I suggested that the house builder should not make an estimate right after hearing a simple statement of the problems. If you are not confident that the user has accurately outlined his requirements in the RD, I suggest that you split the project in two: the Analysis Phase as a first project, followed by the remaining phases as a second project. At definition time your proposal will be for the *analysis only,* and is called the ANALYSIS PROPOSAL. After the analysis there will be a DEVELOPMENT PROPOSAL (see Chapter 3). This is called the two-phase proposal process. The milestone involved here is the purchase of the proposal by the user.

2.2 THE REQUIREMENTS DOCUMENT

The Requirements Document (RD) states the user's problems and the general solutions required. The language is oriented to the user's business, and shies away from computer lingo. The RD is sometimes used as a Request for a Proposal (RFP) when the user tenders the project to outside contractors.

The project team (PT) may be fortunate enough to begin the project after receiving a good RD. In fact, project management really begins after the RD is completed. However, user-written RD's are usually inadequate for estimating and development. The reasons for this are simple. The user may be unaware of what a computer can do, and so the RD is vague. A user may not even perceive his or her own needs correctly. For example, using the 'house analogy'— what if the user requests a bigger tent with a good flashlight? Obviously, this user is not up-to-date with house technology.

We also have communication problems. A non- technical person cannot be expected to learn computer lingo in order to explain his requirements to the computer analyst. It is up to the project team to notice and solve the above problems. My experience is that time has to be spent working with the user to help him write a good RD.

Interviewing the User

Get the proper information from the user and you will have a good RD. A user will tell you anything you ask about —and nothing more (Reference 1). The onus is on the project team's interviewer to learn all about the user's business, understand the user's terminology, and ask all the right questions.

The biggest problem may be getting to the real end-user—the data entry clerk or the shipper in the warehouse. Often a manager or supervisor will tell you that the end-user is busy or unable to give reliable information. Sometimes managers feel that you are treading on their turf if you go directly to the end-user in their department. For those developing products for sale, you may have only the marketing department's interpretation of the user's needs. The solution to this problem is to educate these representatives about the importance of talking to the real end-user. If her input is not taken initially at definition time, changes will occur later and these will be very expensive to implement. Know the politics involved, especially in an internal project. Always get permission from the appropriate managers to interview their people.

Plan the interview. Learn about the business, write down the questions to ask. Here is the logical sequence of the interview:

> First, find out about the flow of information in the company. Start with the outputs: What is the information needed to run the business? How must the data flow among departments and individuals? Determine frequency, timing, and accuracy.

> Second, the inputs are then driven by the outputs: What information is required to produce each of the outputs? What information is available, when, where? What new information will have to be gathered? Remember the five W's of journalism—Who?, What?, Where?, When?, Why? Stay away from 'How' for now (unless unique formulas must be used). Plenty of time for that during DESIGN.

Contents of the Requirements Document

(*Appendix A* contains an example of a complete RD, as well as examples of all the important project documents.)

Examples used in the following topics (and in the remainder of the book) refer to the Amalgamated Basketweaving Courses(ABC) project in Appendix A. The reader is encouraged to refer to the Appendix whenever full detail on that project is desired.

Following are the sections of the RD:

1. *Introduction*   Identify the Company (user) and the vendor(s) to whom the RD is targeted. State the problems that need to be fixed, the history, examples of the problem situation, motivation to fix it, etc. This section is used to introduce the potential vendor to the user company or department if necessary, describing its culture, environment, the way it does its business. Give the project team a feel for the user and his problem.

Example:

> REQUEST FOR PROPOSAL/REQUIREMENTS FOR A MANAGEMENT INFORMATION SYSTEM FOR THE AMALGAMATED BASKETWEAVING COURSEWARE (ABC) CO.

> ABC gives different types of weaving courses. We have classes in ten major cities in North America, each course presented at least 4 times per year per city. Students come from all over the country, but can register by phoning (collect) our main office. We have no computer expertise. All expenditures must be approved by our Fearless Leader and CEO, Mr. Barry Strawman.

> Major problem: General confusion in registration and course administration. Presently, when a student phones to register for one of our courses, the secretary writes the information on a piece of paper, then transfers it to a course file (another piece of paper), which eventually gets collated (on paper).

Last month alone we lost 3 registrations, told 2 students to go to the wrong course, did not have enough material for 2 courses (twice as many people showed up as we anticipated, and we had no way of telling who was officially registered) and we forgot to tell the instructor about one course. We suspect that we are not billing everyone—our revenues are down but the number of students seems to be up.

We also suspect that we should give courses in other cities, and that we are giving the courses at the wrong times of the year.

2. *Project Goals*   A simple statement of why we are proposing the development. Major constraints of time or money can be mentioned.

Example:

Replace existing manual system at ABC with an automated one that handles:

Registration that is fast (on phone), no losses, with timely notification to student, instructor and the company of appropriate information.

Financial system that accurately produces monthly billing, accounting, and course material information.

Warehouse system that allows appropriate course material to be sent to courses and reordered when necessary.

Management information, for better decisions about where and when to hold appropriate courses, available immediately on request.

Project should be done within 6 months of initiation, for under $200,000.

3. *Major Functions*   Simple statements about how the system will function, based on the Project Goals.

Example:

Registration capability by phone in less than 2 minutes. Registrar must be able to see present enrollments (list of students). Automatic confirmation must be sent to student within one week of registering, and summary of all enrollments every Friday to ABC Administration. Two weeks before course, enrollments go to Instructor, ABC, and course material warehouse.

Financial system that invoices student after attending course, keeps Accounts Receivables, roll up of revenues by course type, time period and geography.

Warehouse system notified two weeks before course of items required for the course, where the course is, location of items in warehouse, and automatic inventory decrement and re-ordering.

Reporting system on request or at set intervals, report goes to CEO with number of registrations, courses, revenues. On request, reports detailing courses, enrollments, and revenues by course type, geography, time of year.

4. *General Outputs*   Simple description of information required from the system.

Example:

On-line enrollments by course, input of all registrant information. Printout of student confirmation (The course enrolled in, when, payment information).

Weekly print-out of all enrollments for the week by course and location, revenues associated with courses that ran.

Monthly print out of course sales for the month by type, location, time (for Management). Reports to Accounting on accounts receivables, items invoiced, outstanding and paid.

Two weeks before a course printout of enrollments, location, course material (for instructor and Warehouse). Revenue summary (for management).

One day after a course invoice (to Student), update accounts receivables.

Reports on request on-line reports of registrations, attendance, and/or revenues by course, by geography, by time of year.

Detail every item of *information* (not necessarily screens or reports) required. You may simply state it as general requirements: 'The marketing department needs the number of courses sold by geography'; or as a report if you are certain: 'The President needs a quarterly report of items sold by geography by time'. Remember, it is the job of the computer analyst to suggest what reports will best provide the required information.

5. *General Information Inputs*   (Inputs would not be supplied by an inexperienced user—it would be filled in later by the analyst.) Go through the list of output items above, and see what input data is necessary to produce the outputs. This is a good time to ensure that all of the required data is available at the proper times.

6. *Performance*   How many transactions are to be processed, how much data must be stored, how frequently must reports be produced, etc. State in terms of averages and maxima (in a peak day or hour).

7. *Growth*   This may be difficult to foresee, but try to calculate the increase in business and stipulate the number of years that the system is expected to function. Express the growth as a percentage or as actual numbers. If you are implementing the system in Phases (see Chapter 10), this RD describes Phase One only, and the **Growth** section can describe the additional functions in the subsequent phases.

8. *Operation and Environment*   Where the computer will reside, where the interactive terminals are, if any. Who will use it. Any unusual circumstances such as a hostile environment (intentional or accidental), or endurance requirements. There may be a need for portability, or for special safety or physical security measures.

9. *Compatibility, Interfaces*   State if inter-computer communication is required, any existing equipment that has to be incorporated or if distributed access is required. If the system must go on an existing computer, or must be programmed in a specific language, document these facts here.

10. *Reliability, Availability*   Quote Mean Time Between Failures (MTBF) figures, Mean Time to Repair (MTTR) and percentage up-time required. All manufacturers publish these figures for their hardware. Note that published up-time is rarely over 95%, so no one can guarantee availability greater than that.

11. *Human Interface*   Outline the computer experience required of the user, state how the system is to handle the brand new user. This is just a general description of the human interface; for example, is the system to be menu driven, should on-line help be available, etc.

12. *Organizational Impact*   Which departments will be affected and how must their work be changed. How the new system is to interface to some existing or new manual systems.

13. *Maintenance and Support*   Warranties required: how long, to what extent, how it will be delivered. For example, a statement such as: 'The Vendor will fix any problems with the system for 6 months after delivery, within 24 hours of being notified.'

14. *Documentation and Training*   List the general documents and/or courses that would be required.

Example:

> Vendor must provide documents for Users, Operators, and System Maintainers. He must provide training for the Order Processing Clerks to do their job completely.

15. *Advantages (RFP only)*   If the RD is an RFP in a competitive situation, solicit data from the vendors outlining why they feel they should be chosen. Request data on the vendor's relevant experience, committment, project methodology, examples of successful projects, and references that you may call to verify him. (Be sure to get in the good books of these people first!)

16. *Terms and Conditions (Ts & Cs) (RFP only)*   State the basis for selection, when and how the winner will be announced.

Example:

> ABC company has the right to select among vendors based on its own criteria. Any submitted documents will become the property of ABC. The winner will be announced no later than X. ABC has the right to accept and/or reject any portion(s) of the proposed systems. Pricing for such will be renegotiated with the vendor.
>
> Although T's & C's are formal only for an external project, an equivalent paragraph benefits internal projects as well. State your rights vis-a-vis other departments, such as your right to go out and purchase software, use an outside vendor, and so forth.
>
> The Requirements Document has all information that will be necessary for the project team to assess the limits, functions, complexity and cost of the system.

2.3 THE USER'S RESPONSIBILTY

Even if the user does not write the RD, he or she has the responsibility to provide the project team's interviewer with reliable, timely information. The user must therefore find a person who knows all about the existing system and what is required of the new one.

This person must be *available*. The interviewer will have many questions that need to be answered even after the formal interviews are over. This user person must have *authority* to make decisions about the proposed system and how it will affect the organization. The requirements often involve trade-offs that impact several user departments.

For an internal project a user representative is usually easy to access. For contracted projects, especially ones for Government departments, there may be the occasional 'sealed bid' where no contact with the department is allowed. On the surface this appears to assure equal fairness to all the bidders. In reality these departments are doing themselves a disservice: they would find that much better proposals (and subsequently systems) would be delivered if someone were appointed to answer the bidders' questions.

2.4 THE GO/NO-GO DECISION

Feasibility Study

After the requirements are firm, the next step is to decide whether or not a project is worth doing. To help make this decision, a Feasibility Study is done to answer the question: 'Can this system be built *technically*?' Unfortunately, just about anything is technically possible, so the questions to answer should be, 'At what cost can the system be built, and what will be the cost/benefit?'

In a Feasibility Study we consider all the possible technical solutions, and attempt to estimate a ballpark cost for each solution. For a larger project, we consider the major decision of what hardware to use, and whether to build or buy the software. We evaluate the dollars (pounds, marks, whatever) saved and other benefits of each solution. For a small-to-medium sized project a formal feasibility study document need not be written. It is usually enough to assign someone to study the possible solutions and assess the cost benefits. We then review our findings with some knowledgeable people and together we recommend the best alternative. For details on the contents of the Feasibility Study see Reference 18.

The cost estimate that comes out of the Feasibility Study is a 'ballpark'— it may be off by 200% to 500%. This is not a problem since we use these figures only to see if the project fits into the general budget constraints established for it.

It may be feasible but it should not be done. The project manager (PM) has to answer not only the question ''Is this project technically 'doable'?'' but also the more important question:

Is this project doable NOW by ME?

The PM must ask himself or herself if the project has a chance of success, or if it will fail due to limited resources, knowledge, or risks outside his control. Innumerable projects have failed, completely or partially, because people ignored the obvious signs pointing to failure. Do not make plans on pipe dreams —know the risks involved.

2.5 RISK MANAGEMENT

Historically, the data processing industry has established a terrible reputation for underestimating projects. When asked for the reasons, DP 'professionals' defend themselves with statements such as, ''I estimated correctly based on the facts as presented to me. The reason for the overrun was that:

Fill in one or more: the user changed his mind... never told me about... and the other departments promised... and upper level management dictated the estimate... in other words, it was not my fault!

I feel that the bad estimate was his/her fault. He/she should have foreseen all these things and weighed his estimates with these risk items.

Following is a list of *pipe dreams* on which project managers have based their estimates, and were subsequently surprised when the project ran over:

The Dream World

1. There will be no changes. The user has thought of everything he needs for the next three years. His business will not change. He will not change his mind.

2. Upper Management will do the right things for the project.

   They will protect the team, provide the necessary resources, accept our estimates, keep the politics away, and will not interfere.

3. We will have all the necessary resources.

   We will get enough programmers (from other departments), or hire knowledge-able people; clerical help will be available at the required time; all the computer time we need will be available, etc.

4. No limits on time or money. (This is a good one!)

5. No resources or products need be obtained from a 'third party' (outside of the user and ourselves); we have authority and control over these third parties.

6. The user will agree to the two-step proposal. He is willing to pay us $50,000 up front to do only analysis, and take the risk that he can afford the remainder.

7. The hardware manufacturer will deliver the hardware and the new version of the operating system and language compiler on time and in working condition.

8. The user will fulfill all her responsibilities. We may have to ask the user to provide resources, test data, documentation; to answer all our questions correctly at the very least.

9. Everyone knows that software projects tend to be late.

   PROJECT TEAM: "We'll be six months late."

   USER: "No problem; take your time —we want quality."

10. There is no competition. In a contract environment, the client calls only on us; in an internal department he does not even consider buying packaged software or having another department develop it.

Realities

1. Estimates are by edict.

   UPPER LEVEL MANAGER(ULM): "You will deliver the product by January 15."

   PT: "Why January15?"

ULM: ''Because we have to demo it at a trade show. And you will do it for $100,000.''

PT: ''Why $100,000?''

ULM: ''Because that's what is in the budget.''

2. Management/Marketing signs fixed-price contracts based on your first (ballpark) estimate.

The Salesman has a 30 minute interview with the user's manager, and you are asked to estimate based on the sketchy notes taken. Contracts are then signed in blood based on that estimate.

3. You never get adequate resources.

You will always have to hire more programmers, learn a new language, buy a bigger computer for development, and do your own word processing.

4. Changes take place.

People transfer/resign, user's business changes as do his requirements, your manager (the originator of the project) is fired.

5. Responsibilities remain undefined.

Everyone thinks it is the other person's responsibility and it never gets done.

6. Estimates increase after the analysis and the delivery date slips.

7. When the project slips, management assigns additional programmers, who slow the project down.

8. User is not sympathetic to problems.

9. Management panics, gets involved.

Meetings double, management looks over your shoulder, thumbscrews are tightened.

And the industry standard solutions to all these problems are:

SOLUTION 1.   SEARCH FOR THE GUILTY

SOLUTION 2.   PUNISH THE INNOCENT

SOLUTION 3.   PROMOTE THE UNINVOLVED

SOLUTION 4.   GO TO SOLUTION 1 AND CYCLE THROUGH AD NAUSEUM

If you look at the 'reality' list above, you will immediately be struck by the fact that very few of the problems mentioned are in the jurisdiction of the project manager. But it is the project manager that gets blamed/fired when the project fails. It is therefore very important for the PM to know what his chances are for success, and to be able to say 'NO' to stillborn projects.

On a more positive note, the above problems are risks and contingencies. We will see (Section 2.6) how some of these risks can be reduced, eliminated or priced into the project.

Disqualifying the Project Due to the User or the Project Team

You need to look for major problems in two aspects of the project: the *user* and the *project team*.

Searching for problems in the *user's* area is easy. Ask the following questions:

1. Has the user budgeted enough money for the project?
   You do not want the project to be cancelled halfway through due to lack of funds.

2. Is the problem well defined?
   If the requirements can not be firmed up, make the analysis phase the first project.

3. Are the user's expectations realistic?
   Users may think that the computer will solve all their problems or run the whole business for them. They may not be aware of the high cost of computer software, both in terms of money and time. Educate your user.

It is always harder to find the problem in the *project team*. It is difficult to find fault in ourselves, but there may be problems here as well. Ask yourself these penetrating questions:

1. Is this project in my business area?
   For example, even though our experience is with VAX, VMS, COBOL developing commercial systems, we will bid on a project involving IBM computers running Analog-to-Digital nuclear reactor controllers (We are fast learners!). General Motors will not accept building a new space shuttle for NASA no matter how exciting the project seems. Imagine the liabilities upon failure.

2. Will I have have adequate resources available at the needed time, especially programming staff?
   It is tempting to 'grow empires' by hiring staff. But a company or department should not grow by more than 100% per year. This phenomenal growth can be accomplished if you have three resources available:

Hiring potential	Does your geographical area have good schools, or other sources of good programmers? Is your environment attractive?
Education	It may be difficult to hire people who know your special operating system and languages. Is there training available at your site or within a reasonable distance at the required time?
Good Personnel and Line Management	New employees have to be orientated, made comfortable with management and made aware of company procedures and culture. This should be done by your personnel department and line managers.

There are many cases where larger growth has been successfully absorbed, but there is an optimum size for every organization. A five man company should not bid on a 30 man-year project. It is unfair to the client to use his project as a training ground. We tend to be optimistic about our own capabilities, and it is heartbreaking to turn down a project due to lack of resources, but there are times when saying 'NO' is the best alternative.

How to Say 'NO' When You Do Not Want to Do the Project

It is simple to say 'NO' in a competitive environment: do not bid on the project. It is more difficult in an internal organization. You cannot simply stand up in front of five high level managers and refuse to do a project without good reason. Saying 'NO' requires knowledge of company politics, human psychology, and ample facts and figures for justification.

Obviously, you have to argue that 'NO' is the correct choice. Know the key people to convince, and have your arguments ready. Avoid embarrassing someone who is a great proponent of the project. Present the facts that made you decide to say 'NO' and perhaps that person will come to the same conclusion.

You cannot use the argument that you have a 'feeling' that things will go wrong. Always defend your decision with *financial facts* —most managers think in these terms. If you are turning the project down because of the risks, translate these risks into possible costs (See Section 2.6 on Risk). You must prove that what may appear to be a no-risk $100,000 project *will turn out to be a high risk $500,000* one, once you add up all the problem factors. Don't be afraid to exaggerate the risks a little if necessary. Use the history of what went wrong on past projects (it is usually available) to back you up. Do not get bullied into doing something you do not believe in, and if all else fails, try to negotiate a compromise. (See Chapter 5 on Negotiation.)

The Uncostable Factors that Influence the Go/No-go Decision

Have you ever been in a situation where you present all the above arguments to convince management *not* to do the project, only to have them answer, "Propose it anyway?"

Sometimes there are political factors involved. The client is an 'important user', and this project may be unprofitable but management is looking at future business. Or this may be a high visibility project—the company product will be seen on television, so profit is not a motivator. Here you may find pressure from very high levels—the president of your company has something at stake and has edicted that "The project shall be done!"

You may have ulterior motives. Perhaps you wish to gain experience in a special area. Or you must do this one to stay in business. Sometimes cost benefit arguments just do not wash.

Project Go-ahead Checklist

In this book checklists take the form of a list of questions. Checklists are items to look for, think about, have answers for at specific points in time before proceeding to the next step.

These lists should be used as reminders. Most of the items will probably not be applicable, but there may be something in a list that you have overlooked. Use the lists provided as starting points only. Alter the lists to meet your own needs. The answers to all the questions should be 'yes'!

Here are the questions to ask before writing the Proposal:

1.   Have we looked closely at the client?
    - If we have to program at her site, does she have adequate facilities?
    - Does she have the authority to give us the go-ahead?
    - Is she prone to reorganize? Would this affect the project?
    - Is she cooperative?
    - Is she available and able to answer questions?
    - Does she have funds for the *whole* project?
    - Does she know what she needs? Is she able to communicate this?

2.   Have we looked closely at ourselves?
    - Do we know the application hardware/software?
    - Do we have the necessary resources, and are they free at the required time?
    - Have we looked at the competition? Sometimes there are predetermined winners—do not bid if you have no chance at all!

2.6 THE FOUR STEPS OF RISK MANAGEMENT

Every project would be on time and on budget if nothing ever went wrong. It is imperative to concentrate on things that can go amiss and try to avoid them. This is called risk management. Risk management consists of three steps:

Step   1.   ANTICIPATE THE RISK.
Step   2.   ELIMINATE THE RISK WHERE POSSIBLE.
Step   3.   REDUCE THE IMPACT OF THE RISK.
Step   4.   STAY IN CONTROL WHEN THINGS GO WRONG.

Let us discuss each of these points in detail.

Step 1. Anticipating Risk

The first and most important item in risk management is to be aware of what can go amiss. The best method to identify possible risk items is to look at history and draw up a list of everything that could possibly go wrong. If you do not have history to fall back on, realize when you are in a risky situation.

Let us look at certain situations that expose your project to risks:

General Risk Situations

Inappropriate technical people. Lack of training and experience on the hardware, operating system, software packages or the application area pose risks. Lack of experience in teamwork causes communication problems. Client requirements for excessive security, legalities, statutory regulations (for example ERA) can cause disqualification of your people. I know of a project that ran into difficulty when a landed immigrant was provided as a programmer on a Defense Department project. For security reasons programming had to be done at the client site. *On the day that the programming was to begin,* we discovered that he would not be allowed to enter the client premises: he did not have security clearance. It would have taken 6 months to obtain clearance.

Improper working environment. A proper programming environment is quiet and free from interruption. Be especially careful if the programming has to be done at the user site. A computer with *fast response*, appropriate compilers and good development software is necessary.

Third party supplied resources. If there is anything to be supplied by a party *over whom you have no control*, you are open to risk. Try to obtain authority over these parties. This can be done by penalty clauses in suppliers' contracts, having input into performance reviews for staff, and so on.

Crash projects. You can have it sooner if you overstaff, everyone works overtime, and great gobs of computer power is available. But it will cost twice as much!

Unspecified payment/budget. If the user needs approval for funds quarterly, you stand the chance of being cancelled each quarter. If he is paying you by delivered milestone, you have the hassle of acceptance and payment at each milestone. If you are using the two-step proposal process, the analysis may exhaust the user's funds.

Financial Risk Situations

These are the situations where systems end up costing more than anticipated. Lack of good problem definiton is difficult to estimate especially when the user does not know exactly what he wants or is unable to specify it. *Bad (unstructured) design and coding methods* will cause testing to take longer than anticipated. Acceptance, especially 'Parallel Runs' can go on endlessly. (See Chapter 8 on Acceptance Test Planning where I suggest a solution to this problem.) Lack of project team training, demands for excessive documentation, or unusual standards may cause problems.

Distributed Project Management does not work. It is best to have all the members of the project team, as well as the client, in the same geographical area, otherwise the travel required will be costly.

Overzealous management can 'overmanage' a project. Keep documents to a minimum. Everyone can think of a better way to report his or her activity. Define a certain small set of standard documents and use only those. Keep meetings to a minimum. Use the phone and memos to communicate where possible. Do not interfere with the workers.

Risk is involved when *the user is unable to and has no authority* to answer questions quickly. I saw a project (for a large government department) where the answer to every requirements question had to be decided by a user committee that met once a month. The requirements were estimated at two weeks but actually took six months to complete!

Technical Risk Situations

These are the technical factors that result in bugs or bad performance.

The wrong solution. Are you building a rocket guidance system using BASIC because that is what you know best? Is GM attempting to build a space shuttle? Are you attempting to shoe-horn a large inventory control system into a PC? Is the target computer already 98% loaded and the new Accounting System for 10,000 vendors to be fit into the remaining 2%? Ensure that both the development computer and the target computer match the requirement, will be available when needed, and that both the hardware and system software are supported by the manufacturer. Be especially careful in a multi-vendor environment.

Bad requirements/specification. If anything is unclear or ambiguous, or if the user is unable to give you firm requirements, *changes will occur* during or after development. Changes can be very expensive to implement, and you may not get paid for doing it. Make the analysis the first project in this case.

Not knowing the user. You must be aware *of how he operates*. Union shops may have special rules regarding computer operators. The amount of computer expertise that the client has defines the human interfaces that have to be written. Security, audit procedures, rules and regulations may force a system to be designed in a specific fashion.

Tolerance of data loss defines the backup procedures. Some shops can recover from data that is a week old. Others cannot tolerate any loss, so transaction recording or duplicate files may have to be designed into the system.

It is very risky to specify *response, data volumes,* and *throughput* numbers in a contract. I have been in a situation where a contractor promised that every response would be under five seconds. The user found one circumstance where a certain response took over five seconds, and he refused to pay for the system. If response issues must be addressed in a contract (and most of the time they do), use wording such as: ''95% of the responses...'', or ''We will design toward all responses to be 5 seconds.'' We do our best, but we do not guarantee.

Incidentally, TECHNICAL RISK is the least deadly. This is not surprising since we tend to have many good technicians in this business.

The Risk Quiz. Ask yourself the following risk questions. If you answer 'yes' or even 'somewhat', to any of the questions you are taking a risk. The list is divided into three sections: LOW RISK, MEDIUM RISK, and HIGH RISK items.

LOW RISK ITEMS

AREA	QUESTION
Team Size	Is the project team from 3 to 5 people? (Note that this implies that the only no risk team size is one or two people!)
Software/ Hardware	Are we using a language that was not meant for this application? (COBOL for bit twiddling, or ASSEMBLER for commercial transactions)
User	Is the user a computer neophyte? (It will take time to train him; and as he learns he will want changes.)
	Can she answer questions quickly?
Training	Do WE need training in the target hardware, system software, languages?
Team Member	Do we get along? Are there any individual problems? (Health, productivity, personal issues)

MEDIUM RISK ITEMS

AREA	QUESTION
Team Size	Is the Project Team over 5 people?
Software/	Are there requirements for excessive response/throughout or availablity?
Hardware	Are we shoe-horning into hardware that is too small? Is assembly / macro language involved? (Macro is difficult to learn, difficult to debug, and it is difficult to find Macro programmers.)
	Do we have to modify the operating system? Is there networking involved? (Networking is still the most problem prone area in the business.) Are any of the hardware or software products brand new?
User	Are there any communications problems? (User is uncooperative or far away.)
Team Members	Is there anyone on the team over whom the project manager has no authority? (It is common to have user staff on the team. This is acceptable as long as the PM has input into his/her performance appraisal.)

HIGH RISK ITEMS

AREA	QUESTION
Software/ Hardware	In a proposed multi-vendor environment, are any of the vendors unable to demonstrate compatibility?
	Are we using some hardware, software, design or programming methods that have never been tried before? (Do not be a pioneer. A pioneer is the guy with the arrow in his chest!)
Team Members	Are some of us located a long distance away?
Third Parties	Do some resources depend upon parties over whom there is no control?
Deadline	Is this a 'crash' project? Is the estimate 'edicted?'
Requirements	Does the Requirement Document not exist, is it unfirm, or does one of us (user, project team) not understand it?

In conclusion, you can anticipate the risk by creating lists such as the one above to remind you of possible risk items. Use the history of projects in your company to customize these lists. Remember, the risk lists are dynamic—change them as your environment changes.

Step 2. Eliminating the Risk Where Possible

At this point it is a good idea to prioritize the risk items. Draw up a table such as the one in Figure 2.1.

RISK TABLE

Item No	Risk Item	Probability (1-10)	Impact (1-10)	Priority (PxW)
1	User not communic-Req't will slip	8	7	56
2	Chief pgr leaves-des/pgmg slip	2	8	16
.				
.				
.				

Figure 2.1   Risk evaluation table

Enter into the table each item in the Risk Quiz to which you answered 'yes' or even 'maybe'. Translate the risk items into the actual effect on your project—usually an increase in cost or duration. Decide on the PROBABILITY of the item occurring, and assign it a number from 1 to 10, 10 being the highest probability. Then decide the impact on the project. Assign IMPACT a number from 1 to 10, 1 being an item you can work around, 10 an item that will stop the project dead. The high impact items are the MEDIUM and HIGH risk items on the Risk Quiz, as well as critical path items (see Chapter 14). Multiply the PROBABILITY for each item by the IMPACT to get the PRIORITY.

The RISK TABLE in Figure 2.1 will give you the order in which to attack the risks for possible elimination. Obviously, the higher the PRIORITY in the Risk Table, the more attention that item needs. In fact, approach the items in descending order of PRIORITY.

For each risk item, first attempt to remove the cause of the risk. Exert authority, change staff, come up with better software/hardware, educate yourself and/or the user. Every item will require a unique solution.

Step 3. Reducing the Risk by Contingency
Planning and Pricing

For the items where you cannot eliminate the risk, define contingency plans. Is there another computer in the building or area that you can use after regular hours in case yours is unavailable? Is there a method to simulate some software or hardware for testing if it does not materialize? Is there a backup person who is willing to work on your project in an emergency? For every risk item involving a resource, try to put back-up resources in place.

If there is a high probability that the risk item will occur, you must adjust the price of the project accordingly. Many of my projects were sucessful because the price was marked up by a certain percentage. This is sometimes called a 'fudge factor', because the estimator blindly picks a percentage and increases the total price accordingly.

This percentage is much more accurate if it is based upon calculation of the cost impact of actual risk items.

You can summarize your contingency plans using the table in Figure 2.2.

CONTINGENCY TABLE

Item No	Risk Item	Action	Who	Cost %
1	User uncommunicative	Weekly mtg/ Prototyping	PM PL	$ 5K $25K, 3 mo.
2	Programmer leaves	Back-up pgr.	JR	$20K

Figure 2.2   Contingency and focus table.

Put the contingency plan in the ACTION column of the Contingency Table. In the WHO column put the name of a person who will be responsible for implementing a contingency plan. For those items that you need to have early warning about, put in the WHO column the name of an individual who will keep his finger on the pulse of the problem and warn the team if the dam is about to burst. In the COST column put the cost increase in dollars and/or the time that the risk items will cause.

Step 4.   Staying In Control When Things Go Wrong

And lastly, despite all your efforts, some things will still go wrong. I have seen situations where the poor project manager became so overwhelmed by all the things *outside of his sphere of control* destroying his project that he threw in the towel and resigned. Expect things to go wrong. Do not get paranoid (even if everyone is against you), and keep control as well as you can. Do your best, announce a slip or overrun if necessary, and report to the world the cause of the problems, especially if they are outside of your jurisdiction. Things will eventually settle down, and you will be respected for your ability to keep cool under pressure.

QUESTIONS

1. What is the two step proposal method? Why is it useful?
2. Why can a neophyte user not be expected to write a good Requirements Document? Then how can we produce a good RD?
3. Group exercise. Section 1 (INTRODUCTION) and Section 2 (PROJECT GOALS) of a Requirements Document are shown on page 29.   Write the remaining sections.

Requirements for Bell Family Communications System

Section 1 - Introduction   The Bell clan consists of five families who live approximately two miles from one another. Presently we communicate with each other using smoke signals.

Aside from the obvious problems of smell, delay in starting a fire, and slow communication, the signal is not private and it is hard to make sure that the intended recipient will be watching. We need a better method of communicating.

Section 2 - Project Goals   A communication system that will provide:

   a. Voice communication.
   b. Fast communication - should be able to talk at normal speed.
   c. A fast way of indicating which family we wish to call.
   d. Fast start - less than one minute to start talking.
   e. A way of alerting the specific call recipient.
   f. Privacy.
   g. Indication to the caller if the recipient is already talking.
   h. A way of terminating the call from either side.

4. What three items do we require the user's project representative to be able to do?
5. What is the major question answered by the Functional Specification? Why is a 'yes' answer to this question not enough for a 'go' decision?
6. What two major questions must we ask of the user to qualify a project? What two major questions must we ask of the project team to qualify a project?
7. What is required to be able to grow a business really quickly?
8. Which of the four steps of risk management is most important and why?
9. Group Exercise.

   To help anticipate risk, list at least 10 risk items due to the situation in your company (or an imagined company). Make this list into a 'Risk Quiz', that is, formulate each risk item as a question that will be answered 'yes' if there is a risk. Assign a 'Low', 'Medium', or 'High' rating to each item depending on your opinion of the impact of the item.

10. Evaluate the ten items listed in Question 9 using the format of Figure 2-1. Using Figure 2.2, list the highest risk items, and in the WHAT column list actions that will guarantee elimination of the risk for as many items as possible.

11. For the remaining risk items, put 'contingency plan' actions in the WHAT column.

3

Project Planning

3.1 INTRODUCTION

So you have evaluated the project and decided to go ahead with it! First, you may have to convince some other parties that the project should be built. This is done with a proposal. For an external project, the proposal is written to convince the client to buy the project from your project team. For an internal project as well, *management should insist* that the PT produce a proposal. This forces the project team to plan a little.

A proposal is a document that details the cost and schedule for the project, and outlines the steps that the PT will take to produce the product. How do the members of the team come up with the cost, schedule and steps required? They write the Preliminary Project Plan. A plan for a software project lists the activities required, how long each activity will take, when these activities must take place and how much resources must be spent on each activity to produce the required product.

Planning is an iterative process: the plan will be constantly revised as the project progresses and as you gain better knowledge and understanding. Planning is very difficult but it must be done properly—more projects have gone astray due to lack of planning than all other causes combined. (Reference 3)

If you are using the two phased proposal method (Section 2.1), the plan that you produce here is for the analysis only; otherwise, you will be planning all of the development.

A note on the organization of this book: this chapter will teach the management aspects of planning. It does not detail the use of planning tools such as PERT and Gantt charts. Chapters 13 and 14 will do that. Read this chapter first to learn why we use PERT and Gantt, and Chapters 13 and 14 when you need detail on how to do it.

3.2 THE PRELIMINARY PROJECT PLAN (PPP)

The PPP is the first crack at the steps, resources, cost and schedule required to accomplish the project. It is an internal document: it need not be shown to the user, especially an external one. Lately, however, I find that wise users, especially government departments, insist on seeing the PPP as well as the proposal. They wish to ensure that the PT knows what they are doing, and what better way than to see the detailed plans! Here are the major steps in the planning process:

3.3 WORK BREAKDOWN STRUCTURES (WBS)

The key to any plan is breaking the required activities into smaller and smaller pieces. A WBS begins by listing the major components of the project. This is Level 1 of the WBS. (Level 0 is just the title of the project.) For a software project the best method of breaking the project up into the major pieces is to start with the seven phases. Figure 3.1 shows Levels 0 and 1 of the WBS for the ABC project. Lower levels of the WBS are obtained by breaking down each piece at the level above into its component activities. In Figure 3.1 we see the Definition phase broken down to Level 2.

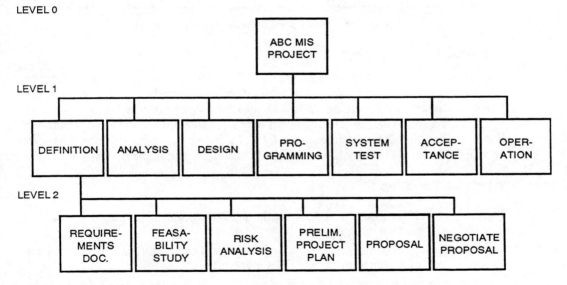

Figure 3.1   Work breakdown structure

If the plan is for the whole project, the above WBS would be completed by breaking each Level 1 entry into at least Level 2, perhaps even into Level 3 components. If the plan is for analysis only, the Level 1 ANALYSIS component is broken out. It may look like Figure 3.2.

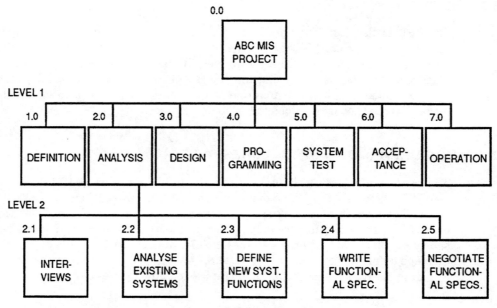

Figure 3.2   Work breakdown structure for analysis

The WBS Numbering System

Number the WBS entries as in Figure 3.2: Level 0, or project title, is 0.0. Each Level 1 item is N.0, ie., 1.0, 2.0 and so on. Each Level 2 item below Level 1 item N.0 is numbered N.1, N.2 and so on. For example, below Level 1 item Analysis, which is 2.0, we have items 2.1, 2.2 and so on. Each Level 3 item adds a dot and digits to the Level 2 number. For example, below 2.1 we would have 2.1.1, 2.1.2 and so on. The algorithm can simply be stated thus: At Level N you have N numbers and the Nth number varies.

When Do You Stop?

The lowest level entries are the tasks, or activities in the project. You can stop breaking down a task if the following is true:

1. Some person (or group for a larger project) can take *responsibility* for the task, or accomplish the activities involved.

2. You can get a *rough estimate* of the effort (person-days) needed to perform the activity (or activities) involved. This will have to be done by the responsible person.

3. You can *schedule* the task. All that you need to schedule an activity is its calendar duration, and its precedents—the activities that must be completed before the task can be begun. The project manager or the responsible individual may specify the precedents.

4. The tasks must be *small* and *able to be completed*. Although this will be used more for controlling than planning, a good 'work package' at the bottom level of the WBS takes approximately one week and there is some method of proving when it is done.

The 'expert' that you assign to a task to may be a programmer, an analyst or even the project manager. She may break each task up further in order to attain the above items, but this is not needed for the planning document yet.

For example, assume that we have an expert analyst in the company. We could give her the WBS in Figure 3.2 and ask her for a rough effort estimate and the precedents for the analysis. She should, of course, insist on seeing the RD.

Depending on her experience and estimating expertise, she may need only the Level 1 WBS. Some analysts could simply read the RD for the ABC project (discussed in the last chapter and in Appendix A) and state, ''The analysis for this project will take 25 days.'' Others may need to break the analysis into Level 2 boxes such as in Figure 3.2, yet others to Level 3 before they could do even a rough estimate.

An example of the Level 3 WBS for the INTERVIEWS and the ANALYZE EXISTING SYSTEMS boxes could be as in Figure 3.3.

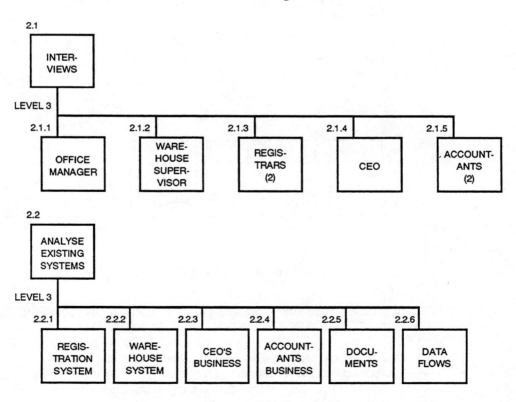

Figure 3.3   WBS level 3 items

The expert breaks down each lowest level box until he is able to estimate the effort required. (See Chapter 13 for estimating methods.) The estimates can be put on the WBS itself as in Figure 3 .4. Note that the TOTAL estimate is the sum of the individual times. This is called DIRECT time. It is the number of actual work days required to do the activity. It is not the ELAPSED or CALENDAR time that it would take.

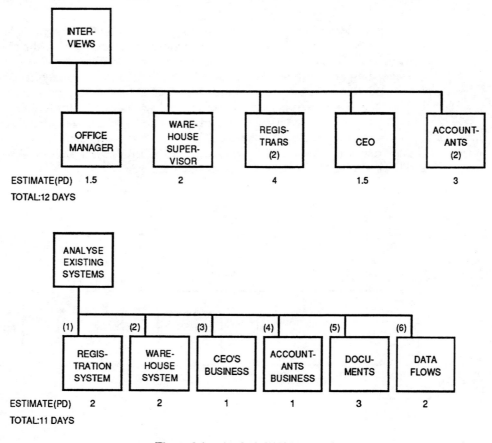

Figure 3.4   Analysis level 3 (partial)

He would similarly break out the DEFINE NEW SYSTEM FUNCTIONS, WRITE FUNCTIONAL SPEC. and NEGOTIATE FUNCTIONAL SPEC. boxes and add up the total time for all of the analysis. He then submits the estimate and the list of precedents required for the whole analysis to the project manager.

The person reponsible for the plan (probably the project manager for a small to mid size project) then collates all the estimates and precedents. He may end up with a list which looks like this:

ACTIVITY	EFFORT	PRECEDENTS
Definition	20	——
Analysis	35	Definition
Design	25	Analysis
Program A (Control)	20	Design
Program B (Registration)	30	Design
Program C (Warehouse)	25	Design
System Test	10	Programs A, B, C
Documentation	20	Design
Acceptance	5	System Test, Documentation
Training	10	Documentation
Operation	10	Acceptance
TOTAL	210 person-days	

Note that in this example only the programming had sub-components. If there are any sub-components of any other major activity available, they would also be listed.

3.4 THE NETWORK DIAGRAM

The second step of planning is to draw a network diagram that shows the sequence of events. The best type of diagram for this is a PERT chart. Figure 3.5 is a PERT chart for the above project. The sequence of events is driven only by the precedents of each activity.

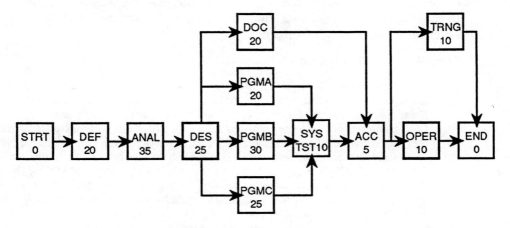

Figure 3.5   PERT chart

This form of the PERT is called a *Precedence Network*. Each box represents an activity. We have written in each box the name of the activity and its duration. You may be familiar with the *Activity on Arrow* format of a PERT, but the precedence network is better than activity on arrow, and most of today's *good* project management computer programs display this format. For details on how to construct a PERT chart see Chapter 14, and for details on how to use computerized products see Chapter 17.

The Critical Path and Project Duration

We will detail PERT charts and Critical Paths (CP) further in Chapter 14, but it should be obvious that a number of paths, or a series of sequential activities can be traced on the above PERT simply by following the direction of the arrows. The length of time that it takes to traverse any path can be calculated by adding up the durations of the activities on the path. The CP is the longest of these paths, and it defines the minimum time it will take to do the project. In the PERT in Figure 3.5 the CP consists of the activities: START, DEFINITION, ANALYSIS, DESIGN, PROGRAM B, SYSTEM TEST, ACCEPTANCE, OPERATION and END. The project will therefore take the sum of the durations of these activities, 135 days.

3.5 CALCULATING PROJECT COST

If the project contract is fixed price, the project manager can calculate a rough price for labour by multiplying the total number of calculated person-days by an average charge per day. Do not attempt to calculate in detail which people at what salary levels will be working on the project—unless you have a good idea of who will be working on it. The charge per person-day is a 'loaded' charge: it should include overheads of heat, rent, clerical support and benefits. To this you must add fixed costs such as computer time, rental of any special equipment and so forth. Fixed costs should be listed by each estimator for his particular activity.

Example of Price Calculation:

If you have one of the project management software products discussed in Chapter17, it is simple to calculate the cost of the project. Figure 3.6 illustrates an abbreviated 'Task Details' screen from the Superproject (TM) software package.(See page 37.)

This computer form can be used to enter for each task all the resources required and their cost. The software calculates the total task cost, as well as the total project cost. If you are calculating costs manually, and you are confident in the total estimate of 210 person-days, price the project by multiplying 210 by an 'average' cost per day, and add the fixed cost items. It would be better to add more detail by costing out at least each Level 1 box on the WBS. For example, the cost of Programming could be calculated as illustrated on page 37.

A price calculation must be done for each Level-1 task or phase, and totaled to get project cost. Note that unique costs such as profit and risk can be more easily accounted for manually than with a computer program.

```
Task Details                  SuperProject Expert                 SOFTWARE.PJ
   View        Edit        Select      File      Output      Help
  ID: 011
Name:AMST0000              SYSTEM STARTUP
                                    ── Start ──    ── Finish ──    ── Totals ──
Duration:   20  Actual Dur:    0  Erly:11-26-89   12-22-89    Var:    8400.00
Strt Del:   20  Finish Del:    0  Late:12-25-89   01-19-90    Fix:     100.00
   Float:    0  Free Float:    0  Schd:12-25-89   01-19-90    Tot:    8500.00
Pct Comp:    0  BCWP:       0.00  Actl:                       Act:       0.00
     Type:ASAP ALAP Must Span      Plan:                       Plc:       0.00
WBS:01.04.00.00.0011 Acct:     0  Scheduled/Crit.  Priority:  Hrs:     400
                                  Dev:0.00                    Plh:     0 Ovr:    0

 Resource   Hrs  Allc Un Ovr Actl    Rate       Var       Fixed      Total     Actual

SENIOR PGR  160  dayx  1   0    0    40.00   6400.00      0.00    6400.00       0.00
JUNIOR PGR   80    4d  1   0   80    25.00   2000.00      0.00    2000.00       0.00
C LANGUAGE  160  dayx  1   0    0     0.00      0.00    100.00     100.00       0.00




Description of this task.                                              CAPS
```

Figure 3.6   SUPERPROJECT task detail screen for task cost calculation

Average Pgr 75 pd @ $1000.00 per pd (loaded)		75,000
Profit 25%		18,750
Risk factors:		
User will change his mind on 10% of formats		
Cost = 10% extra programming time		7,500
PROGRAMMING TOTAL		$101,250

3.6 PROJECT SCHEDULE

The next step is to calculate a delivery date. To do this the planner (probably the PM) must translate the DIRECT days of the estimate to CALENDAR DAYS or duration. One of the difficult tasks here is to allocate resources—who is going to work on what, especially when tasks can be going on simultaneously. Even more difficult to decide is if the duration of a task can be shortened by adding more resources.

On the PERT in Figure 3.5 only one Level 1 activity has more than one resource assigned and is therefore divided into sub-tasks: programming. The PM must ask the appropriate estimators if other Level 1 tasks can perhaps be divided. The PM then redraws the PERT showing the actual duration of each task after it is divided. See Chapter 14 for details on resource allocation.

Then the PM schedules the whole project on the real calendar. The best method to do this is to draw a Gantt or time-bar chart such as Figure 3.7 below:

```
Task Gantt                        SuperProject Expert                    SOFTWARE.PJ
   View       Edit      Select      File      Output      Help

  1 Day Per Symbol                        December 89                    January 90
  ID   Heading/Task    Resource   27      04      11      18      25     01      08

  P1   SOFTWARE.PJ
  001    DEFINITION
  002      REQUIREMENTS DOC
  002                   PM
  002                   USER
  003    PROPOSAL
  004      PRELIMINARY PLN
  004                   PM
  004                   PL
  005    WRITING
  005                   PM
  006  ANALYSIS
  007    FUNCTIONAL SPEC
  008      TECH SECTIONS
  008                   PL
  009    MGT SECTIONS

Name of heading/task or resource.                                        CAPS
```

Figure 3.7   SUPERPROJECT project schedule

First, all the known calendar events such as holidays, vacations, training and non-project meetings are blocked out and all the project activities are scheduled around these. Each activity is then entered on the chart as a bar, starting at the completion of the last precedent activity. The completion of the last activity is the project end. See chapter 14 for a detailed discussion of scheduling.

3.7 PRELIMINARY PROJECT PLAN OUTLINE

Armed with all this knowledge, the PM can write up this crucial document. Here is a suggested outline for the PPP. (Read this together with the example in Appendix A.)

1. *The Project Team*   Detail here the organization of the project team (no names). Show the structure, who reports to whom, who communicates with whom, and so on.

Although Chapter 18 will discuss the organization of a project team in detail, Figure 3.8 gives an example of a typical project team and the major responsibilities of the members on a small to medium sized project.

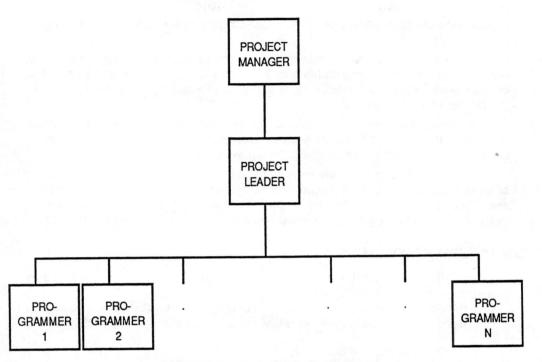

FIGURE 3.8   Typical project team structure

PROGRAMMERS: (No more than 5) Responsible for the programming.

PROJECT LEADER: Supervises Programmers on technical details only. Responsible for (not necessarily does) technical activites such as analysis, design and major programming tasks. Major Goal: Technical quality of the product.

PROJECT MANAGER: Manager of team (leader, motivator, etc. Responsible for all outside communication (reporting, meetings, user/upper level management interface) Major Goal: Successful project. (Plan, Control, Communicate.)

2. *Project Cost*   Include here the WBS's, estimates and calculations that were used to produce the price. You would not want this section in the hands of your competition—it gives the whole project away. This is why this document should be kept private in a competitive environment.

3. *Project Schedule*   The Gantt for the project. If some things are not obviously chronological, document why you did the things in that order. Detail especially how you handle the parallelism—sharing the work if there are simultaneous activities going on.

4. *Reviews*   In this section you relate the approximate dates of the major management and technical reviews (the schedule will provide this!), the purpose of each review and who will attend them. List the responsibilities of the people involved. Try to put reviews after each major milestone. (See Chapter 21 for details on how to do the reviews and reports.)

5. *Reports*   The format and content of the status reports, milestone reports and other project documents are detailed here. List who receives each report and what his or her responsibility is after receiving it. Again the Gantt helps to define when you expect these reports to appear.

6. *Documentation*   There will be two classes of documents in the project: user and project management. Outline which documents will be produced, and the responsibilities involved: who writes, types, edits, approves, distributes each one.

7. *Assumptions*   You are basing a price here upon a lot of assumptions: most of them are facts given to you (sometimes verbally!) by the user. Write down any assumptions still outstanding that would alter your price if it proved to be untrue. For example, ''The system will have at most 10 simultaneous users.'' Protect yourself.

3.8 CONCLUSIONS TO PLANNING

Planning is like horseback riding: it looks difficult before you start. But once you are up there things get progressively easier.

And now for the bad news. The estimates of costs and dates that project managers come up with at this point (in the Definition phase) are, on the average, *50% to 100%* off!

QUESTIONS

1. Group exercise. You are a house builder. You must create a WBS for a house project. The WBS below has Levels 0 and 1, and some Level 2 and 3 items. Complete the WBS below the box 2.0 BUILD HOUSE. Number the items.

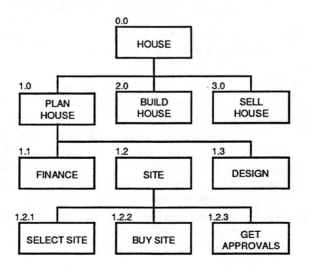

2. List the four properties of a work package item found at the bottom of a WBS.

3. Estimate, in person-days, the build house phase (does not have to be accurate). Start with the lowest level items and work up the WBS.

4. Break 3.0 SELL HOUSE into Level 2 items. Identify the precedents for each task at Level 2 of the WBS for the whole house. Draw a network diagram (PERT) for these tasks only.

5. Estimate the calendar duration for each Level 2 task. Mark this on the PERT. What is the length of the project?

6. Following is an outline of the WBS for PLAN HOUSE. The required resources, days for each and costs are listed. We need a 33% profit margin. What should we charge for the PLAN HOUSE item?

TASK	RESOURCE	DAYS	COST/DAY
Plan House			
Finance	Accountant	10	300
	PM	5	500
Site			
Select Site	PM	5	
	Consultant	5	600
Buy Site	PM	3	
	Accountant	3	
Get Approvals	PM	5	
Design			
Interviews	Client	3	0.0
	PM	3	
	Architect	3	500
Draw	Architect	15	
Blueprint	Architect	2	
	Blueprinter	2	1000 (fixed)

7. Group Project.

   Write a Preliminary Project Plan for the HOUSE project.

4

Proposals

The First Ball Park Estimate and Schedule

4.1 INTRODUCTION TO PROPOSALS

A proposal has three purposes: First, it contains the project team's first estimate of the *cost* and the *delivery date* of the project. Second, for an external project, it is a formal legal document that outlines the project team's intent to provide the required services. Third, it is a sales tool. It must sell the reader on the cost/benefit of the proposed project.

Although formal proposals are usually required only for an external project, one should be written for an internal project as well. Internal organizations benefit from a *formal agreement* between the user and project team regarding deliverables and costs. The sales aspect of a proposal should not be ignored internally. A wise user will insist that the project team 'sell' him on the project: prove to him that it is to his benefit to go through the pain and aggravation of building it.

Proposal War Stories

As promised in the preface to this book, I will relate war stories throughout the book. These are stories about projects that have gone astray due to problems with the particular activity being discussed. Recall that although the stories are based on fact, the persons and events are disguised to protect the guilty.

Proposals fail for two major reasons: First, *no bid* (proposal) where there should have been a bid; and second, there was a bid but *it was lost* to the competition.

42

No Bid

A large soft drink company invited an analyst from Famous Minicomputer Manufacturing Company(FMMC) to do a feasability study on what, if anything could benefit from computerization at the soft drink plant. The analyst did his study, but during the study he had a slight problem with the company accountant. This accountant was afraid of losing his job to the computer, and made the analyst's life difficult by refusing to answer any questions.

The result of the study was typical: The analyst recommended that several computer systems would be helpful. He recommended installing a computer to run the finances: accounts receivables, payables, inventory control, and so forth. He also suggested implementing a personnel system to handle the payroll, taxes and such, and a process control computer to handle mixing the drink, filling the bottles, and automated tracking of items in the warehouse. When asked to quote a price, due to time constraints, the analyst detailed only the accounting system price which came to $150,000.

The reaction of the customer seemed violent. In a nutshell, he stated that $150,000 was much too high for what seemed like a small fraction of his computer needs. He said he would not pay more than $50,000 for the accounting system.

The fatal error, however, was committed by the analyst's manager. Due to the customer's reaction (and probably for personal reasons) the *analyst recommended to his manager that the computer company withdraw its bid.* He felt that this customer would be difficult to deal with, that the customer would not answer questions correctly, and that FMMC and the soft drink company would never reach agreement. Unfortunately, the analyst's manager agreed and dropped the bid.

Comment: All users feel that your software costs are much too high. Perhapsthis user could have been won over by some other approaches. The analyst could have proposed the system in phases — built a smaller portion to get his foot in the door. Maybe the user had the money, and was only negotiating. Never give up a bid after a first meeting. There may have been a personality problem between the fearful accountant and the analyst. The analyst's manager should have detected this and perhaps come on the scene to assist with negotiations.

The preceding situation could take place with an internal project as well—where the user and the client are two departments of a company. Expect the first reaction to any price to be negative. Plan to negotiate. Sometimes your opponent is just testing to see how convinced you are of your proposal. If you withdraw immediately, he knows you were not convinced.

Epilogue: The soft drink factory did computerize, at the price quoted by the first analyst, but not with his company.

Lost Bid

A 'famous' author of Software Project Management (For Small to Medium Sized Projects) books started his consulting career as a microcomputer teacher. He went around the microcomputer stores of his city informing the owners that he would teach anybody anything. Sure enough, he got a call one day from a government aircraft maintenance department. Their job was to track who had training on what type of aircraft across the country.

Six months beforehand a member of the department had bought an obsolete microcomputer complete with an undocumented data base program (at a fantastic price!), but he had left the department before any data base was implemented. No one in the department had any computer experience. So the teacher was hired to train the department well enough to implement the database on that computer. He obtained the appropriate information and successfully taught the people how to use the particular computer and data base program.

About a month later the teacher received a call from the head of the department asking if he could propose the cost for actually implementing their data base. The teacher interviewed the potential users of the database: there were 25 potential users with 50 differing opinions on how to use it. In addition the database program would not handle all their needs—other programs would have to be written (in BASIC). He figured it would take him three months.

The first opportunity he had to present the proposal was at a board meeting of eight department managers. All went well until he presented the price: three months programming, $400 per day, $20,000 total. The managers were aghast. They had spent only $1000 on the hardware and packaged software so far, and here was some idiot telling them it would take another $20,000 to get it going!

Comment: Users are sometimes unaware of software costs, especially in the microcomputer arena where the hardware costs are a small fraction of the total. In this instance the managers' expectations were not set properly for the price range. We will see in section 4.4 how to avoid this problem.

Epilogue: That micro is still sitting there gathering dust.

4.2 THE TWO PHASE SOFTWARE PROJECT PROPOSAL

We in the software industry have established a terrible reputation for estimating. In most environments where software is produced someone comes up with an estimate, which his manager then multiplies by three, then his manager by two and so on. These managers multiply our estimates due to their lack of confidence in us.

As discussed in Section 2.1, we cannot do a proper estimate at definition time because we do not know enough about the problem. Recall that the suggested solution to this is the two-phased proposal process: Make the analysis phase a small front project; propose to do it in an *Analysis Proposal*. After the analysis is done propose the remainder of the development in a *Development Proposal*.

There are obvious objections to this two phased approach. Your user will want to know his total cost exposure up front: he will be reluctant to pay for analysis, only to find out that he cannot afford the remainder. No one likes to fight for money twice. Nevertheless, the two phased proposal is becoming the rule rather than the exception in larger, high risk projects. The Federal Government (which is incidentally the largest victim of software estimators) will usually contract out the Analysis Phase of a large software project to several contractors, and then have one (or more) contractor build the remainder. Government departments have learned that software estimates produced at the definition phase are useless. DEC's Software Services, which is in the business of writing projects on contract, will almost always insist on the two steps.

The sections that follow will address both the analysis and the development proposals.

4.3 WRITING A PROPOSAL

Preparation

Proposal writing is difficult. It has to be done correctly, otherwise you damage your reputation and chances for any future business with your client. Writing a proposal is also expensive: it may take many resources and much of your item, and you rarely get paid for writing it. If it involves several people, treat it as a small project—assign a proposal manager, draw up a plan (use the outline below), assign responsibilities, and control the activities. If you have to produce many proposals, use a word processor and change only the items unique for each proposal, but make sure it appears custom written for every client. Work with the requirements document (RD), especially if it is a Request for a Proposal (REP). The format of the proposal should follow that of the RFP, and if the RD is on your word processor much of the wording can be reused. Leave the door open for further questions to the user as you will have many as the proposal progresses.

Here is a suggested outline for a proposal.

Proposal Outline

(Appendix A contains a full example.)

1. *Cover Letter*   A letter directed to the *decision maker,* signed by the project manager (if an account representative is the primary contact with the client he or she may sign as well). The body begins with introductory text such as, "Thank you for giving XYZ Software Co. the opportunity to propose...for your computer system."

The next paragraph gives a simple description of the system such as "...hardware and software to handle ABC's registration, finance and management information needs for the next three years."

In the subsequent paragraphs explain whether this is an analysis or a development proposal, and explain the two steps if it is analysis only. State *price and delivery* date if it is a 'fixed price' contract, cost per hour and estimated hours if it is a 'cost plus' contract. (A cost-plus contract specifies you will work X hours, and get paid by the hour, plus materials used. See Chapter 5 for the details of these contracts.)

Close the sale—end the letter with statements that force a *quick* decision *in your favor.* You do not wish to wait six months to get an answer. Closing remarks could be expiry dates for the price quoted (30 days is customary), or statements such as, "If we are given a go-ahead in 14 days we can start January 1, otherwise we must do another project, and we can only start yours on June 1." This latter closing works with internal projects as well.

2. *Title Page*   This page contains "Proposal", the title of the system, author, date, revision number, company logo, and so forth.

3. *Table of Contents*   Since the client may not be familiar with your proposal format, give a brief explanation of the purpose of each section. Here is an example of the format:

The remainder of the proposal contains the following sections:

4. *Scope*   See the paragraph above. A lot of this section comes directly from the Requirements Document.

5. *Advantages*   Sell the project team here. Prove how your well planned, well controlled, seven phased methodology will work. Address any requests in the RFP that your team is particularly adept at answering. You may even consider a few remarks about your competition's (inferior) solutions, without names of course.

6. *Financial*   State the total price and the delivery date. If hardware is included, break down the hardware and operating system price. (Your hardware vendor will gladly provide a detailed price list.) If it is a fixed price contract, quote only the final price for the custom software. Although you have by now estimated the software costs down to person-days times costs-per-day, you do not wish to divulge this calculation. As we will see in Chapter 13 (Estimating), we sometimes multiply our estimates by 'fudge factors' due to some inadequacy in the user (or ourselves!), and we do not wish to explain this. Furthermore, those estimates may be very valuable to the competition. Sometimes, though, you *have* to divulge your calculations. Government contracts, for example, usually request such data. You must supply it, but hide the fudge factors. If you are proposing a cost-plus contract, state a nonbinding estimate of hours or days required and the cost per hour or day.

State the expected delivery date (given a prompt go-ahead).

Draw a pay back graph that shows system cost, system cost savings, and the number of months or years it will take for the system to pay for itself.

List any non-monetary benefits, such as job satisfaction, good will, customer happiness, management happiness, etc.

7. *Plan*   Describe the steps you have planned to develop the project. If this is an analysis proposal, detail the reasons for using the two step method. Explain that the analysis phase produces the invaluable Functional Specification document, which will be used by the client and the project team to specify precisely what the system will do.

Describe the Project Team and the project organization. Describe the milestones, especially the ones the user will have the opportunity to review. Show how the user will be informed of project progress.

List the reponsibilities that the user will have. This may be people or materials that he must provide, or a task he must perform. He must appoint a project representative who can answer your questions. He must also provide prompt approvals to certain documents. The Proposal will be a document signed by both sides — make the responsibilities as binding as possible.

Describe the activities in the seven phases. Show that you know what you are doing (remember that this is a sales document).

8. *Deliverables*   List what the user will receive:

Hardware, operating system, packaged softwares: List in detail. State why you chose each one, its functions, capacity, and delivery times.

Custom software: "as detailed above."

Warranties: How long after delivery you intend to fix any problems, and how you will provide the support.

Documents: List the manuals (User, Operator, Manager, Maintenance) with a brief description of the purpose and the reader.

Training: List the courses (User, Operator, Manager, Maintenance) with a brief description of the purpose and the audience.

Describe the method of delivery: When you will deliver, where it will be delivered and how it will be done.

9. *Acceptance*   One of the greatest problems in the computer industry is system rejection. The user refuses to accept the system (and to pay for it) because she feels that it is not what the PT agreed to deliver up front. We must implement an acceptance method that *proves* unequivocally that the PT has met its commitment. In Chapter 8, we will discuss a very thorough acceptance method tied almost verbatim to the promises made in the functional specification (FS). In the proposal we warn the user that we will agree on (sign) the FS, we will build an acceptance test plan (also signed) based on the FS, and if the acceptance is run as prescribed in the acceptance test plan the *user must accept and pay.*

10. *Alternatives*   Sometimes you find that an RFP has been written with a certain vendor (hardware and/or software) in mind. This is fine if you are that vendor, but what do you do if you are not? You must then detail the other vendor's solution as an ALTERNATIVE SOLUTION, and prove why your solution is better.

11. *Terms, Conditions and Assumptions*   List here all conditions that you desire to work under (even for an internal project). These are here to protect you. Be especially careful about cost plus projects: you promise to deliver only the hours, not products.

List all assumptions. There will always be questions that the user was unable to answer precisely, and so assume the answers. If these assumptions affect the cost of the project you must protect yourself.

12.   *Terminology*   Even though the proposal must be written using the user's language as much as possible, some computer terms may have crept in. If you feel that these are unfamiliar to the client, define them here.

4.4 THE INFORMAL PROPOSAL

Proposals should not be made in boardrooms. They should be made informally in a telephone call, on a golf course, over coffee or beer. Recall the war story about the consultant who shocked his customer when proposing a costly system for the first time in the boardroom. This is what he should have done, and will do the next time:

After a few days of interviewing the potential users he should already have an idea of the complexity involved. He should arrange an informal meeting with the client and say, "You know, this is going to be very complex; fifty screens, 2 to 4 months of programming. By the way, did you know programming costs run around $400-$600 per hour?" The initial jolt is delivered.

Then a week later the consultant has a more accurate estimate. He calls the manager again, and informally states: "I feel this may be as much as 4 months of programming. But I would only charge $400 per hour." In other words, if you know that the news will be shocking, inform the user in slow, easy installments. He will have time to digest it, maybe even take a second look at his budget. At worst, the client will calculate that even two months at $400 is way out of line with his budget and tell the consultant to stop wasting his time on further analysis.

A formal boardroom presentation will still have to take place, but the user should already know what major items will be proposed.

4.5 INTERNAL PROPOSAL APPROVAL

There is a rule at DEC Software Services which states that no proposal may go out before it is approved by a higher level manager. The level of management approval is tied into the amount being proposed. This rule has averted countless disasters. Take, for example, a case where a PM is bidding on a rocket guidance system for the military, and he needs VP level approval. The PM may ask, "What does a VP level manager know about such a highly technical system?" Indeed the VP may know nothing about the system, but he has *worked with the military* countless times and can warn the PM of risks that may add to the price, or give advice on how to sell a project to the military. Even in small companies where few levels of management exist it is wise to show a proposal to someone else before sending it out. *Getting a second opinion is an excellent risk-reducing tool.*

4.6 PRESENTING THE PROPOSAL

Always prepare the presentation. A dry run is best. Prepare and schedule all the required resources: transparencies, projectors, screens; possibly a terminal and a modem to log into a system similar to the one you are proposing. Make the presentation in a proper room, at *your* site. At the customer site there will be more interruptions.

The order of events in the presentation should be: First, make the opening remarks. Introduce everyone, and state the purpose of the meeting. Introduce your proposal by paraphrasing the cover letter (see Section 4.3). Then distribute the proposal. Allow time for everyone to read it quickly. Then emphasize the advantages section. Lastly, close the sale: get the user to buy, and buy quickly.

Prepare for the inevitable negotiation. Have all the pertinent facts at hand. Beware of the 'hostile user'. There may be individuals on the client team who are against you. This may be due to fear or ignorance, which can easily be dealt with. The most difficult issue to deal with is the client who is convinced that your solution is wrong. The classic example is the user who has always used a certain brand of hardware, and objects to a different brand. The best defense against this person is to anticipate the objections and be prepared to answer. Typical objections may be, "Brand X is better hardware, or better support, or better reputation or will network better with our existing Brand X mainframe." Have the facts ready that disprove these arguments.

4.7 CONCLUSIONS TO PROPOSALS

Proposal writing and presenting is an art. You may be fortunate and not have to write proposals. You may be able to simply go to your managers and say, "Let's build this system; we will make money, everyone will be happy. Trust me." Most people have to convince their manager using some sort of proposal. Do not fill the proposal with extras. Emphasize quality, not quantity. Do not promise anything that was not requested by the client: who do you think will pay for this? Avoid the "We will cross that bridge when we get to it" attitude when you hit a major stumbling block. That is being dishonest with both yourself and your user. Plan a solution for all the problems. And finally, for an external project, a proposal is a legally binding document. It should be treated similarly for an inside project—with as much respect and formality as if it were an external contract.

QUESTIONS

1. What are the three purposes of a proposal?
2. What arguments would you expect from a person trying to talk you out of the two phase proposal? How would you counter these arguments?
3. Group assignment:
   Write a proposal for the 'HOUSE' project developed in the QUESTIONS in Chapter 3.
4. What is the main purpose of the informal proposal process? Can you think of any disadvantages to proposing informally?
5. What is the advantage of getting higher levels of approval for a proposal?

5

Negotiation and Contracts

The Legal Aspects

5.1 NEGOTIATION

Why is it that when people go to the marketplace in Mexico they will negotiate for hours on a price of a few dollars, but when they are dealing with a product worth hundreds of thousands of dollars they are reluctant to 'haggle'? Never be embarrassed to negotiate. Learn how to do it correctly and you will be able to use the skill in situations ranging from the world of projects to your neighborhood garage sale.

The Science and Art of Negotiating

The key to successful negotiating is knowing the facts. First and foremost, know the product you are trying to sell or buy. For example, if your management (or user) is trying to 'bargain down' your price estimate for a software project, have at hand the details of the methods and formulas that you used to calculate the price. In Chapter 13 we will discuss estimating and pricing methods, but the major point that we will learn is that you must break the project into small pieces and estimate each piece. Armed with these details, you can turn the tables on those who try to reduce your estimate by saying, "Which piece do *you* feel can be reduced?" In fact, there should be little or no haggling on an internal project. If you establish a reputation for accurate (and honest) estimates, you can stand firm on your first proposal.

   Before you embark on a negotiating session, decide two things: what you absolutely need out of the deal, and what you are willing to give up. If you are the software vendor and the item under negotiation is price, have a good idea of the minimum price you are willing to accept. If you are the buyer, know the maximum price you are willing to pay. It also helps if you know your opponent's needs as well as his flexibility.

You should also anticipate how much negotiation there will be. If you feel that the opposition will believe you without argument, prepare an accurate estimate and state it as an unnegotiable fact. This is the best way to approach a closed bid contract or Government RFP where a bid is either accepted or rejected as it stands. In a competitive situation or when management is inexperienced, negotiation will usually take place. Pad your estimate to allow for a slight reduction. Depending on your opponent, there may even be a psychological benefit in allowing him to bargain you down a little.

The Three Negotiables of a Project

The item most often negotiated is the *price*, but the project *duration* and *functions* provided can also be put on the bargaining table. As the saying goes, "You can have it cheap, fast or good: pick two." You can sometimes save money by taking a little longer. Or if the price is absolutely unacceptable, consider proposing fewer features. You can even deliver the product in releases. Release 1 contains the basic functions for a basic price, and the subsequent releases add more and more functions. This piecemeal implementation has advantages for both parties. The user does not have to exceed his present budget, and also has a margin of safety by not having to commit to the whole thing up front. The project team gets the first job, and unless they bungle it completely they will usually do the subsequent phases as well. (See Chapter 10 for programming and integrating a system that will be built piecemeal.)

You Get What You Pay For

If you are the buyer of the product, beware of bargaining the project team down too far, or accepting an unusually low bid. Imagine the following situation:

ABC company puts their software requirement out to tender. They receive two bids: The first is from Smart Software Co.(SSC). SSC has done an accurate estimate and bid a price of $200K, to be done in twelve months. The second bid is from Unscrupulous Software Co.(USC). They bid $100K, six month duration. They may be dishonest, estimating it to be $200K and twelve months, but bidding low to "get their foot in the door." Or they may be stupid and have estimated wrongly. Trying to save money, ABC of course accepts USC.

Six months later, and after payments of $100K to USC, the following scene takes place:

ABC:	The system will be delivered today, right?
USC:	Well, we have some bad news.
ABC:	What bad news?
USC:	Unfortunately, we have spent the $100K, but we have only half the system written. You have two choices: give us another $100K (maybe more,) or take your half a system.
ABC:	But we have a contract!

| USC: | I have to pay my programmers, otherwise they will leave. If you don't pay me I will declare bankruptcy. Please forward all my mail to Brazil. |

The neophyte customer can do nothing with half a system, so he has little choice but to pay the extra amount. Note that this scene could just as well have taken place on an internal project. Recall the 'estimate by edict' scenario? The dialogue went between the PM and the upper level manager (UL) like this:

PM:	We estimate this project will take $200K, 12 months.
UL:	You must do it for $100K in 6 months.
PM:	Why $100K?
UL:	That is what is in the budget.
PM:	Why six months?
UL:	That is what marketing promised to the customer.
PM:	I'll do my best.

The results will be the same. A twelve month project cannot be done in six months no matter what you do. Justify your price by demonstrating your well planned, well controlled management method. Prove that you know what you are doing. If the user is confident that she will get a quality product, she will wait patiently and pay a fair price.

5.2 CONTRACTS

The contract for the software product obliges the project team to provide certain deliverables, by a certain date, for some kind of remuneration. Unless the project is done on a very formal basis for an external organization, a special "contract" document does not need to be written. Instead, the following items are addressed in the proposal. Recall that the proposal is a signed document, and it should be treated as a formal contract. These items could appear within the text of the proposal, or better, under a topic titled "Terms and Conditions."

Items To Be Contracted

In addition to *price, delivery date* and *deliverables*, the contract can include other terms and conditions such as *non-disclosure* or *reproduction, price holding, licensing,* or *warranties*. If failure of the software can cause loss of life or other critical situations, the *liability* of the authors must be clarified. If the estimates quoted are based upon verbal input from the user, an "*escape clause*" should be included. This allows the project team to walk away in case of false information. The *user's responsibilities*, such as providing accurate and timely information, or even doing some of the work such as documentation, should be written down.

The Fixed Price (FP) Contract

This is the most common type of contract. In the FP contract the project team quotes the total price for the project up front. The PT, however, assumes most of the risks in a FP contract. What if certain items beyond their control cause the project to exceed the quoted price? Use a FP contract only if you can quantify and price in the risks. (See Section 2.5 on Risk.) A FP contract is appropriate if:

1. You are confident that no major changes will occur.
2. You are working with known software and hardware products.
3. You have good communication with your user.

In fact, the user usually prefers a FP contract. She knows her total exposure, and can budget better up front. But watch-out, the user will try to get as much for her fixed price as possible (which indeed she should!)

The Cost Plus (CP) Contract

If the risks are too high to quote a fixed price, the PT should opt for a CP contract. In a CP contract the PT gets paid a fixed amount per hour or day worked, plus expenses incurred. Usually no firm promises are made as to how long they will take. The CP contract is appropriate if:

1. You feel that major changes will occur. (The Requirements Document does not exist or the requirements are not firm or unclear.)
2. You are working with an unknown operating system, packaged software or hardware, or you will have to write special development tools, such as simulators, test beds and so forth.
3. Communication between you and the user is weak.
4. The majority of the activities are human oriented, for example, interviews. (Try to estimate the task of 'Interviewing someone until all his/her problems are written down.') This is why large software companies such as DEC will usually try to do the Definition and Analysis Phases in a separate CP contract.

Terms and Conditions

If you are on a CP contract, make sure that the terms and conditions are clear. The following is quoted from a DEC CP contract:

COST PLUS CONTRACT DISCLAIMER

[We estimate the project to take X hours. This] ...is based upon the project team's present understanding of the requirements. The project team will provide such service up to a maximum of X hours [at a cost of $Y per hour]. If additional service is required, the project team will resume work only after written authorization from the user, at which time a new estimate will be mutually determined.

Note how DEC states the extents and limits of their service in a simple paragraph.

Include all of your terms and conditions—the legal aspects of the way you want to work with the client. This provides protection to both you and the client, and avoids difficulties later. Legal items that have to be clarified up front may involve payment issues, copyrights to the sources and the documentation, liabilities, warranties, and problems with hardware and software provided by a manufacturer.

Contracts in an Outside Organization versus an Inside Organization

Contracts are widely accepted if an external organization or company is providing the project service. Why is this not so for an inside project? Even in the closest of PT and user relationships there should be some sort of formal, written agreement describing the services the PT will provide. This can be a letter of intent or a formal proposal. Write it down and you will avoid endless hassles later.

5.3 REVIEWING THE RETURNED PROPOSAL

The user may return the accepted proposal with 'minor' changes. Schedule time for the technical members of the PT to review the changes—minor 'wording' changes may mean major effort. Even the price may have to be renegotiated. Watch out for disagreements in the Terms and Conditions. Let higher level management or perhaps the legal department handle them. Do not start work until all agreements are final. I know of one project that was cancelled six months after the PT started it due to disagreement on copyrights to the software. It may even benefit you to let your user know about your terms and conditions before writing the proposal.

5.4 CONCLUSIONS TO THE DEFINITION PHASE

This brings us to the end of the definition phase. Let us review the key milestones that have been reached. Recall that these milestones were used to plan the project, and control its progress.

1. The Requirements Document is complete and agreed to by both the PT and the user. Look for a formal sign off, such as a memorandum stating acceptance.

2. A Proposal document, either for analysis or for the whole development, is completed and bought by the user. Written agreement is required.

3. Although not considered a milestone (perhaps a yardstone, or meterstone in Canada?), approval of the Preliminary Project Plan by those providing the resources is necessary.

QUESTIONS

1. What must you know before you can begin negotiating?
2. What three items can be negotiated in a software project?
3. List three major items (and as many minor items as you can) that may have to be formally and legally contracted in a software project.
4. What are the differences between fixed-price and cost-plus contracts? Describe two situations where you would use a fixed-price contract, and two where you would use a cost-plus one.
5. The client has changed something in the proposal when reviewing it. Under what circumstances should the project team review the impact of these changes?
6. What are the milestones of the Definition Phase?

6

The Analysis Phase

Detailing the Promises

6.1 INTRODUCTION

The objective of the Analysis Phase is to define exactly what the system will do for the user and how it will fit into his/her environment. The major activity (and milestone) of this phase will be to produce the document that defines the system behavior, called the *Functional Specifications* (FS). (See Figure 1.1.)

After the FS is done, you are armed with more knowledge than at the Definition Phase, so you should revisit your preliminary project plan and initial *estimate*. Statistics taken at DEC and other places show that your estimates are on the average twice as accurate after the analysis as those done before. If using the two phase proposing method, you plan and estimate the remaining phases at this point.

The third activity, writing the *development proposal*, will be done only if the two phase proposing method is used. It will be written after the FS. We will not detail how to write the development proposal. The content and outline is the same as that for the analysis proposal, except that it proposes to do the remaining five phases of the development.

Note in Figure 1.1 that one of the milestones of the Analysis Phase is the top level design (TLD). If this book were strictly theoretical, I would state, ''In the Analysis Phase you must deal only with *what* is to be done; stay away from *how* it will be done because the Design Phase will deal with that.'' But this is a practical book, so I suggest that by the time your analysis is done you must know how the system will do the *major functions.* In other words, the TLD must be done. In fact, you have already done some of the design in the Definition Phase when you wrote into the proposal the hardware and major *software* packages that would be used.

56

Having an idea of the TLD is crucial so that impossible or extremely difficult commitments are avoided. The following could be a (exaggerated!) demand of your user at analysis time: "I wish to twirl a dead chicken about my head, strike the terminal with it, and have the main menu appear." You may want to talk the user out of this on the grounds that the chosen hardware and Fourth Generation development language (part of the TLD) does not support chickens. Would he take a mouse?

Analysis War Stories

Story 1.   There once was an Arts Programming Committee whose job was to schedule and run cultural events in the theater of a large city. The Committee consisted of 27 individuals with 8 subcommittees. The individuals were not technical except for the Treasurer, who was also the Vice-President of a Famous Minicomputer Manufacturing Company (FMMC). All of the committee's income came from government and private donations, and since there was always a bit of fighting among the members, there were a lot of 'politics' involved in every aspect of this committee's business. Needless to say it was very difficult to make decisions.

A few years ago this committee decided that they should get a small computer to assist with the organizing, advertising, and accounting. The VP from the FMMC immediately recommended a computer—in fact *he gave them a computer free of charge* (good publicity, tax deductible, etc.). So the committee hired an analyst from the FMMC to help them decide how to use the computer.

The analyst began to interview the members to get the system requirements. He received a set of suggestions from the first member. The second member asked, "What are the suggestions of the first member?", then proceeded to disagree with the first member. The third one disagreed with the two previous ones, and so on. But worse than that, the previously interviewed members were constantly changing their minds! An interesting phenomenon takes place when a person goes through his or her first computer analysis discussion. He usually gets turned on to computers. After the discussions, the committe members began to read computer magazines and articles.

The poor analyst found himself barraged by requests such as, "Hey, I just read an article about a computer that could do mouses. Can yours? Yes? Then I want the function I requested last week changed to..." Four weeks and 27 interviews later only three pages of 'final' specifications were written.

Comment: In the industry this is known as "analysis paralysis." The problem is that you cannot go on to the next step, design, until the majority of the analysis is done. Although analysis paralysis is usually caused by users who cannot make up their minds, I have known analysts, managers and even programmers who delayed progress due to indecision.

Epilogue: There was some bad publicity about receiving their 'free' computer. After six months of analysis paralysis the committee realized that they were taking too long to decide. They gave the computer back. As far as I know, they are still at it...

Story 2.   This story took place in a large data processing shop that was responsible for all the programming for their company. An analyst was assigned to do the FS for a certain project. He wrote it and gave it to the user for approval. The user read the *first page*. It was full of computer jargon and technicalities that he did not understand. He filed it. There was a meeting set up for the analyst to get together with the user to explain and approve the FS, but this meeting was constantly postponed. Finally the deadline for approving the FS arrived. It was returned to the analyst with a note to the effect, ''Go ahead and build it, and we'll tell you what's wrong once we see it.'' At acceptance time the following scene took place:

ANALYST(A):	Here is your system. The first report we will demo is the ''Sales by Geography Report.''
USER(U):	This report does not give me the information I need to make a marketing decision based on geography. It is useless.
A:	What do you mean it's useless? We described this report on page 10 of the FS and you signed off!
U:	(Never having read page 10) I did not understand a word the FS said.
A:	How come you never told me that?

Comment: I feel that this problem is the analyst's fault. We will see how to better ensure that the user understands the FS.

Epilogue: The DP department had to rewrite the system.

6.2   THE YOURDON DATA-FLOW/BUBBLE CHART METHOD OF ANALYSIS

Edward Yourdon invented a graphic method for documenting and driving the analysis process that has become very popular (Reference 11). Following is an application of that method (modified somewhat) to the ABC project.

Defining the Users

The analyst, together with the user, develop a diagram such as Figure 6.1 below. They begin by listing in circles all the users that will have any interface to the system. Note that even the indirect users, such as the STUDENT, are listed. Then they draw arrows for all the inputs from and outputs to each user, marking on the arrows the information or data that is passed. Note that the arrows can represent *information flow* (STUDENT -> REGISTRAR by telephone), *data flow* (REGISTRAR -> COMPUTER via terminal) or even *physical movement* of items (WAREHOUSE -> CLASSROOM ships material). This is why the diagram is called a 'data flow' chart. Next, the analyst and the user identify the general information kept by the system (course information, student information, material information) and write it into the circle. These are not (necessarily) files, just items of information that need to be kept.

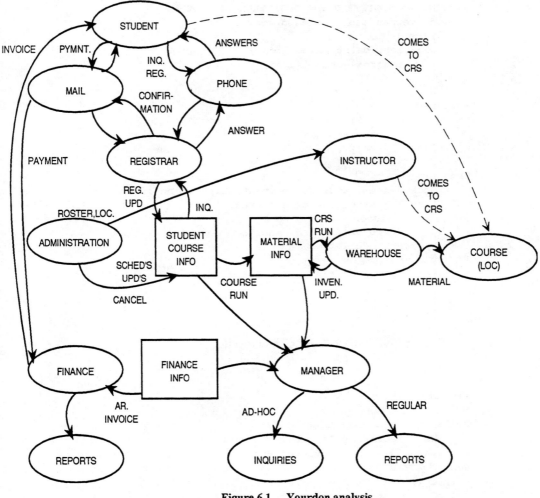

Figure 6.1   Yourdon analysis

Defining the User Interfaces

The user and the analyst detail each item represented by the arrows, which are the data flows between the users and the system. This will drive the description of all the menus, forms, reports, commands and messages—in other words the 'user interface' to the system. The purpose of this process is two-fold: first to detail the computer interfaces, and second, to gain a common understanding of the user's business. Sometimes even the user learns about her own business from this type of analysis.

For example, analysis of the STUDENT to REGISTRAR data flow may result in the following *mutually agreed upon* detail:

```
STUDENT -> REGISTRAR and REGISTRAR -> STUDENT
Method: Verbal over phone, or mailed in
Inquiries
      Location, dates of courses
      Number enrolled/maximums
      Cost
      ...
Responses
      Course locations, dates (next 6 months)
      Number enrolled (next 6 months); maximum allowed
      Cost
      ...
Changes
      Update name, address, payment information of student
      Cancel a student from a course
Register a student
      Obtain and enter name, address, course (by number)
      Payment information
Performance
      Must handle up to 3 calls per minute
```

Analysis of the REGISTRAR to ABC may result in:

```
REGISTRAR -> ABC
Method: Terminal input
Automatic registrar menu
      When registrar logs in with specific account number, menu of
the format in the Functional Specification Figure 3.9 is pre-
sented. To make a choice on this menu, the registrar can use
either the UP and DOWN arrow keys followed by RETURN, or move the
mouse up or down, followed by press on mouse button.
If student wishes information on course
      Registrar chooses 1.
      Menu of format FS Fig. 3.10 appears.
If student wishes to enroll...
```

Thus all of the possible system interfaces are addressed. The next step is to detail all the appropriate menus, forms, reports, and commands. All the menus such as the Registrar's and the Inquire on a Course must be detailed. Granted that some things cannot be made absolutely final, and changes will have to be made later. But the more detail you can agree to at this stage the more stable your project definition will be.

6.3 THE FUNCTIONAL SPECIFICATIONS (FS)

The remainder of the analysis effort will be to fill in all the detail required for the functional specifications document. The FS describes, in narrative and picture format, all system behavior. The user interfaces defined above—the menus, commands, responses, reports, and messages are detailed as much as possible. All performance requirements are addressed. Any changes in the user's environment due to the new system are explained. All the deliverables, including hardware, software, training, documentation and warranties are detailed. The FS is *what* the system will do for the user.

In addition to the proposal, the FS is also a contract between the user and the PT. Large sums of money may be at stake, and the user requires more detail about his deliverables than what was in the proposal. The FS will probably be negotiated and revised, and when agreement is reached it must be signed off by both parties.

Outline of the FS

(See Appendix A for a full example)

1. *Title Page*   Title 'Functional Specifications,' system name, author and date. Do not forget version number: this document will be revised!

2. *Table of Contents*   Section names with page numbers.

3. *System Overview*   Describe the system. Keep in mind that the FS is a technical document intended for a non-technical reader (the user). The best way to describe such a system is to use pictures. Let us take the example of the Amalgamated Basketweaving Course system described earlier. The basis of the system is data pertaining to Courses and Students. The user requires certain *inquiries* on this data, such as enrollments, course availability, schedules, accounting details and so forth. She also requires update capability, such as registration, defining a new course, cancelling a course, adding new students into the data base and so forth. She requires *reports* to be generated, such as invoicing, material order, confirmation, numbers of students enrolled by course or geography. All of these parts must interface to the user, so a mouse driven menu system is to be provided. To explain all this, you should start with the diagram as shown in Figure 6.2.

Figure 6.2 is truly worth a thousand words. The user can easily see that the five major functions to be written are INQUIRY, UPDATE, INVENTORY CONTROL, REPORT GENERATION, and *and* a mouse driven MENU interface.

4. *Major Objectives*   List the objectives of the system, relating each to the main modules. For example, INQUIRY will allow *immediate* response to questions such as ''How many students enrolled in a course.''

Describe how the new system will affect the user's environment: where terminals will be placed, who will use them, what reports will be generated, when—how all this will change each person's job. You must warn the user if this system will affect any aspect of his life. What if the system will put three clerks out of a job? Although this is not your problem, you should warn the user now.

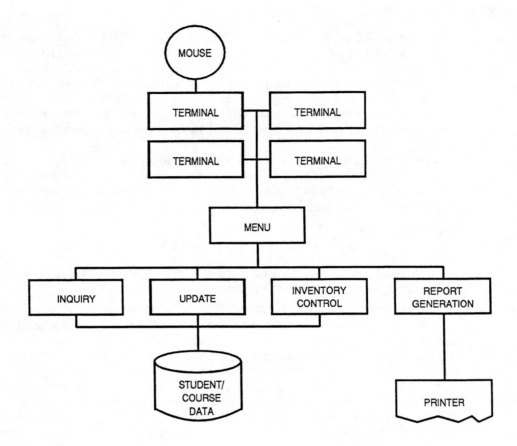

Figure 6.2   Major functions of the system

5. *Special System Requirements*   This section addresses system requirements such as networking, compatibility, security, reliability, and ease of use.

Tricky issues such as response (number of seconds it takes for the computer to 'answer,') throughput (total amount of work that goes through the computer in a period of time) and growth (requirements several years from now) can be addressed here. These issues are difficult because you cannot make ironclad promises about them, nor can you adequately test for them. For example, what if the Requirements Document contains a statement such as, "The system must respond to every input in 5 seconds." Even the fastest computer ever manufactured will under certain circumstances take longer than 5 seconds to respond to certain requests. The FS can make promises such as, "The computer will respond to 95% of the requests within 5 seconds in a 24 hour period (or the peak period of 11:00 to 12:00 AM)" or, for a critical system such as a nuclear power generator, "The crucial requests involving shutting down the reactor will be responded to within one second," or even, "The main design objective will be system response."

Similarly, do not make ironclad promises about throughput or growth. Promises *can* be made in terms of numbers of users, size of files, transactions per minute or the expansion of the hardware, but these may be difficult to prove at acceptance time. It is much too expensive to plug in all the possible expansion devices, or fill a disk full of 'garbage' data just to prove that the system will handle it.

6. *Component Descriptions* Include here a detailed description of each box, or function, shown in the system diagram in Figure 6.2. For example, when detailing the MENUS, the use of the mouse as well as a picture of all the proposed menus is shown.

For INQUIRY, all the possible inquiry types and system responses are listed. Similarly for UPDATE and REPORT GENERATION.

For INVENTORY CONTROL detail only the functions visible to the user. There is no need to detail how the system does the calculations. Do not make the FS technical —remember, the user *must understand every word*. (See Section 6.4, Technical Writing for the Non-Technical Reader.)

For the DATA kept, list only the *data elements*. For example:

> Course Data: Course title, date, number enrolled, material required, location, instructor, status (running or cancelled).

Do not describe file oriented information such as file organization, record and field—the Design will do all this. Do state limits however, such as the maximum number of courses the system will handle.

7. *Other Deliverables* **Documentation**. State the number of documents to be produced, the intended reader and use, the approximate size and table of contents if possible. For example:

The User's Guide will show all the appropriate users how to sign into the system, use their menus, do their work, respond to error situations and sign off the system. The User's Guide should serve two purposes: first, as a learning tool since all the commands will be presented in the order that the user will see them in his/her work situation. Second as a reference since at the end of the guide all the commands and messages will be presented alphabetically. The following is the Table of Contents (not final):

```
1.0    Registration
1.1    Sign into system
       ...
6.0    Warehouse
       ...
15.0   Reference of all Commands
       Indexes
```

Training. Detail the number of courses, their length, the intended students, and the skills each course will teach. List the modules or topics to be covered in each course, and the training material to be used or produced for each one. A well written User's Guide can be used as the basis for the training.

8. *Specification Changes*   Nothing kills projects as quickly as changes. The FS is a 'baseline'—subsequent items will be built based upon it. Changes to the FS may cause changes to all of these other items, which may cause expensive overruns and delivery delays. Changes must therefore be minimized. Since you cannot stop changes altogether, put in place a procedure to control the changes, to assess their impact and to receive payment for making any changes. I propose the following change control procedure:

Form a 'change control committee', consisting of at least one person from the user side (usually the user project coordinator) and one person from the PT (usually the Project Manager). Inform the user community that all changes must come to the PT through the user coordinator. Each week, or as necessary, the committee meets and all changes are presented to the PM. The user should prioritize his changes from a rating of 'critical' to 'desirable'. The PM then takes the changes to the technical members of the PT, who classify the changes as 'easy' or 'hard'. An easy change is one that can be implemented by a person in a few hours without *altering a baseline document.* (So far the only baseline we have seen is the Functional Specification. We will see one more: the Design Specification.) The PT usually implements the easy changes without further ado.

A hard change usually involves a large cost—in dollars of effort and/or project delay. The PT calculates this cost and presents it to the user, usually at the next meeting, perhaps sooner if it is a 'critical' change. The user must give written go-ahead to any change, accepting the impact of a price increase or delivery date slip.

9. *Acceptance*   As we saw earlier, one of the greatest problems in the software world is that the user is often reluctant to accept and/or pay for the system. She may feel that problems will crop up later and that the PT will not be around to fix it if she pays for it all up front. I have even heard of a case where the FS stated that the system would handle the user's growth for the next five years. The user said, ''I will pay you in five years if it still works.'' We do not buy cars on those terms. We pay for them and the problems are suppose to be fixed under warranty.

I will propose a method for acceptance that minimizes ''mistrust'' as well as any surprises, and ensures acceptance and payment. This method will be detailed in chapters 8 and 11, but it is essentially a step-by-step demonstration of all the functions that the system is supposed to do. In the proposal we outlined the general acceptance method to the user (and told her that if all the tests work she must accept and pay). In the FS we detail the acceptance method, and get sign off here as well.

10. *User and Project Team Interfaces*   The user and the project team must communicate at both technical and management levels. A technical user representative is required when the PT needs fast and accurate answers to technical questions. These questions do not stop at the Analysis Phase, but become more and more complex as the project proceeds. The user should appoint at least one person to be available to answer questions. This person must know the user's business well, and have authority to make decisions for every department that the proposed system will affect. The user and project team must communicate at management level as well. This will be done at least by the user project coordinator and the Project Manager. They will discuss issues such as budgets, schedules, major changes or people problems. This section contains the four (or more) names and the lines of communication. Note that this section, as well as several other sections in the FS just refine items in the Proposal and the RD.

11. *User's Responsibilities*   In order to save money and time, or if the user wishes to be more involved, the PT may ask him to perform project tasks such as providing test data, writing the User's Guide or even planning the acceptance test. List in this section all such activities, and the due dates. Remember that the user signs this document so he is committed to do these things.

12. *Terms, Conditions and Assumptions*   List here any new rules and regulations by which everyone is to abide. Repeat any important assumptions for protection.

6.4 TECHNICAL WRITING FOR THE NON-TECHNICAL READER

The FS is extremely difficult to write well. Since it describes a technical system it is a technical document, but it is written for a non-technical reader. In addition, the *bonus of ensuring that the user understands it is on the analyst.* How can you ensure this?

Write from the user's point of view—use his terminology. You must therefore learn the user's business and language. Use simple subject-verb-object constructions: "You do this, the system does that." Use diagrams wherever possible.

One of the greatest reasons for misunderstanding a document is that the words are ambiguous. Avoid mamby-pamby words such as "can be, could, usually, probably, most, etc." It is tempting to make no commitment, but remember that if you use the word "some" and mean "minimum," the user will assume "maximum." Similarly, avoid implied commitments that are difficult or impossible to prove. Words such as "any, all, every", superlatives (words ending in "est") may cause problems later. For each promise you make in the FS, ask yourself, "How am I going to prove it?"

6.5 OTHER USES FOR THE FUNCTIONAL SPECIFICATION

A good FS can be used to introduce new members of the PT to the project. The user can use it to introduce the new system to his or her management, or to other interested parties. But most important, the sections describing the menus, forms, queries and reports can be used in the User's Guide. If you intend to use these parts of the FS in the User's Guide, write everything in the present tense. It is tempting to write in the future tense. Writing "When the user will type 'X' the following menu will appear (we hope)..." leaves you an escape route. But be brave, use the present tense and you will be able to use these sections of the FS *verbatim* in the User's Guide.

6.6 CASE SOFTWARE TOOLS FOR ANALYSIS

Computer Aided Software Engineering (CASE) is using a set of software tools in each phase of the system life cycle. These tools should allow you to produce the required documents, as well as computer readable products that can be used as input to the CASE tools of the following phases.

A word processor is all the software that you need to do the Definition Phase. There are several excellent software products available to help you do analysis. The examples presented here are based on a personal computer product called Excelerator (Reference 2.2). This product, introduced in 1984, has become the most popular analysis tool in the industry. Excelerator can be used to draw the high level data flow diagrams as in Figure 6.2, then to 'blow up' the DFD's into lower and lower levels of detail.

The parameters among the diagrams can be detailed, and Excelerator ensures consistency—all parameters passed and received among diagrams must have the same attributes, and the parameters used by a diagram at a lower level must be the same as the corresponding parameters at the higher levels.

Analysis tools provide menu, screen and report painting facilities to help describe the user interfaces to the system. In Chapter 15 we will see how this can be used to prototype a system. Input and output screen forms can be painted using mouse input. Similarly, reports and on-line queries can be quickly mocked up (Figure 6.3).

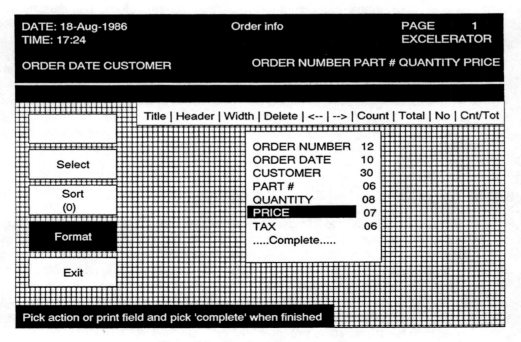

Figure 6.3   Excelerator report mock-up

And the icing on the cake is that these products can then print out all the menus, screens, forms, and reports. This is most of the Functional Specification! Excelerator even has a word processor built in which can be used to produce all the other required documentation, index them, and so forth.

These tools are truly CASE tools because they integrate into other tools used in subsequent phases. For example, design tools can use the analysis DFD's to draw the design structure diagrams (or at least ensure that all the analysis DFD items are designed), and again ensure that all the defined parameters remain consistent.

Tools such as Excelerator can keep track of all the records and fields defined in your forms and reports and store these in a Data Dictionary (DD). This is how the tool ensures consistency in the Definition Phase, and assists in the design of data and files in the Design Phase.

On mini computers, tools such as DECDESIGN support the Analysis Phase by drawing data flow or entity relationship diagrams, as well as the Design Phase by drawing structure charts and state transition diagrams. Context checking is handled through the data dictionary. All of these tools are mouse and window graphics driven.

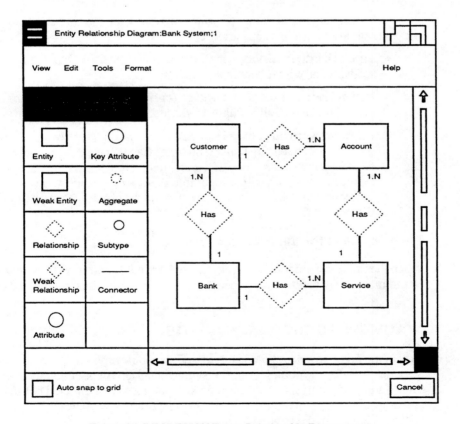

Figure 6.4 DECDESIGN Entity Relationship Diagrammer

6.7 REVISING THE PLAN

Planning is an iterative process. Revise the preliminary project plan (PPP) right after analysis. Remember, weeks, possibly months have passed since you wrote the first plan and much has been learned in this period. Re-assess the work breakdown. Are the tasks still able to be estimated, assigned, scheduled and completed? Most important, ask if the resources assumed for each task are still available when needed. This is an excellent time to do contingency planning. For each resource needed ask, ''What if it is late or unavailable?'' Suggest alternative plans. The following is a short list of problems that can occur in the next three phases (Design, Programming, System Test) along with suggested contingency plans:

- A key programmer or designer leaves. Can you train a backup? IBM has successfully used a *buddy system* where a programmer is assigned as a buddy to a key 'guru' programmer. The buddy's job is esentially to 'carry the water' for the guru, but also to learn enough from him to be able to take over in case he leaves.

- The development computer is unavailable. Can you find another in the building/city to use, perhaps after regular hours?

- Special hardware device does not materialize on time. Can you simulate it with software, or with a Personal Computer?

- New release of a software package (or hardware) does not work. Can you use the old release? Call it Phase 1; Phase 2 comes out when it all works.

- A resource provided by a third party does not materialize. Can you exercise some control to ensure that it is on time? Can you negotiate penalty clauses, get on their board of directors? If it is an internal project and the third parties do not report to you, can you get input into their performance reviews? Can you get someone who has authority over them on the project Steering Committee (see Chapter 21)?

Training Plans for the Project Members

When the final staff is decided, check to see who needs training. Your programmers will be the most likely candidates. Schedule all training to be done by the end of Design.

6.8 CONCLUSIONS TO THE ANALYSIS PHASE

Expect the FS to be renegotiated and revised; schedule time for approvals and revision. Set a deadline for the completion. If disagreements among individuals or departments cause 'analysis paralysis,' get everyone into one room and threaten not to adjourn the meeting until the issues are resolved. And last, let us review the major milestones achieved in the Analysis phase:

1. The Functional Specification was agreed to and signed off by both parties.

2. If the two step proposal was used, the Development Proposal was written and bought by the user.

3. The Preliminary Project Plan was revised to include new estimates and schedules; resources are still committed for all activities.

4. The Top Level Design was done. It may not be obvious, but you have done a TLD when you thought up and drew Figure 6.1. It may not be the best TLD, nor the final one that will be used, but it is a first stab at how the system will work and the major pieces that will have to be produced.

QUESTIONS

1. Why is the Analysis Phase the most important phase in the user's eyes?
2. Draw the analysis data flow diagram for the 'Bell Family Communications' (BFC) system.
3. Group Exercise.
    Write the Functional Specification for the BFC system.
4. What are some methods to ensure that the user will understand the Project Team's technical documents? Ensure that the FS produced in Question three meets these criteria.
5. What functions should a good CASE tool provide for analysis?
6. Why should you review the Preliminary Project Plan after the analysis is done?
7. What milestones are achieved in the Analysis Phase?

7

The Design Phase

How It All Works

7.1 INTRODUCTION

For those readers who are technically inclined and who have been less than enthusiastic about all the 'planning' activities discussed previously, we have finally arrived at one of the most fascinating technical activities—system design. We can get down to solving the real problems with real solutions.

The major activity of the Design Phase is creating the top and medium levels of the system design and documenting it in the Design Specification. The second activity in this phase will be starting the Acceptance Test Plan (ATP). The ATP is a document listing the tests that will be used to demonstrate all the system functions to the user in the Acceptance Phase.

A major milestone is reached when the Design Specification is walked through (reviewed) and declared error-free. A minor milestone is the user sign off of the ATP, although this may not occur until later.

Note the levels of effort in Figure 1.1. The manager's effort diminishes, but total effort and therefore cost increases since several designers and walk-through personnel are involved.

Designing a software system consists of two major steps: First, you divide the system into its functional components, and second, interconnect these components. There are many design methods published. Some of the better known are Warnier (Reference 6), Orr (Reference 7), Nassi-Shneiderman (Reference 9), and lately Object Oriented Design is becoming popular (Reference 8). Note that Reference 10 is a paper titled ''A Survey of Software Design Techniques.'' We will not detail any specific *design* method in this chapter except for the simple, hierarchical functional breakout. It does not really matter which method you use, as long as you *make one method the standard for everyone.* We will, however, focus on how to do file design because the way you do input and output will impact your system performance drastically.

Those who are not at all technical may find this chapter a little too involved. If you are strictly on the management side and have good designers working for you skip this chapter. If, however, you wish to know how they do their jobs, or you are a technical manager who has to know about everything related to the project (not uncommon for a small to mid-sized project) read on. In any case read the War Stories (these are amusing) and the conclusion.

Design War Story

This story involves two young men who who became good friends while taking a Computer Science degree at a well known university in Ontario, Canada. After graduation one became Data Processing Manager for a famous publishing company, the other became a System Designer for a Famous Minicomputer Manufacturing Company (FMMC). A few years ago the publishing company decided to install a new computerized order processing system. The DP Manager could not handle the work load alone, so he hired his friend from FMMC to help do the design and programming.

I am not certain of the exact details of this story, but I assume the following occurred: After they did the top level design together, they divided up the major modules, each one doing the medium level design of specific modules. The Designer from FMMC designed the first module. Wishing to show off his design talents to his friend the DP Manager, he made the design very 'elegant' to save a few bytes of storage or a few nanoseconds of CPU time. He even added a few 'esoteric' features: the ones that no one requests or understands or ever uses.

The DP manager was responsible for designing the second module. When he saw his friend's wonderful design he probably thought, "I can do better than that!" So he made his module a little more elegant than his friend's, and added a few 'bells and whistles' of his own. He took longer than scheduled and the module was bigger than planned. The Designer, accepting the challenge, made the third module even more 'perfect,' adding more bells and whistles until the module became twice as large as it should have been. And the race continued through the Design as well as the Programming Phases.

The system was supposed to handle 16 users. When the system was finally turned on (50% late!) it worked well for up to 4 users. When six users signed on it became *very slow.* With eight users on, it crashed—the programs were so large that the operating system was unable to handle them.

Comment: Technical people can get carried away by the technical challenge. There is always a better way to solve the problem, but the foremost challenge must be to meet the goals of time and budget.

Epilogue: FMMC gave the user a larger CPU at no cost.

7.2 STRUCTURED DESIGN

The major goal of structured design is to break the system into small, manageable, buildable pieces. Several excellent methods have been documented to do this (References 10, 11). The approach we will take is more basic than those methods: we will simply break the system into smaller and smaller functional components until it is broken down enough for the programmers to code.

Top Down Design

Top down design begins with the top level design (TLD) such as the one developed for the ABC system during the Analysis Phase (Section 6.3), reproduced here as Figure 7.1.

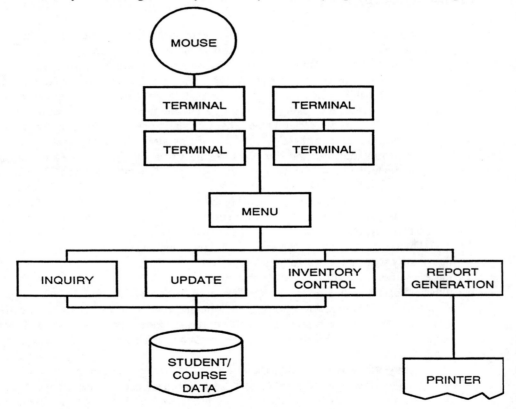

Figure 7.1   Top level design

Each major component, or box in the TLD is then broken down into sub-pieces, starting with the top most level, working *down* to the next level and so on. In our case we would start with the MENU and design it before going down to INQUIRY, UPDATE and REPORT GENERATION which would be followed by further levels, if any.

Bottom Up Design

In certain cases it may be easier to approach the design from the bottom level upward. This is often the case in process control systems where the hardware device controllers at the bottom levels determine how the system is put together. For example, let us design an automobile engine test system. We must begin with the basic hardware involved— the sensors on the engine (Figure 7.2A).

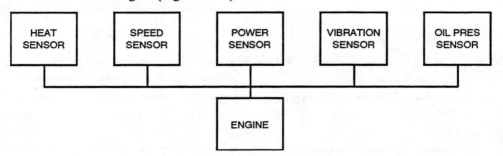

Figure 7.2A   Bottom up design

The sensors are usually attached to special analog-to-digital devices, which are attached to unique device driver software modules (Figure 7.2B).

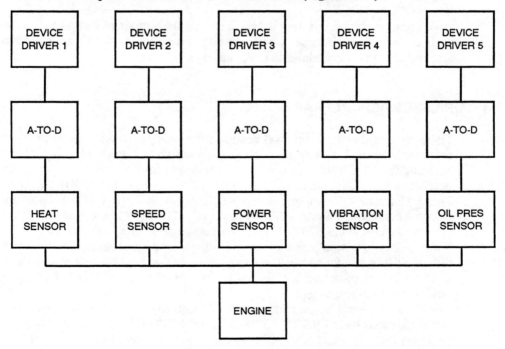

Figure 7 .2B   Bottom up design (continued)

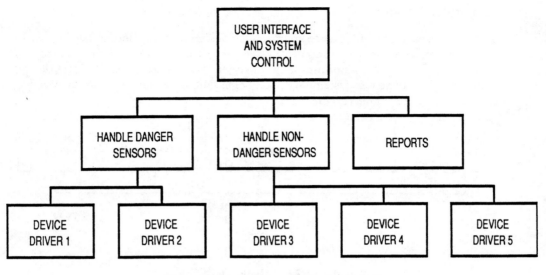

Figure 7.2C   Bottom up design (continued)

The software to control the device drivers is then designed 'on top' of the these drivers (Figure 7.2C).

Thus the software system is designed from the bottom levels upward. Bottom up design is also better in cases where existing software components are combined and assembled with new modules to make up a system.

7.3 TOP LEVEL DESIGN TRADE-OFFS

There are usually many top level designs that could accomplish the same things in a software system. For example, the top level design in Figure 7.1 is just one way of breaking the ABC system into major components. Another method could be to use a purchased Data Base Management System (for example DATARIEVE, SQL, or a Fourth Generation Language) to replace the INQUIRY and UPDATE portions, or a Forms Management System (FMS) to do the MENU, perhaps a Report Generation system (RPG) for the REPORTing, or a combination of the above. This is a typical 'build or buy' decision, and there are advantages and disadvantages to each combination of built or bought items. The more packages you buy, the less programming you have to do; but packages are expensive, and usually less efficient than the custom written program equivalent.

Other top level designs may suit as well. One suggestion may be to remove the file access portions of INQUIRY, UPDATE, and REPORT GENERATION and have a common FILE HANDLER routine to do all file accesses. The TLD would look like Figure 7.3.

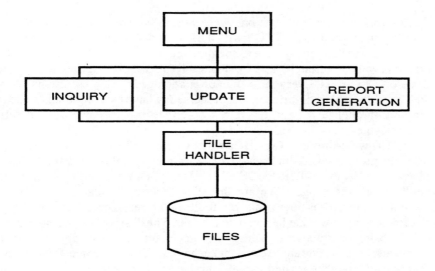

Figure 7.3 (Another) Top level design

Here five programs would have to be written, and slight performance degradation may appear due to the frequent calls to the FILE HANDLER, but the system would be smaller. Each choice of TLD has advantages and disadvantages and involves trade-offs and compromises.

Design Priorities

Your choice of TLD will affect the following:

> System Cost
> Time to Build the System
> User Friendliness
> Performance
> System Size
> Reliability
> Modifiability

These items must therefore be prioritized, *together with the user* at system planning time-during definition and analysis. This makes the choice of TLD much easier.

7.4 DESIGN WALK-THROUGHS

When deciding among several technical approaches to a problem, make the decision easier by asking the opinion of others. Call a meeting of several experts to do a top level *design walk-through.* At least one week before the walk-through give the attendees copies of the FS and all the TLD's with the list of advantages and disadvantages for each one. Tell them that the purpose of the meeting is to choose the best TLD. This will be done by 'walking through', step by step, each suggested design, ensuring that the list of trade-offs is correct. Everyone should be encouraged to suggest alternative designs, as well as additional trade-offs that the authors may have overlooked. Let each person on the walk-through team know that they are—as a team—responsible for determining the best design.

TLD walk-throughs (and later when we discuss lower level design, documentation and program walk-throughs) can be extremely valuable if the following rule is obeyed: "LEAVE YOUR EGOS OUTSIDE." (This was the sign on the door of the studio when the songs "We are the World" and "Tears are not Enough" were recorded.) The idea is not to point out faults in the designer, nor is it an opportunity for the attendee to prove that he could do it better. The designer must also be aware that all criticism is constructive—he must not get defensive. The objective is to find all problems, suggest alternatives and make the best possible choice. Some people suggest that managers not be invited to walk-throughs. Managers can inhibit the free flow of ideas and discussions.

7.5 MEDIUM LEVEL DESIGN

After the TLD is chosen, you must break each major function or component down to the sub-functions or components. Let us see how this could be done for the Amalgamated Basketweaving Company system. Begin by assigning a number to each major component on the TLD.

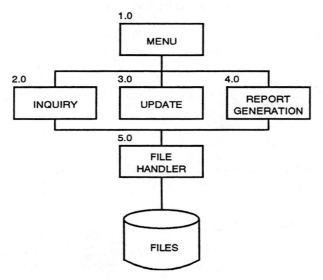

Figure 7.4   Numbering system for the TLD

Top down design dictated that the break down must begin with the MENU box. Let us assume that this component is called when the whole system is started and it presents the following 'main' menu to the registrar.

```
MAIN MENU

1. INQUIRE ON A COURSE/STUDENT
2. UPDATE COURSE/STUDENT DATA
3. REGISTER STUDENT
4. WAREHOUSE
5. REPORTS
6. QUIT


USE UP/DOWN ARROW TO HILITE  YOUR CHOICE THEN
PRESS RETURN,
OR MOVE MOUSE TO HILITE YOUR CHOICE, THEN PUSH
BUTTON ON MOUSE
PRESS HELP KEY TO GET HELP ON HILITED ITEM
```

Then the program waits for the user to move the mouse. The major sub-functions of the MENU component can be:

1. Start the system up and present the main menu.
2. Handle movement of the mouse.
3. Handle the button on the mouse.
4. Go to INQUIRE, UPDATE, WAREHOUSE or REPORT when chosen.
5. Handle errors as well as on-line help messages for the whole system.
6. Shut down system if QUIT is chosen.

The next level of breakout diagram (or *structure diagram*) for the MENUcomponent could look like this:

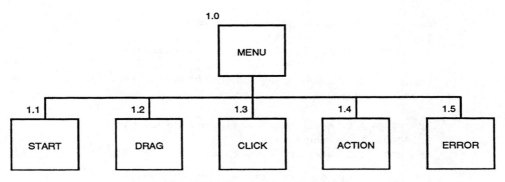

Figure 7.5   Second level of breakout

The third level of breakout can be seen in Appendix A—Design Specification. You may consider breaking it down even further. Remember, you go down to a level from which the programmers can start module breakdown and programming. The lowest level boxes represent modules. A module is the smallest testable, compilable piece. See Section 7.7 for what constitutes a good module.

Note that on the structure diagrams (Appendix A) we can show control flow: solid lines show module calls. We can also show data flows: the dotted arrows show the parameters passed. The direction of the arrow shows the direction of the data movement.

Naming Conventions

Modules are named to indicate system, function, or subfunction as necessary (See Appendix A, Design Specification, Section 6 for the ABC system module naming). For languages where more characters are permitted, establish a detailed naming system that clearly indicates the function of both modules and variables. Do not try to save paper by shortening names to obscure acronyms.

Numbering Conventions

The number on each box is constructed as follows: On each lower level add a dot plus an integer to the number of the box above. The integer can be sequenced left to right. The number shows the path down the break out tree, as well as the level at which the box is found.

7.6 DESIGN DICTIONARIES

Module Dictionaries

As you progress through the design, build the following three dictionaries:

Dictionary 1. Numerically ordered by component number, gives the routine name and a short description for every module. For example:

```
0.0   A0000000   Amalgamated Basketweaving System
1.0   AM000000   Menu system
1.1   AMST0000   Startup, disp first menu, shutdown etc.
```

Dictionary 2. Alphabetically ordered by component name, gives the routine number and a short description for every module. For example:

```
A0000000   0.0   Amalgamated Basketweaving System
AM000000   1.0   Menu system
AMST0000   1.1   Startup, disp first menu, shutdown
```

This can easily be created from Dictionary 1 using a sort program.

Dictionary 3. Alphabetically ordered by the short description, gives component number and the routine name. For example:

```
Amalgamated Basketweaving System    0.0  A0000000
Menu system                         1.0  AM000000
Startup, disp first menu, shutdown  1.1  AMST0000
```

This can also be created from Dictionary 1 using a sort program. You can use these dictionaries during design, programming, or subsequent testing and maintenance—anytime you need to find a module, its calls or its parameters.

The (Common) Data Dictionary (CDD)

List in alphabetical order all the parameters that are shown on the data flow arrows. For each item list the type, length, restrictions and the modules that use it. This CDD will later contain all other parameters defined in lower levels of design and programming, as well as the fields defined in files. The CDD ensures that the parameters will be consistent throughout the whole system. Some operating systems such as VAX VMS provide a Common Data Dictionary.

7.7 STRUCTURED MODULES, OR HOW FAR DO YOU BREAK IT UP?

How do you know if a box at the bottom level is broken down far enough—or if you have broken it too far? A box at the bottom must represent a *structured module.* It will be coded into a program or sub-program module. A structured module has the following properties:

1. It performs a single function completely. For example, it could receive, edit, reformat, and pass on a single parameter.

2. It is small. Some rules of thumb for size state 50 to 100 lines of executable code, or at most 2 pages of listing.

3. It is predictable. All behavior is visible from reading the code. It is not affected by hidden flags in other modules or in the operating system.

4. (Most important!) It is independent. A change in the module or in the parameters that it uses does not affect anything else in the system. For example, the US Postal Service is changing (1988) the ZIP code from five to nine digits. Imagine all the programmers that will be employed for years accommodating systems to this change! Perfect module independence would allow a programmer to make a change in one module that handles the ZIP code, and no other part of the system will be affected. Or how about changing only the Data Dictionary?

5. Although this is not in the strict definition of a structured module, look for reusability—a module that is complete enough and general enough so that

you can use it in other applications with as little modification as possible. For further detail on modularity read the original article in Reference 20.

Leave Something for the Programmer

If you break the modules down further and further, eventually *you will end up describing the program code in English.* Programmers do not enjoy translating this 'pseudo-code' line for line, into program lines. That is boring. Leave several levels of breakout for the programmer. See Section 9.3 for details of this process, called Module Design.

7.8 FILE DESIGN

Getting Real Performance

The design of the files will make or break your application. This is especially true when using Fourth Generation Languages (see Chapter 16). Some designers even advocate designing the files before anything else. Let us design the ABC file system using an indexed sequential file system such as IBM's ISAM or DEC's RMS. You begin file design by looking at the results of the Analysis Phase, the requirements and the top levels of design produced so far. I recommend going back to the data flow diagram (Figure 6.1,) and drawing all the 'information types' that are mentioned. The result of this would be the boxed items in Figure 7.6.

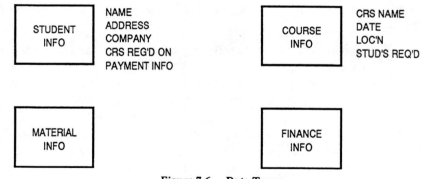

Figure 7.6   Data Types

Now go to the detailed requirements (see Requirements Document in Appendix A) and try to allocate each data item mentioned (or implied) in a requirement to one of the boxes. Add more boxes if necessary. For example, the requirement "Register a student on a specific course" would result in adding the fields listed beside each box in Figure 7.6. Next, consider the processing logic needed to handle the requirement. If the STUDENT INFO and the COURSE INFO are separate files, they would need to be related by a key. Add the keys STUD_NO and CRS_NO, and the access logic can be added as arrows, as in Figure 7.7.

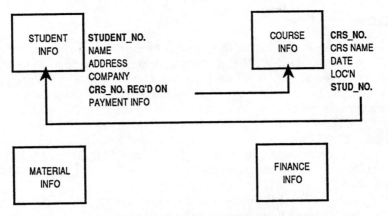

Figure 7.7   Data types, keys, and access

Now we can handle registering a student, as well as inquiries such as, "Given a student name, find all the courses he is registered in." (Access STUDENT FILE by name, get CRS_NO, access COURSE FILE by that CRS_NO.) The diagram is continued until all the requirements are handled. The result could be Figure 7.8. (For the sake of clarity the arrows are not shown.)

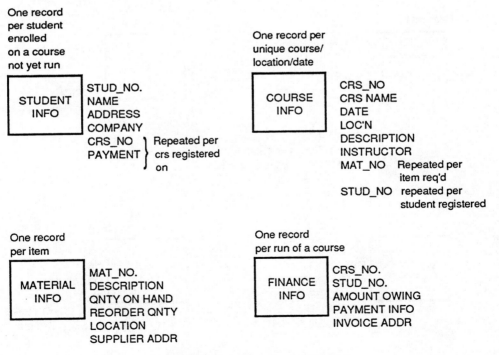

Figure 7.8   Data types, key, and access

Optimizing Files

The next step is optimizing disk storage by eliminating redundant fields and files.

In the STUDENT FILE, if many students have the same address, such as the same company, the address fields are repeated. Consider an ADDRESS file with one record per company, and a COMPANY_NO on the student record pointing to it. This file could also contain the invoice addresses needed by the FINANCE FILE.

In the COURSE FILE items such as DESCRIPTION, INSTRUCTOR, and MATERIAL NO list would be constantly repeated since they are the same for each run of the same course. Split off into a new file called SCHEDULE FILE the items unique to each run of a course, leaving COURSE FILE with only course type dependent information.

FINANCE FILE can only be keyed by STUD_NO or COURSE_NO. There are already files using those keys, which usually indicates that the fields in this file could just as well be combined into other files, if payment and invoicing information can be associated with the student. The FINANCE FILE will not be needed. The resultant file design could be as in Figure 7.9.

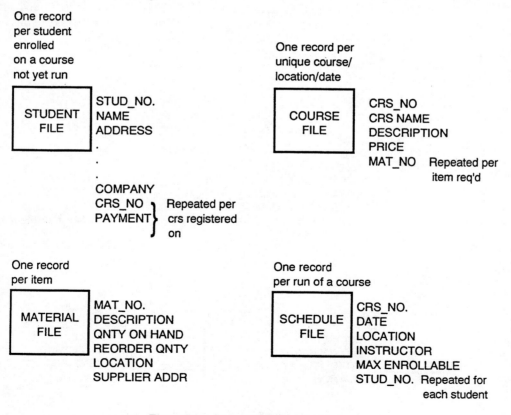

Figure 7.9   Data types, keys, and access

Optimizing a Variable Number of Items

In the STUDENT FILE there are two fields, CRS_NO and PYMNT information, that are repeated for each course in which a student enrolls. Similarly there are repeated fields in the SCHEDULE and COURSE files. These can be programmed using variable length files. As items are added or deleted the length of the record changes accordingly. This method saves disk space.

Alternatively, if the maximum number of the variables is known, a fixed length record can be used. For example, if no more than 30 students will ever be enrolled in any course, each record in SCHEDULE leaves room for 30 students. This method uses more disk space than the previous one, but it will require less processing time. Futhermore, fixed length records are easier to design, understand, and therefore maintain than variable length records. Disk space is getting so inexpensive that I suggest that you use fixed length records whenever possible.

A problem may arise if the limits cannot be set: for example, why should the number of students in any course be limited to the same number? To solve this, a separate file can be used to hold only the variable information. A file called ENROLL-MENT can be set up for each run of a course, and each file would contain one record per enrolled student (Figure 7.10). This may be very expensive both in disk storage and file handling.

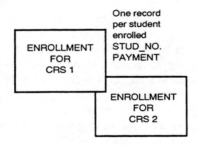

Figure 7.10   Handling variable information

A simple way to handle this would be to make a file called ENROLLMENTS, which would contain one record per student registered per course. The fields would be only the STUDENT_NO and COURSE_NO. (Question 8 at the end of this chapter asks you to design this.)

History Files

What do we do about data on students who have taken a course? Neither the accountants nor the marketing people wish this information to be erased, but we do not want working files to be cluttered by obsolete information.   The solution is to define a STUDENT_HISTORY file, and after a student takes a course his record from the STUDENT file is transferred to the History file.

Testing the File Design

In a design walk–through, each requirement that involves data access must be 'processed' using the file design. This may indicate improvements as well. For example, a requirement states, "List all occurrances of an XYZ course, location and price." Let's go through the access logic. The Registrar converts the course name to CRS_NO (how??). The records in SCHEDULE are accessed by CRS_NO to give the date and location of each course, and the COURSE file is accessed by CRS_NO for price. If this kind of request is common, perhaps the course name should be made a key on the SCHEDULE file. Maybe the price can be added to the SCHEDULE file to save accessing the COURSE file each time. To save disk space a price code could be used.

Ensure that all requirements are feasible. Look for possible future enhancements, even if the user did not request it. For example, how would you process a request such as, "List all courses that use material X," or "Handle a price increase six months from now by charging one price up to that date, and the new price afterwards." We do not fix the problems in the walk-through. Someone is asked to take notes and the problems are addressed later.

7.9 RELATIONAL DATA BASE MANAGEMENT SYSTEM (RDBMS)

In Section 7.8 we assumed that you can get a record from a file given a key. In reality, there must be a DBMS to accomplish this. Most mini and mainframe manufacturers include a DBMS with their operating system. RMS and RDB are common for VMS. The examples used in Section 7.8 made use of an indexed DMBS such as RMS. As a manager you need not understand how a DBMS works, but you may have to decide which one to use. Let me make a case here for the relational system.

Relational data organization is extremely simple to understand and to set up (one of the pros). In an RDB every item is expressed as part of a table or relation. The rows of the tables (tuples) can be compared to records, the columns (domains) to fields. The rules for setting up the tables is that each tuple in one table must be unique, and no field needs to be repeated in any of the tables unless they are needed to 'join' one table to another. Joining means looking up a record in one relation by a field found in another. Figure 7.11 is an example of the relations (tables) that could be defined for the ABC system. Note how close this is to the file design of Figure 7.9 and Question 8. The file names became relation names, the records and fields became rows and columns. In fact entering the tables such as in Figure 7.11 is all that is required to create the data base.

```
Student relations:
Stud-No      Stud-Name    Company-No  all items unique to student
1            JOHN BLAKE   999
2            JANE SMITH   999
.
```

```
Run of a course relations:
Course-No     Course-Date     Location      Instructor    Cost
123           1/1/90          OTTAWA        RAKOS         1000
123           1/2/90          NEW YORK      RAKOS         1500

Enrollment relations:
Course-No     Stud-No     Pymnt
123           1           0

Course relations:
Course-No     Crs-Name     Desc     Mat-No     items unique to a course
123           WEAVING      INTRO    001

Company relations:
Comp-No     Addr          Ship-To      Bill-To      Tot-Owing
999         FIRST ST.     X Y          A B          10000

Material relations:
Mat No     Desc      Whse     Source     Cost
001        STRAW     1-1      X Co       1.00
```

Figure 7.11   Relations in the ABC relational data base

As in the nonrelational method, the DBMS will retrieve a field given other fields. For example, if you require a list of students on COURSE_NO '123,' the relational system will search ENROLLMENT for the course number, build a table of the associated STUD_NOs, then search STUDENT by the STUD_NOs to build the table of STUD NAMEs. The beauty of the RDBMS is that this may be done for you automatically. It is wise, however, to set up the relations knowing the requirements ahead of time because there is a lot of overhead associated with constantly creating tables.

The format for this kind of ad-hoc data base query has actually been standardized, and it is called Structured Query Language(SQL). Most relational data base products have SQL built in. Oracle (Reference 2.6) is the most well known product for this. For example, the following will instruct SQL to list what courses 'Smith' is registered on.

```
SELECT CRS-NAME FROM COURSE
WHERE COURSE-NO IN
      SELECT COURSE-NO FROM ENROLLMENT
      WHERE STUD-NO IN
          SELECT STUD-NO FROM STUDENT
          WHERE STUD-NAME = 'Smith'
```

Unfortunately, SQL as originally defined by IBM has many shortcomings so the newer products have to extend the language to provide additional features. You could simply ask a lot of new 4GL's (that support Query By Example[QBE]) to fill in the following form:

```
STUD_NAME  =  Smith
CRS_NAME   =  _____
              _____
              _____
              _____

                        "

                        "
```

The major advantage of an RDBMS is flexibility. For example, if you need to access the same data differently from several applications, the system will accommodate. If you anticipate ad-hoc queries, (and it is difficult to foresee the exact format), RDBMS is the best tool to use. In Section 16.6 on Computer Aided Software Engineering, we discuss using a Fourth Generation Language together with an RDBMS to automate almost all of the classical computer applications!

The only drawback of an RDB is performance. There is a lot of space and time required for storing, tracking, and traversing through all the tables. But computer cycles are getting cheaper—the time saved in user friendliness and flexibility makes an RDBMS on a powerful CPU a worthwhile investment.

7.10 BENEFITS OF STRUCTURED ANALYSIS AND DESIGN

Reducing the Number of Initial Errors

The following statistics are quoted from surveys done by TRW for large projects, and DEC's Customer Services Systems Engineering (the department responsible for ensuring that DEC products—both software and hardware—are as bug free as possible).

USING UNSTRUCTURED METHODS

	ANALYSIS AND DESIGN	REMAINING PHASE	AFTER OPER.
EFFORT SPENT:	10%	23%	67%
PROBLEMS INTRODUCED:	64%	36%	
PROBLEMS FOUND:	19%	27%	54%
DOLLARS SPENT(AVG) (TOTAL=250K)	25K	57.5K	167.5K

USING STRUCTURED METHODS

	ANALYSIS AND DESIGN	REMAINING PHASE	AFTER OPER.
EFFORT SPENT:	20%	50%	30%
PROBLEMS INTRODUCED:	32%	68%	
PROBLEMS FOUND (1):	30%	33%	37%
DOLLARS SPENT(AVG) (TOTAL=190K)	40K	50K	100K

(1) There were half as many as before

Figure 7.12   Causes and costs of problems

Figure 7.12 proves that *even though the up front cost increases,* structured methods reduce the overall cost of a system. There are other benefits to finding errors up front instead of later on in the cycle. Statistics have shown that it is up to 100 times as expensive to correct an analysis error after acceptance than at analysis time.

7.11 THE DESIGN PROCESS

The Design Team

Choose your best people for the design team. The best designers are *not necessarily your best 'bits and bytes' people*. They are the people who can conceptualize the whole thing. Avoid a perfectionist on the design team. There is always a better way to do it given enough time—but the limits of time and cost must always be kept in mind. Since many trade-offs and decisions are made during the design, it is best to have an odd number of people on the team, or at least a good moderator.

The Design Meeting

Designing is like brainstorming: several people get together in an undisturbed, quiet room. Everyone is encouraged to 'burst out' their ideas for all the functions to be performed and how to perform them. Since the ideas will flow in random order, provide a facility to capture the ideas. Write down each idea, and at the end organize all the ideas and suggestions into unique modules.

7.12 TECHNICAL DOCUMENTATION

The design specification is a very technical document. It is intended to be read and understood by the programmers. The user is welcome to see it but you need not ensure that he understands it. Consider the following points when writing technical documents:

1. Use formal, precise language. The second largest source of errors in a software system is when the programmer misinterprets the design. (The largest source, incidentally, is when the analyst misinterprets the user's needs.) Read a law text. It is not gobbledegook. Lawyers try to use language that can not be misinterpreted.

2. Use pictures—structured diagrams and such.

3. Make the intent of the design clear on the first few pages. Then elaborate.

4. Be consistent in the graphics language and sentence structure. It is best when one person writes all of it. If deadlines force you to use several people, be sure that they use a common style.

7.13 STANDARDS 'DICTATED' AT DESIGN TIME

Certain things must be done the same way no matter who does it. This is especially true in the programming phase where the most parallelism can take place. You may get frowns for imposing 'bureaucratic' standards but establish rules for the following:

- *Design Conventions.* Methods of break-down, structure diagram formats. Module and variable naming conventions. This must be used for all the lower levels.

- *Parameter passing.* Detail order, length, format, place holder if missing and so forth.

- *Error handling.* Strictly structured standards suggest that a single error handler be used. Every module passes context (situation where the error occurred) and an error number to this handler. The handler displays the error message. This guarantees consistent error handling, but the performance may suffer due to all the additional calls to the error handler.

- *Programming standards.* Structured programming standards such as code appearance (white space, indenting, comments), constructs allowed, organization, module size, and interdependence is detailed. Create a 'template' or skeleton containing comment lines for the following:

  header (title, author, purpose, date, modification history)

  parameters (received, sent)

  entry (one only)

  variables used

  subroutine calls

  error handling

  exit (one only)

- The programmer starts with this template and fills in the process code. SeeSection 9.4 for programming tools that help format programs consistently.

If you set these standards well you will be able to use them for many other projects.

7.14 OUTLINE OF THE DESIGN SPECIFICATION

As with other project documents, Appendix A gives an actual example.

1. *Title page and table of contents*   All sections with page numbers.

2. *Overview*   Although the programmers are urged to read the Requirements Document and the Functional Specs, the Design Specification (DS) should begin by summarizing the problems, the general solutions and how the system will fit into the user's environment. This makes the DS into a stand-alone document.

3. *Hardware/Software*   List the hardware on which the system will run; list the operating system and version, as well as any packaged software, utility programs and languages that will be used.

4. *Design Priorities*   List, in descending order of priority, the design priorities discussed in Section 7.3. Emphasize the trade-offs that may have to be made.

5. *Design Diagrams and Module Dictionary Conventions*   Explain the structured diagramming conventions: how each box refines the function of the box above, and how the data passing among the boxes is indicated. Tell the programmer that as she breaks down further during module design, she must follow the same diagramming and dictionary keeping conventions.

6. *Module Naming Conventions*   Explain the naming convention such as the one discussed in Section 7.5.

7. *Parameter Passing and Data Dictionaries*   List the rules for parameter passing among modules. Indicate where the data dictionaries are to be found and how they are organized. So far the DD contains all the parameters defined for the TLD and MLD. The programmer will have to add any new parameters he defines for submodules. Give examples of typical CALL formats.

8. *Error Handling*   Describe how errors are to be handled. If there is a system wide error handler show how the programmer calls it and gets control back. Give examples.

9. *Structured Programming Standards*   List the standards discussed in Section 7.12. Indicate where the 'template' program can be found.

10. *Programming Tools*   Coding and testing tools such as Editors/Language Sensitive Editors, Compilers, Debuggers, Automated Testers and Source Code Analyzers will be discussed in Section 9.4. These all make the job of programming and debugging easier. If these tools will be available indicate how they are to be accessed and used.

In Section 9.4 we will discuss a Code Management System (CMS) to store source code and track the changes to sources. If a CMS is to be used, indicate how.

List any source or object code subroutine libraries available, as well as existing modules that may be reused—do not re-invent the wheel.

If specific packaged software such as Data Base Management Systems or Forms Management Systems are used, explain how and when to use them.

11. *Top Level Design*   Include the TLD structured diagram such as Figure 7.1. Briefly explain the TLD, and the general functions to be performed by the five major components. Explain how the other components fit together, referencing all appropriate sections in the medium level design.

12. *Medium Level Design*   Include all the MLD structured diagrams. Explain the general function of each module or box. For example:

> Module AM000000 gets control when the operator types ABC at command level. (May be automatically started by a LOGIN file.) It first calls AMST000 to open all system files and do some initializing..., and so forth until all the general functions of the modules are detailed.

For the outline of the lower level modules, use the following format:

Module name:	
Called by:	list all callers
Subroutines called:	(to be filled in by programmer)
Input parameters:	list
Displays:	the I/O with the terminal or user
Returned parameters:	list
External variables used:	list
Files used:	list
Functions:	List in English statements. If you have pseudocode for each module, it can go here.

And so on until all the medium level modules are detailed.

13. *Module and Data Dictionaries*   Explain the construction and use of the three dictionaries discussed in Section 7.6. Explain where the CDD will be—for example if the operating system provides one—and how to use it. Show how to list it to see what is already in there from the top and medium level design and what is added as the design proceeds.

14. *Files and Tables*   Recall that in the Functional Specs we listed the data elements that will be kept. In the design we show how these elements fit into files. For the ABC system we must provide the details for the files COURSES.DAT, STUDENTS.DAT and so on. For each file show Organization (e.g. RMS), attributes, record length, keys and what modules in the system use the file.

Include a record map that details each field name, length, restrictions, and so forth. Indicate which modules access that field and for what purpose.

Do not forget to include when the file will be created, how large it will be, and how expansion will be handled.

Explain any other data structures that are to be used, such as in-memory tables and arrays.

7.15 TESTING THE DESIGN

When the design is done, the whole thing must be walked through. The purpose of this walk through is to ensure the following:

1. All the Functional Specification requirements are met.

    Do this by stepping through the FS, sentence by sentence. For any function promised in the FS, the designer must be able to point to a module and say, "We handle that here." Conversely, all design functions need to be called for in the FS—ensure that no bells and whistles were added by the designers.

2. The design is easy to program and maintain.

    This will be the case if a structured, piece-by-piece approach was used. Look for small, independent, well understood pieces.

3. It can be implemented on time and on budget.

    This is a subjective question that only the Design Leader can answer. Questions to ask are:

    - Have all the software and hardware components that were designed around been *shown to work previously*?

    - Is it a simple, straightforward design?

    - Are the pieces still estimable? Are the estimates still within the original ballpark?

7.16 CHANGES TO REQUIREMENTS DUE TO DESIGN

Some of the detailed design will invariably lead to requirements changes. You may have to go back to the user now and convince her that she does not really want what she asked for before. As before, your argument has to be based on cost/benefit. If the change can be shown to save money in development or maintenance due to the simplified design that you are suggesting, the user should agree. If you are stuck in a fixed price contract use the argument, "We can do it the previously agreed way, and we know we can't raise our price, but we'll take three months longer." That is why I suggest that you should not get into such a contract until after the design is done.

7.17 PLANNING THE ACCEPTANCE

Although Acceptance is a phase on its own later on, planning for acceptance can be begun after the medium level design is done. Preparing the Acceptance Test Plan is therefore presented in the next chapter since it is the next chronological activity. It can be done anytime after this point, as long as it is completed by the Acceptance Phase.

QUESTIONS

1. What is the purpose of the Design Phase?
2. What is structured design? What is top-down design?
3. What is bottom-up design? What type of systems are typically designed bottom-up?
4. What may be the adverse effects of setting 'user friendliness' as the highest design priority?
5. What is the purpose of the top level design walk-through? What can be a major problem in a walk-through and how can you avoid this?
6. What is a Common Data Dictionary? Why is it useful?
7. Why break a system into structured modules?
8. Referring to the file design in Section 7.8, assume that the two most common requests to the system will be "How many students are registered on course no. NNN?" and "What are the courses that student no. SSS is registered on?" Can you describe a file design where both of these questions can be answered with access to only one file?
9. What are the advantages and disadvantages of using a relational data base management system?
10. What is the benefit of structured analysis and design?
11. What personality traits would you look for in a system designer?
12. What items must be standardized by the designers and why?
13. What is the purpose of the medium level design walk-through?
14. Group Exercise:

    Write the Design Specification for the 'Bell Family Communication's systems'.

8

The Acceptance Test Plan

Agreeing to Agree

8.1 INTRODUCTION

The goal of acceptance is to get a *written* statement from the user that the product was delivered as promised. Getting this statement—and payment if it is a contracted project —may be difficult unless the user can be convinced that the system works exactly as promised. The user may be apprehensive at acceptance time: he has to take over the ownership and responsibility for the system. He may be reluctant to hand over the check—what if something goes wrong?

8.2 THE TRIAL PERIOD OR PARALLEL RUN

The trial period or the parallel run are the most common approaches to acceptance. Using the 'trial period' approach the project team simply installs the new system for the user to try. The 'parallel run' approach adds the dimension of leaving the old system running as well for comparison and backup. In both cases the client uses the new system for 'X' days. If there are no problems the user accepts; if there are any problems the project team is supposed to fix them and rerun the trial for another 'X' days.

These approaches are simple, but they have several major flaws:

1. Small problems can force you to rerun for 'X' days indefinitely. Sometimes a complex software system is *never 100% debugged*. You learn to live with the faults. (Document them as features!)

2. It may be difficult to trace the cause of a problem. If ten users are on an interactive system and it crashes it is a challenge to find exactly what caused the crash.

3. There is no guarantee that all the features will be tried within 'X' days. I have seen one accounting system that was implemented at the start of a new fiscal year. It ran well during the trial period (six months) only to fail at the end of the fiscal year when the accountants attempted to close the books. Unfortunately the warranty was over and the vendor would not fix the problem.

4. Letting the end user access a system on the first day that it is implemented is not always beneficial. Would you test airplanes that way? As in romance, first impressions are important.

8.3 SOLUTION: A THOROUGH BUT PIECEMEAL ACCEPTANCE

A better approach is to devise a series of tests that demonstrate all of the promised functions. The acceptance will be a formal run through of these tests for the customer. Successful tests are signed off one by one. If a test fails, the PT fixes the problem—hopefully on site; if it is a major problem then the tests are adjourned until the problem is fixed. In theory only failed tests are repeated; however the user has every right to rerun previously accepted tests after a 'fix.' The set of tests and the order in which to run them is called the acceptance test plan (ATP).

This approach has the following advantages:

1. You can demonstrate all the promised functions.
2. The action causing a problem is always known—you know exactly who was typing what when the problem occurred.
3. The user will be less apprehensive about many, 'small' signatures than about a single 'binary' signature that accepts all or none.

The major disadvantage of this approach is that it takes a lot of work to write the ATP. In addition the user may not be familiar with the approach. But you can familiarize her with this new method beforehand. It is mentioned briefly in the Proposal, which is a signed document. It is detailed in the Functional Specification, another signed document. She will also see and sign-off the ATP before acceptance. There should be no reluctance to accept *and pay* if this method is used.

8.4 ENSURING THAT ALL THE PROMISES ARE TESTED

To ensure that all promises are tested go through the FS page by page, paragraph by paragraph, and list all the functions that are testable. Consider a table such as Figure 8.1 as shown on the next page:

FS REF SEC/PAR	FUNCTION TO BE TESTED	TEST METHOD	TEST NUMBER
3.1	Main menu appears at start-up	T	1.0
3.2	Registrar menu appears when...	T	2.1
3.3	Manager menu appears when...	T	2.2
7.7	Store 10,000 student records	I	7.8
10.2	Students by course by city report	T,A	4.5

T - test   I - inspection   A - Analysis (Hand calc,or use another pgm)   N/A - not applicable

Figure 8.1   Functions vs tests table

Note that some things will not be tested (N/A). It is not worth breaking a disk just to prove that the 'Parity error handling' works. Some things such as item 7.7 in Figure 8.1 will be tested by inspection (I) — for example, you can look at the OPEN statement in the code or the directory listing for the size of a file . The results of calculations, formulas and totals should be double-checked, perhaps by hand. Reuse tests if possible. Often a test defined for one function can be reused as it stands or with a slight modification.

8.5 USING THE DESIGN

You may be wondering why I suggest doing the ATP after the design is done. Strictly speaking, you need only the Functional Specification to produce the ATP. However, the design helps to group the tests into *test sets* that demonstrate major functions of the system. You can run the tests in the same top down order as the TLD, which is well understood by your user. Approaching the ABC system in the order of the TLD (Figure 7.1), you can demonstrate all the menus, then all the inquiries, followed by all the updates and so on. Another way to group test sets is by function. Go through all the Registrar's functions, followed by the Administrator's and so on.

The TEST NUMBER assigned in the Functions vs. Tests table (Figure 8.1) can follow the same numbering convention as the Medium Level Design (see Appendix A).

8.6 WRITING THE TESTS

You have already determined how you will test an item when filling in TEST METHOD in Figure 8.1 above. The following is an example of test number 4.5, 'Students by Course by City' report. [Notes in square brackets would not appear—these are the explanations.]

TEST NO: 4.5

TEST PURPOSE:	Demonstrate the production of the Students by Course by City report.
F.S. REFERENCE (SEC/PAR):	10.2, 12.8, 11.3 [Note how one test can demonstrate several functions.]
SETUP:	Ensure files STUDENT.DAT and COURSE.DAT contain data.Start system.
INPUT:	Choose Selection 1. from Main Menu using mouse click and drag method.
OUTPUT:	'CHOOSE REPORT TYPE' menu (format per FS pg 17,Figure8.15) appears. [Refer to the Funtional Spec. whenever possible.]
INPUT:	Choose Selection 5. (Students by Course by City report) by UP/DOWN arrow and RETURN method.
OUTPUT:	Message 'Report being prepared.' appears. No longer than 60 seconds later, message 'Report being printed' appears and the printer starts printing. The terminal can be used to enter any other command. User will try up to 3 commands of his choice.[There is danger in stating, "User may type any number of commands." He just may!] When the report is complete (printer stops,) inspect it to ensure it is of format FS pg. 23, Figure 12.12. Total columns will be checked by hand calculated addition of the attendance figures printed.

USER SIGNATURE_____

PROJECT TEAM SIGNATURE_____

DATE_____

COMMENTS_____

Figure 8.2   Typical test

8.7 THE ACCEPTANCE TEST PLAN CHECKLIST

Use the following as a checklist for all the activities required to plan the acceptance:

- Functions vs. Tests table produced and all the FS promises are *addressed*.
- Tests and test sets are defined.
- Responsibility for writing the tests is assigned.
- The client and the PT are aware that the ATP will be reviewed, revised if necessary, and signed off by the user. The client is aware that successful

completion of the tests constitutes acceptance of the system. Look at the sample form in section 10 of the ATP in Appendix A.

- Responsibility for test data is assigned. Test data should be provided by the project team and the user. If the user can provide data that is true to life, the system will get a better test, plus the user will feel more comfortable with the accuracy of the tests.

8.8 CONCLUSIONS TO THE ACCEPTANCE TEST PLAN

Encourage the user to write the ATP if he can. It will give him a feeling of control—the project team must build the system to meet the tests. The project team must have a signoff on a user written ATP; what if the user tests for something that the PT does not intend to provide?

You can overdo acceptance testing. Consider the cost of the test versus the cost of the risk that there is a problem. You can never test everything, especially in a multi-user interactive system.

8.9 CONCLUSIONS TO THE DESIGN PHASE

At the end of the Design Phase we have reached to the following milestones:

1. The Design Specification document, containing the final top level design and medium level design is walked through.

2. ATP responsibility is assigned and started. It need not be finished until the Acceptance Phase.

3. The project plan, especially the estimates, are revisited. Although you are estimating only the remaining four phases, the Programming Phase will probably be the most expensive and time consuming in the whole project. The design gives you an approximate count of the number of modules and their complexity. By now you probably know who the actual programmers will be so you can factor their productivity into the estimates. With this information the amount of programming time required can be easily estimated (see Chapter 13). Statistics show that at the end of the Design Phase *estimates should be no more than 10% off.*

QUESTIONS

1. What is the goal of Acceptance?
2. What are the advantages and disadvantages of a 'trial period' as the acceptance method?

3. What are the advantages of the piecemeal approach to acceptance over the trial run approach? Are there any disadvantages?

4. List three ways of testing a function. Give examples of functions that would be tested by each method.

5. Write a 'Functions vs. Tests' table for the Bell Family Communications (BFC) system.

6. Write a test for 'Call a family and communicate' function of the BFC.

7. What are the milestones of the Design Phase?

9

The Programming Phase

Building the Pieces

9.1 INTRODUCTION

Programming is usually the easiest part—that is what we 'technical types' are most familiar with. In fact, as Project Manager you may find yourself restraining your staff from starting to program too soon. There is always pressure to 'do something concrete', not only from the project team but from higher level management as well. Be careful of a management disease called WISCA: Why Isn't Sam Coding Anything? (Constantine) It worries managers when the programmers are sitting around idle. Never start coding until the design is firm enough that no rework will be necessary.

The activities in this phase will be writing the programs. The milestones will be the tested programs, the System Test Plan, and at least a start on the user's documentation.

This chapter is fairly technical, so those who are strictly managers may consider reading the War Stories, the Conclusions, and then going on to Chapter 10.

Programming War Stories

This story is about a large grain farming co-operative. For those who are not familiar with the grain farming business, a farmer ususally delivers his grain to the nearest grain elevator. He gets a receipt for his delivery and payment depending upon the type of grain, tonnage, quality, and price based on grain futures. The headquarters of the grain company must keep track of the grain in all the elevators under its jurisdiction, so that when a large amount of grain is sold the trucks and trains that pick up the grain are sent to the right locations.

A few years ago this grain company, headquartered in city 'A', decided to computerize its operation. They were going to use FMMC (Famous Minicomputer Manufacturing Co.) hardware and networking software, so the grain company sent its programmers to FMMC's training center, located in city 'B,' to learn the networking software.

The grain company was so impressed with the FMMC course instructor that they hired him as a consultant to design the system. The design was excellent. The Instructor/Designer suggested that PC's be placed in each elevator (very little computing power was needed there) to handle the farmers' transactions and receipts. A minicomputer at headquarters would keep the transactions and grain stocks and automatically dial up each PC at midnight to get the transactions. It took the instructor three weeks to design this and he went home.

But the grain company was so impressed with this design that they hired the instructor as a consultant to do the programming as well. The programming was to take place in city 'C,' since it was home to most of the programmers. The picture at this point was: instructor/programmer was in city 'C;' The Project Leader (the instructor's manager) was in city 'B;' and the Project Manager, who was the account representative from FFMC, was at the grain company headquarters in city 'A.' This is called 'distributed project management.'

The instructor began to program. Despite a schedule of one module per week, the first module was not done for eight weeks. Finally the PL received the first module—mailed electronically to city 'B'—and panicked. The programming was awful: unstructured and full of bugs. He phoned the instructor at once, and the following conversation took place:

PL: What took you so long? And why is this program so bad?

PGR: John (not his real name,) I have not programmed for six years. I thought it would be fun to get back to it. But I hate it, and I hate city 'C.' Get me out of here!

Comment: The instructor was not even reprimanded. He was an excellent instructor and designer, but a terrible programmer. This is common. The problem was that the PL was not supervising. Had they been together, the PL would have noticed the problem at once and replaced the programmer immediately. For any new or unknown resource, walk through their work within one week of starting. This is especially important with outside contractors.

Epilogue: The instructor was moved back home, another programmer was moved to city 'C' to replace him, and the project was successfully completed, albeit ten weeks late.

About three months later FMMC noticed that their new grain control computers were enjoying an inordinate amount of popularity. After a little investigation FMMC discovered that the PC's, which were idle 90% of the time, magically grew games and compilers such as BASIC. Informal computer courses were sprouting up. The farmers—and especially their children—were enjoying the new system immensely.

9.2 PRE-PROGRAMMING CHECKLIST

Before you start programming, answer the following:

- Did the design reviews suggest any rework? If so, schedule the time and delay the start of programming.

- Are the planned resources and programmers still available? Do not be too optimistic about other people's projects finishing on time. If there have been any staff changes, have you re-estimated for the productivity of the new people? Industry statistics have shown that the best programmer can be as much as eight times as productive as the worst.

- Are the people trained? Programmers need to know the operating system, the languages, packaged programs, and programming tools that will be used. They should also be familiar with the user application and business problem. Ensure that they read the Requirements Document and Functional Specifications.

- Is the programming environment good? You need easy-to-use development software and programming tools (see Section 9.4). The development computer must provide fast response, must be available when needed, and must be reliable. Be sure that the warranties provided by the manufacturer as well as all the development software documentation are up-to-date. Provide a quiet enviornment isolated from interrupts.

9.3 THE PROGRAMMING STEPS

Step 1. Plan the Integration

Common sense dictates that you cannot program it all and then throw it all together—that a step-by-step assembly will be required. Plan the order in which you will put the pieces together. Chapter 9 details several methods for assembling the pieces, but you must plan this order of integration now, since *you should be writing the programs in the order that they will be integrated.* This is called the System Test Plan.

The remaining steps pertain to each module:

Step 2. Design the Module

The programmer receives *some* level of design from the Design Phase. His job is to break it down to lower and lower levels of detail until he reaches a stage that he can program. This is called *module design*. The medium level design such as Figure 9.1 below, was developed in the Design Phase.

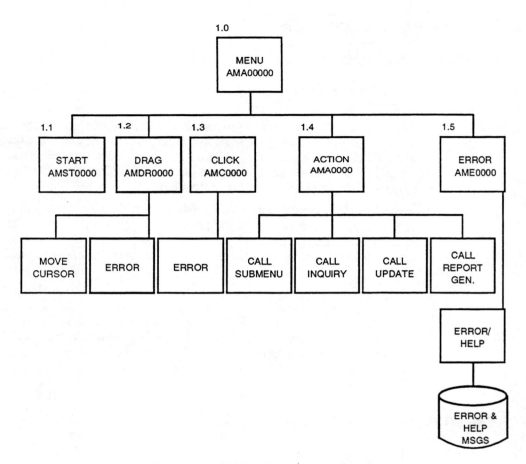

Figure 9.1   Medium level design (3rd level)

The programmer receives from the designers a description of the module such as the one below (see Appendix A):

```
Module name:  AMST0000
Called by:  AM000000
Subroutines called:  to be filled in by programmer
Input parameters:  none
Displays:  none
Returned parameters:  if no errors exit code 0. If error, exit
code   is error number
External variables used:  (list)
Files used:  STUDENT.DAT (open), COURSE.DAT (open), MATERIAL.DAT
(open), SYSTEM.DAT (open)
Functions: Open the files STUDENT.DAT, COURSE.DAT, MATERIAL.DAT,
SYSTEM.DAT. If error, exit with code... Initialize variables...
```

```
Check for abnormal shutdown by checking Record 1 of SYSTEM.DAT
file. Byte 1 = -1 means proper shutdown (See module AMSHUT00). If
not -1, do following ... On error exit with error code ...
Ensure correct status of
     Mouse by checking...
          On error exit with error code ...
     Screen by ...
          On error exit with error code ...
     Network by ...
          On error exit with error code ...
     Normal exit error code 0
```

The programmer first draws a structure diagram for the module. It may look like Figure 9.2.

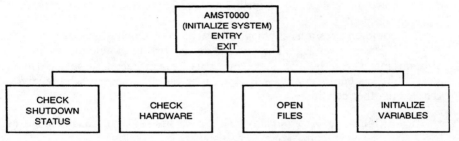

Figure 9.2   Fourth level module breakout

The module design is approached top down starting with the topmost box, AMST000 and break it into the appropriate sub-components as in Figure 9.3.

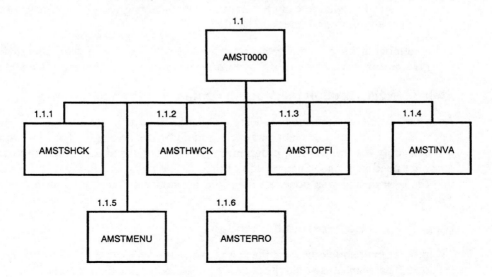

Figure 9.3   Fifth level module breakout

Then each sub-component can be further divided as in Figure 9.4.

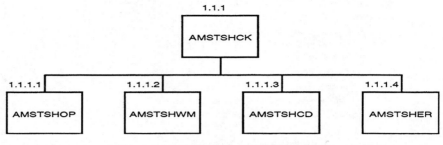

Figure 9.4   Sixth level module breakout

And so it is broken down further and further until a level is reached where it can be programmed.

A common question is, ''At what level does system design stop and module design begin?'' The answer is, ''The system design breaks down to the level where the programmer can begin.'' This level may vary from project to project and even from one part of the system to another—depending on the programmer who receives that part. There are other considerations:

- If module breakout is crucial to meet priorities such as response, user friend-liness or consistency, the designers may go lower.

- The level of breakout of the design may be dictated by the contract. Government departments such as the Military specify the number of levels.

- If the programmers are not known at design time, a median level of programmer knowledge can be assumed, and the design is taken to a level that a median programmer can handle.

But remember that *programmers detest receiving a design of such detail that programming is simply translating English-like statements verbatim into a program language.*

Step 3. Walk Through the Module Design

As in the top and medium levels of design, tradeoffs have to be made in the lowest levels as well. Walk through the design of each module before coding it. This walk-through is small: only the appropriate programmer, his supervisor and perhaps another programmer need to attend. The purpose of the module design walk-through is to ensure that the best design was done, all functions are addressed and all contingencies are handled.

Step 4. Plan How to Test the Module

The programmer should prepare the test plan and the test data for the module before it is coded. Test plans done after the code are prejudiced. They tend to test only the 'hard' parts of the code. The Project Leader may insist on a test plan walk-through along with the module design walk through. Do these two walk-throughs together.

Step 5. Code Each Module

Coding standards were set up during system design (See Section 7.12). We will not discuss here how to program—consult References 12 (this paper discusses design as well as programming) and 13 for some insights. Here is a summary of what constitutes a structured program:

- It is small. Rules of thumb suggest approximately 100 lines of executable code, less than two pages of listing.
- One entry, one exit.
- Minimum global references.
- Structured constructs to use: Sequence, IF/THEN/ELSE, CASE, WHILE, UNTIL, CALL (not GO TO).

Step 6. Test the Module

The programmer tests a module by setting up the appropriate environment, providing some input, letting the module go through the processing logic and observing the results. The input may have to be faked, especially if the module that will actually provide this input is not available.

Modules should be tested in two phases. Phase 1 is called 'white box' testing. The programmer knows what is inside the module, and supplies test data so that each logical path in the program is executed. After this, Phase 2, or 'black box' testing can be done. In black box testing the programmer ignores the innards of the module—data is supplied in the order and frequency that approximates real use.

Step 7. Test the Lowest Levels of Integration

If a main module calls sub-modules, the programmer must integrate and test all these modules working together. Even if he is not responsible for writing the sub-modules, he must test the CALLs to and RETURNs from these modules. The best method to do this is to create a 'program stub' in place of the sub-modules. A stub may be a four line program which indicates that control was successfully received, shows the parameters received, and passes control back with some fake parameters if necessary.

Step 8. Save the Results of All Tests;
Submit Finished Modules to Integration

Test results are used to gather statistics on the causes, cures and costs of correcting errors. The Project Leader is usually in charge of integration in a small to medium sized system. Software such as CMS (Code Management System) is very useful for configuration management—keeping track of versions and changes to source code (See Section 9.4).

Step 9. Get Started on the User Documentation

Whether the programmers are responsible for user documentation or not, this phase is the best time to begin producing it. The following documents may have to be written:

User's Guide.   This document can be written by the programmers, a technical writer or even the user. Recall that the FS has sections that detail the menus, screens, forms and other user interfaces—do not re-invent the wheel.

A good USER'S GUIDE is divided into sections that represent different users' jobs. In the ABC system USER'S GUIDE, for example, there should be a chapter labeled 'Registrar's Functions', another labeled 'Warehouse Functions' and so forth. The material should be in the order that the user will normally use it. This makes the USER'S Guide useful for learning the system. Another popular order for USER'S GUIDES is by a logical trace down the tree of menu commands. At the end of the guide provide reference sections where each command, menu, form and message appears in alphabetical order.

Maintenance Guide.   How do you get programmers to document the details of their programs for subsequent maintenance? Most PM's find this very difficult to do: programmers are reluctant to document before the program is written; and good luck getting them to do it after everything else is done. Programmers think that maintainers require a detailed explanation of program logic. This is boring to write and totally unnecessary. There is a simple solution to this: *A good, detailed module level design specification with structured, self documented code is enough for system maintenance.* The MAINTENANCE GUIDE will consist of the Design Specification, the program listings, and an explanation of how it all fits together, how to approach changes, and how to link and test it all.

Operator's Guide/System Manager's Guide.   This is the equivalent of the USER'S GUIDE for the person who brings the system up in the morning, shuts it down, does backups, handles major problems, does the accounting and so on. The documentation provided by the manufacturer of the hardware and the operating system may be enough—only the procedures unique to the custom software will have to be written down.

Training Documentation.   If you will provide courses on how to use the system, plan what form of training material will be required. A good USER'S GUIDE should be adequate in most cases. You may have to produce training aids such as overhead transparencies, hands-on exercises, tests and so on.

9.4 PROGRAMMING CASE TOOLS

The following are software products that help the programmer do his or her job better. These are called CASE (Computer Aided Software Engineering) tools because they help to automate the programming process. See Reference 2.1 for actual products.

The Programming Language

The programming language and compiler is the most important tool. If it is simple and well-suited to the application the programmer will be able to learn it quickly, use the exact construct required, and program without awkward work-arounds, the short comings of the language. The compiler should be fast, and the error messages clear.

Language Sensitive Editor (LSE)

An LSE provides templates for every statement in the language. For example, in PASCAL, the user can type 'FOR' and the LSE produces

```
FOR %{ctrl-var}% := %{exp}% %{TO|DOWNTO}% %{exp}% DO
      %{statements}%
END;
```

The programmer merely fills in the variables and the LSE ensures that the syntax is correct. The LSE can also call the compiler. If an error is found by the compiler, the LSE gets control back, and the programmer is back in the editor—with the compiler error message and the source line that caused it *on the screen*. The LSE can produce the program header from a template.

An LSE aids in syntax checking, compiling and ensuring consistent source format throughout the system.

Debugger

A debugger helps detect and correct errors. It should provide program stop, trace, and step. A good debugger allows setting and displaying of variables at any point, as well as executing specific parts of a program.

Code Management System (CMS)

Sometimes called a configuration manager, CMS is invaluable for any programming effort. CMS is the 'librarian' that owns all sources. It can police who updates what and ensures that conflicts are avoided if two people are updating the same module at once. CMS keeps track of all changes to all the modules so that a history of a module is easy to see. And for the icing on the cake, CMS provides easy regression to previous versions of the sources.

CMS can handle any ASCII file. It is therefore useful not only for tracking source files, but for storing and tracking documentation files, test files, and system build files as well. Imagine the situation at a hardware/software manufacturer such as DEC, where there are usually 20 to 30 versions of an operating system supported, each varying slightly depending on hundreds of permutations and combinations of hardware and software flavors. A CMS is absolutely necessary to track all of these versions. (Excuse me for sounding overenthusiastic, but CMS has saved my life many times.)

Module Management System (MMS)

An MMS is used to automate the compile and link process, or the system build. It can rebuild only those components that were changed since the last build. MMS can be used to automatically run a set of tests against a module. MMS is very useful when you are building a 'release' of a system: assembling all the appropriate sources and executable images, as well as all the documentation in a package. MMS works hand-in-hand with CMS where all the sources, document files and command files that run MMS can be stored.

Test Manager (TM)

A TM is used to automate the testing of a module. To use the TM you define a set of tests to be run against the module along with the expected output. TM will run the tests, and inform the programmer if the results vary from the expected output.

9.5 COPYRIGHTS

The subject of copyrighting software is still in the courts, but a recent ruling states that not only is the piece of software copyrightable, but also the 'look' and 'feel' of it (whatever that means). If you wish to protect your code, add a copyright notice to each source module and document. ''Copyright © 19nn, Company Name'' is all that is usually required.

9.6 CONCLUSION TO THE PROGRAMMING PHASE

Here are some thoughts on programming:

> Programming used to be considered to be an art. Programmers were allowed to "do their own thing." It was very quickly discovered that it is too expensive for that. It has to be considered as a science—rigorously dictated.

> Programming is fun—debugging it is not. Watch out for statements such as "Coding is done; all that's left is to debug it, so I am 90% done!" Statistics show that the programmer is only 50% done after coding.

Here are some thoughts on programmers:

> Programmers will always underestimate a task. Teach them pessimism—things will go wrong.

> Programmers will enjoy their job if you motivate them with a challenge. Each task should be just a little bit harder or different than the last. If you wish to learn how to motivate programmers, read G. Weinberg's book, "The Psychology of Computer Programming" (Reference 14).

> Programmers are easily abused—they will work overtime when requested. But beware of

constant overtime. After a while no extra productivity will be gained and the programmers will burn out.

At the end of the programming phase look for the following milestones:

1. The module designs have been walked through and signed off.
2. The individual programs have been coded, tested and signed off by the project leader.
3. The order for the integration has been decided, written in the System Test Plan (and programming is progressing in that order).
4. The responsibility for the user documentation has been assigned, and if you are lucky it has already been started!

QUESTIONS

1. Why do programmers always start coding too early (before the design is completed)? Why is this inadvisable?
2. When does system design breakout stop and module design begin? What factors would override this?
3. Why should programmers plan the module test before writing the code?
4. What is white box and black box testing? Why use both?
5. List five attributes of a structured program.
6. What two things would a good User's Guide be used for? Why provide both?
7. What is the traditional program maintenance document, and why is this disliked? What could replace this?
8. List, in order of importance, six programming CASE tools. Explain why you chose the first three as most important.
9. What are the milestones of the Programming Phase?

10

The System Test Phase

Putting it all Together

10.1 INTRODUCTION

The System Test Phase has two activities. First, the pieces will be integrated into a composite or system; and second, this system will be tested. The testing is there to ensure that the pieces work together, and that the system functions as it should.

It is difficult to estimate how long system test will take. You cannot state that there will be X number of bugs, each of which will take 4 hours to resolve. A rule of thumb is that system test will take one eighth the amount of time of all that has happened before. In addition, if the activities so far have taken longer than planned, system test will take longer as well. Good project managers allow lots of contingency when scheduling system test.

System Test War Story

On one large telephone switching system project the Chairman of the Board of the client company was present at system test time. This switch was supposed to handle 200 lines. When we first turned it on it crashed after 20 lines were plugged in. The CEO panicked and suggested an immediate halt to the whole project! He said, ''Looks like you have only one tenth of the system ready after all this time and expense, and I cannot afford another ten fold expenditure!''

It was only a DIMENSION statement that was wrong, but it took the President of my company to calm this CEO down.

Comment: I am usually reluctant to allow the client to be present at the start of the System Test Phase. If the user (or even the PM for that matter) is watching the integration and test activity, and is not used to the nature of the exercise, *panic may result.* It always appears to be in terrible shape at first: hundreds of problems, nothing works. But things soon fall into place. You may have only one module working on the first day; but by the end of the second day you will have five more working, and by the end of the week most of the system may be ready.

10.2 THE SYSTEM TEST PLAN

How do you assemble a large system comprising of many programs and modules? You do not first write all the programs, then link all of them together at once and turn it all on. Obviously some sort of piecemeal integration is needed. We will see the different orders in which you can integrate the sytem, but in all cases this order has to be planned in the System Test Plan (STP).

The STP documents not only the order in which the pieces will be integrated but also the tests that will be run at each stage of the integration (as each module is plugged into the 'package').

Contents of the STP

1. Test schedule, staff, resource requirements.
2. Configuration management, integration and testing tools to use.
3. Order of integration.
4. Checklist of tests to run at each step of integration, source of these tests.
5. Checklist of 'bad' data and procedures to try.
6. Regression process.
7. Load and perfomance tests.
8. List of deliverables (sources, documentation, etc.)

Getting *Something* Going as Quickly as Possible

The System Test Plan should be written before the programming begins because the programs can then be written in the order that they will need to be integrated. This implies that you do not have to program everything before you can start integrating. In fact, there are advantages to bouncing back and forth between the programming and the system test phases. Program several integratable modules, then integrate and test these, and you have something working to show the user and your management. Then go back, program another set of modules, integrate and show off again. Another advantage to this is that the experience gained during integration helps in approaching the subsequent programs.

The Order of Integration

There are three common orders in which to approach integration:

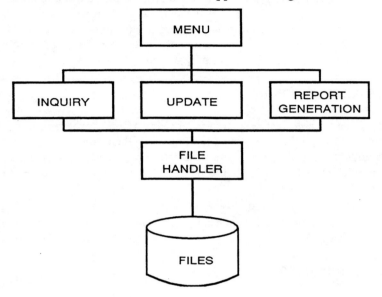

Figure 10.1   Top level design

Top down order. The order of assembling the pieces can be done top down according to the TLD. For the ABC system whose TLD is shown in Figure 10.1, top down integration would assemble the modules or programs comprising the MENU portion first. When the MENU is working, the programs comprising INQUIRY are first integrated, then plugged into the MENU. Then UPDATE followed by REPORT GENERATION are added to complete the package.

If you wish to get something going as fast as possible, you would first program the MENU modules, integrate them, and show this to your management. This could be a small milestone. Then go back to programming the INQUIRY, and show it off when it is integrated, and so on with the other components.

Bottom up order and program stubs. It is very tempting to integrate bottom up, starting with the FILE HANDLER and working upwards on the TLD—after all, the FILE HANDLER is probably the least complex component. The MENU is the most complex, and it is psychologically difficult to begin with the hardest piece. But a major problem will crop up. When integrating and testing components without the other components in hand, you must 'stub out' the other components by fake routines that simulate the presence of these components (See Section 9.3 Step 7 for an explanation of stubs.) Working top down, when MENU is being integrated, the INQUIRY, UPDATE, and REPORT GENERATOR must be stubbed out in order to test the CALLs these components. For example, the stub for INQUIRY is probably a four line routine that indicates it received control, shows the parameters it received, pretends to get a record from the data base by delaying a few milliseconds (if timing is important) and sends a fake record back in a buffer. This is relatively simple to do. But working bottom up from the FILE HANDLER, you would have to stub out the MENU as well as the middle levels. The stub would have to open the files, initialize many things—you would spend almost as much time stubbing the higher levels out as you would writing them!

For certain systems, especially real time systems, integrating bottom up may be necessary. For example, the automobile engine test bed discussed earlier (Section 7.2) had the TLD shown in Figure 10.2.

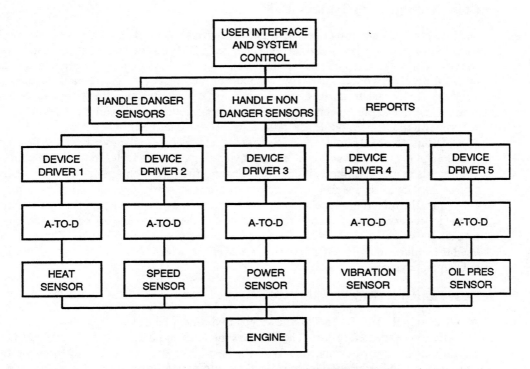

Figure 10.2   Top level design for engine test bed

In this case you would probably start integrating bottom up—not because the stubbing problem is any less serious—but because the heart of the system is the engine sensors and drivers, and you need to get that portion going first.

Systems that are in large part created by re-assembling existing components or modules also should be designed and integrated bottom-up.

Sub-function or Release order. This method is best for getting something *useful* going as quickly as possible. For instance, assume that there were 20 different menus, 50 inquiries, 50 updates and 25 reports promised in ABC. How about getting 10 menus, 20 inquiries, 20 updates and 10 reports going first of all? This sub-system would be *accepted* and *implemented* for the user as Release 1. Then go back to programming additional menus, inquiries, updates and reports and implement as Release 2. This approach is used in very complex systems such as operating systems, because the developers (and users) can start with something simple, learn it, then go to more and more complex systems.

10.3 SYSTEM TEST TOOLS

Code Management System (CMS)

Did you ever have several developers try to change a module at once? Did you ever wish for a way of policing the 'midnight code changer'? Did you ever have a module that was 'almost working', and someone applied a change (then a change to the change, and so on until nothing worked) and you wished you had a way of going back to the old version? CMS assists in all of these areas by controlling and tracking changes to sources. CMS can prevent changes entirely, warn a developer that another developer is working on the same module, or indicate where the changes conflict.

The most useful feature of CMS is ease of regression. CMS never burns its bridges. If a change is made to a source it is done by coding a 'change file', containing change commands somewhat like edit changes. Change files are then applied to the original source. A 'level' is reached when a set of sources work. Changes can be applied subsequently, but if these changes 'break' something that worked previously, the Project Leader can easily regress to the old level of the code. A history of all the changes to a single source module, a level, or the whole system can be produced. This can be used to produce statistics on the cost of the test effort, which will be useful for estimating subsequent systems.

Test Manager (TM)

As we saw in Section 9.4, a TM allows you to define a set of test procedures and data, as well as the expected results. The TM runs the tests and indicates if any of the results do not match what was expected. With the best TM systems you can even create the testing files (procedures, data and results) automatically by running the tests once interactively and storing the results.

The TM makes regression testing (going back to tests run previously because something 'broke') very simple. TM also allows you to easily organize, summarize and examine the test results. For those interested in problem causes, solutions and costs (and who isn't!) TM provides a history of the whole process.

Source Code Analyzer (SCA)

An SCA is a tool for finding a character string throughout many source files. For example, you can find all the occurrences of a variable name or a routine name. This is useful when a variable is suspected of causing a problem somewhere, or when all the CALLs to a routine need to be traced.

Performance Coverage Analyzer (PCA)

A PCA traces the sections of the system which are executed and their frequency. This measurement can be used to improve performance—optimizing should take place in the sections of code that are executed most. The trace is also useful to ensure that your tests forced all parts of the code to be executed.

A good PCA can be used to analyze the crucial interfaces from your system into the operating system such as Input/Output and system function calls. One of the most important items to optimize on a virtual memory computer is paging. PCA shows where page faults occur.

Module Management System (MMS)

An MMS automates the building of the whole software package. It does the compile and link of the sources, as well as assembling the appropriate test sets, data files, and documentation. MMS saves incredible amounts of time in system test since it can be programmed to rebuild only the pieces that changed since the last build.

10.4 THE INTEGRATION PROCESS

The first tests in the system life cycle were done by the developer, who developed a set of tests—procedures plus data—to thoroughly test the module. When submitting the program to integration, the programmer should provide a smaller set of *crucial* tests to the integration manager. This is shown as TESTA in Figure 10.3.

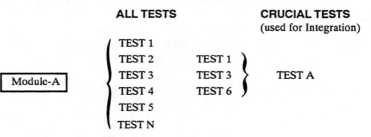

Figure 10.3   Crucial tests retained for system test

When integration begins—for example MODULE-A is integrated with MODULE-B tests are defined that test the CALLs made from A to B, the parameters returned, and the functions in A that depend on B (and vice-versa). Let us call this TESTAB (see Figure 10.4). You must also run tests to ensure that nothing was broken in A or B when the two were plugged together. The total tests for the lump A-B (called a 'build') will be the tests TESTA, TESTB (the crucial tests for MODULE-B), and TESTAB.

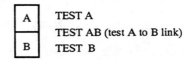

Figure 10.4   Integration test for MODULES A and B

Figure 10.5 extends this to many modules. When module C is plugged in, TESTC is run to check out MODULE-C, TESTABC is run to check out the CALLs to C from A and B (and vice-versa). To ensure that A and B did not break when C was plugged in, some or all of the tests in TESTA, TESTB, and TESTAB should be rerun. The braces in Figure 10.5 show the order of the integration and the test sets to be run at each stage.

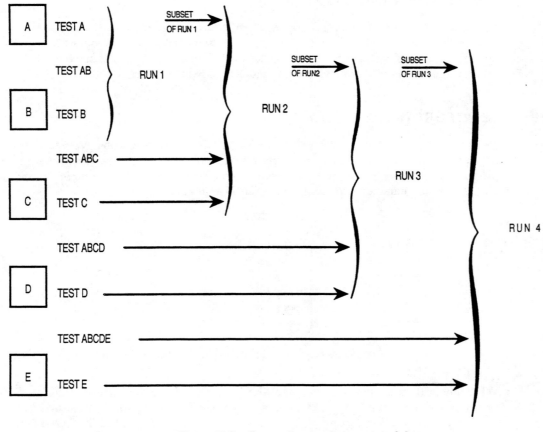

Figure 10.5   Integration test for many modules

The Test Manager (TM) software discussed above can be programmed to run any of the test sets automatically.

10.5 REGRESSION TESTING

The TM can also be used for easy regression. For example, what if the tests comprising Run (3) in Figure 10.5 show that TESTABCD failed? The problem may be in any one of MODULES A, B, C or D! If the project team cannot identify the cause of the problem, they must first go back and rerun the Run (2) tests against the build comprising of Modules A, B, C and D. If the problem still persists, the cause is in MODULES A, B or C; if the problem is gone then it was in D. They may have to go as far back as Run (1) or even to individual module tests if necessary. The TM can make this process very simple, especially if a CMS is used to store all the test files.

10.6 THE FINAL, THOROUGH TEST

The System Test

When the system is all integrated, someone runs through a thorough set of tests to ensure that the system functions as promised. Following is the order of the tests that should be run:

1. Unless nothing has changed since integration (hardware, software, environment, test personnel), run through some of the tests used toward the end of integration.

2. Devise a set of tests that are true to life—emulating how the real user would be using the system. Here you would log several users on a multi-user system to check the interactivity. Try to approximate the typical system load by issuing the commonest commands. Do not forget to test the operation functions such as system startup, shut-down, backup, restore, and so on. The best source for this data is the user.

3. Try to overload the system to ensure that the promised performance requirements are met.

4. Try to break it by entering wrong inputs, out of range values and simulating error conditions.

5. The Acceptance Test Plan should be finished at this point. (See Chapter 8.) Run through the acceptance procedure privately. This provides another thorough test and ensures that there will be no surprises when the tests are run publicly during the Acceptance Phase.

6. Do not forget to test the user documentation as well. Make sure the manuals are clear, useful, and structured according to the format and standards agreed to up front.

All of the above is documented in the System Test Plan.

The Case for an Independent Tester

For a small to medium sized project, the person in charge of system integration and testing is the Project Leader. For a larger project, or for any project where you can afford it, put a separate, *independent* person in charge of a final, thorough test exercise. Sometimes called IV&V (Independent Verification and Validation), the independence is needed because developers are prejudiced testers. They look for specific things to go wrong and test only the 'hard parts' of their code. They look for things working; a good tester looks for things not working. An independent tester will also exercise the system as the user would.

10.7 CONCLUSIONS TO THE SYSTEM TEST PHASE

Keep the PM informed of the progress of the system test. She/he is waiting with baited breath to announce to the world the major milestone when an integrated, tested system has been reached.

The milestones to achieve at the end of the system test phase are:

1. The pieces are all problem free and work together. The PM signs off, agrees that this is so, and calls a party to tell the world that we have a system!
2. The System Test Plan is updated with the results of the tests. Write down the type of tests that you had to run, the causes of the errors and the cost to correct these errors. This is not done to police your people; it is done to gather statistics so that you can better estimate the test effort on subsequent projects.
3. The acceptance test plan has been run (privately) and any problems found were corrected.
4. The time and place for acceptance has been verified with the user.

QUESTIONS

1. What are the two purposes of the System Test Phase?
2. Why have a System Test Plan? Why write it before programming begins?
3. List the advantages and disadvantages of integrating top down.
4. What types of systems are usually integrated bottom up?
5. What is the benefit of integrating by releases?
6. Which features of CMS are the most useful in the System Test Phase?
7. Which feature of PCA would you consider most useful when testing a system?
8. Modules A,B, and C need to be integrated. Tests A1 and A2 ran successfully against Module A alone; tests B1 and B2 ran successfully against Module B alone; and C1 and C2 against Module C alone. Modules A and B were integrated into Section AB and tests

A1, A2, B1, B2 and new tests AB1 ran successfully. Module C was integrated to make Section ABC, but tests A1 failed. Is the problem with Module A or Module C? Defend your answer with examples of error types.

9. Why is an independent tester better than testing by one of the developers?

10. What are the milestones of the System Test Phase?

11

The Acceptance Test Phase

Demonstration to the User and (Hopefully) Payment

11.1 INTRODUCTION

We saw in Chapter 8 that the goal of acceptance is written acknowledgement from the user that the project team has delivered what was promised. We also saw that the major problem in the small to mid size contract is the user's reluctance to pay—not because the system is bad, but because the user is afraid to lose the control he holds over the PT when he hands over the payment. To avoid this problem we suggested developing an Acceptance Test Plan (ATP) which is approved by the user ahead of the acceptance test phase. In the acceptance test you will merely run through the tests defined by the ATP at a formal, ordered session to demonstrate the promised system functions.

The obvious but major milestone is the user's signature of acceptance—on the bottom of a check.

Acceptance War Stories

Story 1. There is a large city in North America that has recently and rapidly grown to a population of 700,000. The inhabitants of this city still think that they live in a small town—for example, traffic moves like molasses. Recently, the city council decided that they needed a rapid transit system. They invented one: buses. Not ordinary buses, but computer scheduled buses! They gathered statistics on bus use and traffic in the city by geography and time. Then they hired programmers to write a statistical analysis system in COBOL on a large mainframe computer at a time-sharing company. About one year later they decided that it would be better to have their own computer, so they bought a *microcomputer* and attempted to install the software, still in COBOL. They very quickly realized that the micro would not handle the load, so they bought a computer from our Famous Minicomputer Manufacturing Company (FMMC) and hired programmers from FMMC to convert the system to run on the new computer.

Everything went well until acceptance. When the acceptance test procedure was run all the tests went smoothly except that the statistical results of several calculations were not the same as on the old system. The results were only different by one digit in the third decimal place, but the client refused to accept.

The FMMC programmers spent hours poring over formulas and algorithms in their programs but could find no errors. Finally one of the programmers took a hand calculator and analyzed some data manually. Lo and behold, the FMMC calculations were correct. It turned out to be a bug in the COBOL compiler on the old system.

> *Comment:*   Never assume that anything is correct.

Story 2.   There once was an Account Representative (also known as *salesman*) whose job was to negotiate the Functional Specifications (FS) for a project with the client. During the negotiations the client asked, "Could we have additionally the functions A, B and C for our fixed price?"

"Of course you may!" answered the Account Representative, came back to his office, and updated the FS to contain the new features A, B and C. He thought, "The project team has not started the design yet; when they do they will print out this FS and build the right thing." He neglected to tell anyone about the changes, or even put 'VERSION 2' on the front page of the FS. Unfortunately, the PT had already printed the FS and were busy designing.

At acceptance time the following scene took place:

Project Team:	Here is your system, Mr. Client.
CLIENT:	Very nice, but where are our functions A, B and C?
PT:	What functions A, B and C?
CLIENT:	The ones on page x of the FS.
PT:	Our page x doesn't have that!

> *Comment:*   First of all, only the technical people may make commitments. Second, be sure that all communications are clear among the members of the PT (even the Account Representatives).

> *Epilogue:*   Guess who had to add functions A, B and C free of charge? Oh yes, that Account Representative no longer works for the company.

11.2 ACCEPTANCE CHECKLIST

Here are the items that must be done before acceptance can begin:

- The ATP has been written, reviewed by the user, and revised as necessary.
- A specific time has been set aside and confirmed with the client's signing authority as convenient to run the acceptance.
- The PT personnel required to run the acceptance has been advised. These include the PM, to handle any negotiation and sign off, and at least the Project Leader to handle technical issues, fixes, and so forth.
- Any resources required for the acceptance run have been prepared. These are the software and hardware needed, forms for sign off, and copies of the acceptance script.
- One copy of the user documentation is available. Remember that this is part of the deliverables. Do not photocopy it yet—there will be changes.
- The PT has run through the ATP thoroughly ahead of time and made all the necessary corrections.
- The acceptance procedure has been agreed upon. This includes the order of the tests, who will enter the inputs, which terminals will be utilized, and so on. Remind the client of the agreement: he will sign off each successful test and the whole thing if all the tests work.

Prepare for the acceptance test well. This may be the first time that the user sees the system. If you are disorganized and ill-prepared, the client will become apprehensive about paying you.

11.3 RUNNING THE ACCEPTANCE

I usually suggest to the client that a member of the PT type while the client watches. Invariably the user answers, "*I* want to type and *you* watch!" This is understandable because by now the user is dying to play with the system. So I schedule extra time for typing. (Whereas I can type with two fingers, the user types with fewer.)

What happens if a test fails? (See next section for the types of problems that may be encountered.) If the problem is minor and it can be fixed within 30 minutes, the project team applies the fix and the acceptance is continued. If it will take longer to fix, the acceptance may be stopped and resumed later, perhaps the next day. In the case of any changes to the system, *the client has the right to rerun all previously performed tests*, although you can probably make the case that you do not need to regress to a previously completed test set. (See Chapter 8 for what comprises a test set.)

Leave time for the user to try to 'break' the system after each test. The ATP tests only for things working. You must also test for things not working, and this is difficult. Encourage the user to enter wrong things, use bad procedures, and so on.

11.4 CONCLUSIONS TO THE ACCEPTANCE PHASE

Problems encountered during acceptance will be *very minor* or *very major*. Since you have run through the acceptance procedure beforehand, all the obvious problems should be corrected when the user runs it. Minor problems that you may run up against are incorrect spelling of commands or messages, wrong abbreviations, and so forth. These problems are easily corrected, or the documentation may be updated to reflect the change—if the user agrees.

Major problems could be serious misinterpretations of the requirements. The client may reject a screen or a report because he did not understand the description in the FS, or despite agreeing to the FS, he realizes only now that it does not solve his problem. He may have changed his mind about something, or the problem itself may have changed since the FS was written. Most of these problems are caused by poor definition or analysis. If the FS was correct, these changes must be part of a new project. If indeed the FS was incorrect, or ambiguous, or incomprehensible, prepare to make the change.

The acceptance phase has one milestone—the most important one of the project—the client signature.

A Success Story

I wish to conclude this chapter with another story to demonstrate how pleasant acceptance can be.

The FMMC was hired at a recent Olympiad to provide a computer system for the news media. The system was to provide reporters with immediate event results and to compare the results to previous ones. There was to be a facility to word process reports and send the articles electronically to their respective newspapers and TV stations.

FMMC prepared the ATP meticulously—it was extensive. The environment was set up to do the acceptance and everyone showed up. But the client representative (the head of the Olympic committee) smiled and said, "FMMC, if you wish to provide a faulty computer system to dozens of newspaper and television reporters throughout the world, go ahead. We know that there will be no problems with your system." The checks were then signed.

QUESTIONS

1. List the people and things to bring to the acceptance session.
2. Why are the tests defined by the ATP not adequate for a thorough test?
3. Discuss several problems, caused by poor definition or analysis, that only become visible during acceptance.

12

The Operation Phase

The Proof of the Pudding

12.1 INTRODUCTION

So you are finally ready to turn on the system and let the real user begin to use it to solve real problems. The key issue here is that the whole project team may not leave town yet. There will always be problems found by the user, at least there will be questions which turn into problems if they are not answered quickly.

The major activity of this phase is the warranty: a period of time when the PT fixes any problems still left in the system. A minor activity is a post project review meeting to ensure that any mistakes made in the project are not repeated.

The milestones are a fully operational system and the sale of the next project (probably Version 2 of the old project).

Operation War Stories

There are so many cases where we turn the system on only to find major surprises, that I will not relate a particular story here—I am sure you have several favorite ones. These stories usually show that you just cannot test everything and that faults always remain in systems. There are documented cases where elections results reporting systems elected the wrong parties or candidates; where reservation systems showed trains full only to have no passengers riding on them; where rocket guidance systems sent rocket ships into the wrong orbits and so on. Software has been known to kill people. Recently there was a case where the software in a cancer irradiating treatment machine (kemo-therapy) produced a lethal dose of radiation when the back-arrow key on the operator terminal was hit too quickly. The manufacturer's fix (temporary, I hope) was to pry the cap off the back-arrow key. I collect horror stories. Please send me yours. My address is in the Preface.

12.2 PROVIDING WARRANTY

Warranty means fixing the problems *caused by the authors* free of charge for a certain period of time. Six months to one year is a common warranty period in the software industry. Providing warranty can be handled in one of three ways:

1. Have someone reside at the user site to address any problem. This person should be the project leader or a senior member of the team who knows every aspect of the system.

2. Have someone who can address the problem be accessible by phone. Preferably all of the authors of the software should be accessible.

3. Have someone who can address the problem available within a short period of time after a phone call is received. Again the actual authors are best.

You may consider a combination of the above. How about someone at the user site for two to four weeks after delivery? She could also do any user training required in this period. For the next two months guarantee that someone will be available by phone. For the following three months guarantee to address the problem within 4 hours after the problem report is phoned in.

Note that in all cases the terms of the warranty state that someone will *address the problem, not fix it,* in a certain period of time.

Manufacturers such as DEC have the following warranty available for both their software and hardware: When a problem is called in (and it cannot be fixed remotely) they promise to have a low level technician at the user site within a certain amount of time, for example four hours. If he cannot fix the problem within eight hours, someone at the next higher level is called in. This can progress up the hierarchy until the actual author of the software is called in.

12.3 SELLING THE NEXT PROJECT

A major mistake project managers make is to ignore the fact that one project will usually lead to another. If the project team is in the business of selling projects, the Operation Phase provides an excellent opportunity to sell the next project—Version 2 of the first project. If there were changes requested but turned down during the development, Version 2 of the product can incorporate these changes. This is why it is so valuable to write down all change requests on a form such as the Change Request Form discussed in Chapter 21. If there were no changes, or the PM sees no new opportunity for another project with the user, he could offer to do maintenance on the old project.

12.4 MAINTENANCE

There is always a need to change a system in order to improve it, add new features, or fix any problems still left after the warranty is over. Most of the time, the user's business will change with time and so will his requirements. These changes or enhancements are called maintenance.

Several software development methods include a Maintenance Phase. Maintenance may go on for a long period of time. Statistics from TRW, NASA, and DEC have shown that maintenance costs could be as much as seven times the cost of the original development. In order to have a clean ending point to the project, maintenance should be considered as a separate project that begins after the warranty period is over. See Section 22.5 on how maintenance projects can be treated as any other project.

12.5 POST PROJECT REVIEW

You should close the book on the project with a meeting called the post project review. Although this meeting will be detailed in Chapter 21 on meetings and reviews, the purpose of the post project review is to *write down* what went well, what could have been improved, to make suggestions for future projects, and to gather statistics on actuals versus plans in order to improve your estimating formulas. Do not let this be a 'chat over coffee in the cafeteria' type of get together—it should be a formal meeting with a written report.

12.6 OPERATION PHASE CHECKLIST

You are done with the whole project when:

- The new system is up and running smoothly.
- Conversion or cutover from any older systems is complete. Cutover should be done in phasesif possible.
- The end users are trained and comfortable on the new system.
- Warranty is provided. The PM should make sure that whatever technical resources were promised are actually made available. This is especially difficult when the warranty resource is supposed to be available by phone.
- (Optionally) The next project is sold.
- A post project review is held and all items that can benefit future projects are documented.
- The responsibility and method of ongoing maintenance is defined.

12.7 CONCLUSIONS TO THE OPERATION PHASE

Include the price of the warranty in the first proposal for the project. It is much more difficult to get additional funds for six months of warranty after the system is delivered. Proper operation is essential for user satisfaction. Remember that first impressions are critical—hold the user's hand at the start.

12.8 CONCLUSION TO PART 1 OF THE BOOK

This wraps up the 'theoretical' aspects of the business. At first glance it may seem 'bureaucratic' to do all these steps, write all these documents, and have all these meetings. But each phase, step, junction, document, and review provides a tool to do one or more of the following:

1. Plan a smaller chunk.
2. Complete a work package to measure progress. Progress reporting is needed to make both the client and your upper level management happy.
3. Involve the user at a review point. It bears repeating that the more the user is involved, the more succesful your project will appear to be, even if it is late or over budget!
4. Provide a point to stop and look for problems. We must ensure that each step correctly interprets the intent of the previous one. This is called Validation. Following are the six major transformations of information in the system development life cycle, and validation must be done at each transformation:

    I   The user perceives his own needs. (Mental transformation!)

    II   The user relates the needs to the analyst. (Verbal transformation.)

    III   This is written down as the Requirements Document. (Written transformation.)

    IV   The requirements document is transformed into the Functional Specifications. (Written transformation.)

    V   The Functional Specifications are transformed into design. (Written transformation.)

    VI   The design is transformed into code. (Written transformation.)

Validation is difficult. There are no (good) tools available to ensure that information is transformed correctly. The step-wise method allows us to intersperse reviews, walk-throughs, and inspections throughout the development to ensure that a problem introduced in one phase is caught as soon as possible, before it is carried on to the following phases. The next section of the book details the practical tools that make the development activities easier.

QUESTIONS

1. What are the ways to provide warranty?
2. Why is the Operation Phase a good opportunity to sell the next project?
3. Why should maintenance not be part of the project?
4. Why have a post project review? What is the result of this review?
5. What are the milestones of the Operation Phase?

PART 2
Practical Methods

13

Estimating

The Weakest Link in the Chain

13.1 INTRODUCTION

Estimating is an iterative process. Recall that the first estimate is done during the Definition Phase, when you write the preliminary project plan. It is necessary to do it at that point because you need an estimate for the proposal. But statistics from DEC, NASA, TRW, and others have shown that an estimate done at that point is 50% to 100% inaccurate. After the Analysis Phase you re-plan. You have to revisit the estimates and revise the preliminary project plan into the final project plan. At this point the accuracy of your estimates should double: You should be only 25% to 50% off. After the medium level design is done, you revise the estimates again. With the knowledge gained by that time you should be within 10%. Although not mentioned as an explicit activity in any other phase, plan to revise your estimate each time some new knowledge alters it.

All of the techniques that we will discuss are crucially dependent upon granularization: breaking things into small pieces. It is therefore essential to have a good work breakdown structure (discussed in Chapter 3), before any estimating is attempted.

13.2 ESTIMATING TECHNIQUES

There are three major techniques used to estimate: professional judgement, history, and formulas.

Use of Professional Judgement

Let us say that you know a person who has extensive experience programming report generation modules. You approach him or her with the design of a report generation program and ask him or her to estimate how long it would take to program it. After studying the design for five minutes, the programmer closes his eyes for another five (he is not asleep—he is calculating), and then replies, "Fifteen days." This is pure professional judgement.

The advantages of this method are that it is fast, and if the person is truly an expert, the estimates are amazingly accurate. The main disadvantage of the method is that you need an expert who has experience in the appropriate area and experts are *usually hard to find*. Furthermore, the estimate that you get is for the length of time it would take the expert to do it. It may not be dependable if someone else must perform the task. It is also dangerous to rely solely on the subjective knowledge and opinion of a few experts.

Use of History

To get away from depending on a few people and to make the estimate more scientific, you should keep history. *Write down* how long each task took to complete and who was responsible for it. You can then compare the task to be estimated with the actuals of similar tasks done in the past, and come up with an estimate. This implies that you should break the project up into tasks that are usually repeated and are easily compared. For programming this may be the generation of an input form, a report, calculation of a complex formula, and so forth. Companies or departments tend to build similar types of projects. Find the basic building blocks and document the actuals required for these. If you are really intelligent, take this one step further and build these blocks in a reusable fashion. You can estimate a re-use much more accurately than a re-write.

In order to compare apples with apples, you should also write down who performed the task. Statistics from IBM and DEC have shown that there can be as much as an 8 to 1 productivity ratio between the best and worst computer professional.

Use of Formulas

There have been many formulas published on software estimating. The best known is called COCOMO (Reference 15). COCOMO can be used to estimate project cost, effort (person months), schedule (months), and staffing (number of staff) for each of the following four phases:

Preliminary Design (PD)	-	our Analysis Phase
Detailed Design (DD)	-	our Design Phase
Code and Unit test (CUT)	-	same as ours
System Test (ST)	-	our System Test and Acceptance phases

There are three types of input to COCOMO: First, the monthly cost of the staff involved. Types of staff can be programmers, analysts, designers, test staff, administrators, and technical writers. Figure 13.1 shows an input screen that prompts for the second type of input. These are factors indicating the general level of complexity of the software, the size and availability of the computer used for development, the capability and experience of the staff, and the programming practices and tools used.

```
┌─────────────────────────────────────────────────────────────┐
│                    Estimation Mode Form                        │
│                                                                │
│  Name:Test                                                     │
│  Mode:   Simple (Intermediate Complex)                         │
│  Outputs:                                                      │
│  PDCOST:   5500     (Prel. Des. = Analysis Phase)              │
│  DDCOST:   5500     (Detail Des.= Design Phase)                │
│  CUTCOST: 5500      (Code&Unit Test)                           │
│  ITCOST:   4800     (Int. & Test)                              │
│  Inputs:                                                       │
│  Line of Source Code: 10000                                   │
│  Factors (1 - low through to 5 - extra high)                  │
│  Relability:       3    Exec time const:  1   Analyst cap.  1 │
│  Data base size: 2      RAM constrained:  3   Applicat'n exp 3 │
│  SW complexity:  3      VM volatility     1   Progrm'r cap   2 │
│                         Turnaround        2   VM experience  3 │
│                                               Lang exp       4 │
│                                                                │
│  Modern programming practices:            3                   │
│  Software tools:                          4                   │
│  Schedule constrained:                    3                   │
│                                                                │
└─────────────────────────────────────────────────────────────┘
```

```
                      The Factors are:
1 - Very Low  2 - Low   3 - Nominal 4 - High 5 - Very High
```

Figure 13.1 COCOMO parameter prompt screen, as implemented by VAXSPM (Reference 2.1)

At this point you probably feel that COCOMO will do a wonderful estimate, since these items seem to be exactly what determines the length of a project. But here is the rub: the last item COCOMO asks for is the number of lines of source code (LOSC). I feel that by the time you have enough knowledge about the system to accurately predict the LOSC, you do not need any formulas — you can probably accurately estimate the whole project.

Function point formulas. The COCOMO approach can be improved vastly by products that calculate the LOSC given the functions that a product does, and feeds the result into the COCOMO formulas. One such product is Before You Leap (BYL) by the Gordon Group (Reference 2.5). Figure 13.2 is the BYL screen that prompts the user for the function points as well as the language used. The results given by BYL are similar to those of COCOMO, except that the output can be presented as graphs such as pie or bar charts.

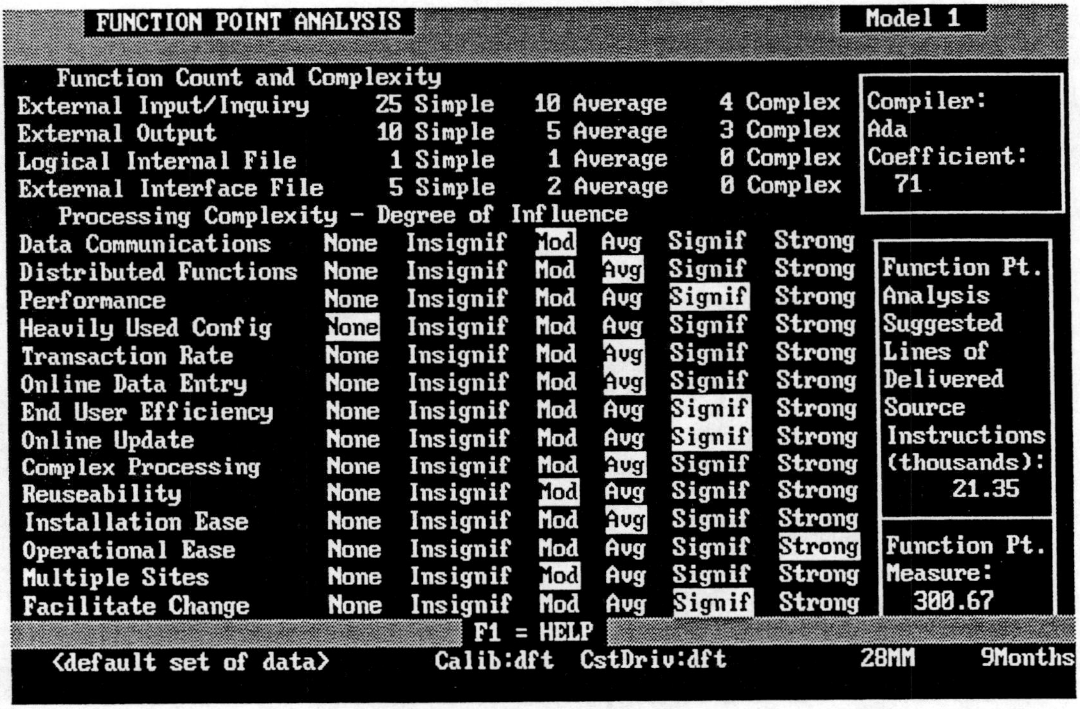

```
╔══════════════════════════════════════════════════════════════════════════╗
║ FUNCTION POINT ANALYSIS                                          Model 1   ║
╠══════════════════════════════════════════════════════════════════════════╣
║  Function Count and Complexity                                             ║
║ External Input/Inquiry      25 Simple    10 Average    4 Complex  Compiler: ║
║ External Output             10 Simple     5 Average    3 Complex  Ada       ║
║ Logical Internal File        1 Simple     1 Average    0 Complex  Coefficient: ║
║ External Interface File      5 Simple     2 Average    0 Complex  71        ║
║    Processing Complexity - Degree of Influence                             ║
║ Data Communications    None  Insignif  Mod  Avg   Signif  Strong           ║
║ Distributed Functions  None  Insignif  Mod  Avg   Signif  Strong  Function Pt. ║
║ Performance            None  Insignif  Mod  Avg   Signif  Strong  Analysis  ║
║ Heavily Used Config    None  Insignif  Mod  Avg   Signif  Strong  Suggested ║
║ Transaction Rate       None  Insignif  Mod  Avg   Signif  Strong  Lines of  ║
║ Online Data Entry      None  Insignif  Mod  Avg   Signif  Strong  Delivered ║
║ End User Efficiency    None  Insignif  Mod  Avg   Signif  Strong  Source    ║
║ Online Update          None  Insignif  Mod  Avg   Signif  Strong  Instructions ║
║ Complex Processing     None  Insignif  Mod  Avg   Signif  Strong  (thousands): ║
║ Reuseability           None  Insignif  Mod  Avg   Signif  Strong    21.35   ║
║ Installation Ease      None  Insignif  Mod  Avg   Signif  Strong           ║
║ Operational Ease       None  Insignif  Mod  Avg   Signif  Strong  Function Pt. ║
║ Multiple Sites         None  Insignif  Mod  Avg   Signif  Strong  Measure:  ║
║ Facilitate Change      None  Insignif  Mod  Avg   Signif  Strong    300.67  ║
║                            F1 = HELP                                        ║
║ <default set of data>       Calib:dft  CstDriv:dft        28MM    9Months  ║
╚══════════════════════════════════════════════════════════════════════════╝
```

Figure 13.2 BYL Function Point Analysis screen

Another product worth considering is Estimacs by Computer Associates. CA-Estimacs allows you to explore cost, effort, schedule, and staffing as in COCOMO, but adds suggested hardware required (IBM oriented), financial break-even analysis, risk analysis, and maintenance cost for both single and multi project environments. CA-Estimacs can take into account modern system development tools such as code generators and prototypers. It can even estimate for purchasing existing or customized packages. The types of factors input to CA-Estimacs are listed in Figure 13.3. Note that these are more detailed and sophisticated than those of COCOMO.

INPUT FACTORS	AFFECTED ESTIMATE
Business costs	Payback
Tool costs	
Hardware costs	
Customer complexity	Effort, Function point,
Customer geography	Maintenance
Developer's familiarity	
Business function size	
Target system sophistication	

Target system complexity	
Development strategy	Staff, Cost
Skills Deployment	
Rates	
Work week	
Machine cost	
System type	Hardware required
Application category	
Operating window	
Transaction volume	
Background workloads	
Number of terminals	
System size	Risk analysis
Project organization	
Customer/developer relationship	
New technology	
Deadlines	Multi project aspects
Other projects	
Background Workloads	

Figure 13.3 Table of some CA-Estimacs inputs and outputs

The only fly in the ointment is the cost of CA-Estimacs: over $20K MSL.

Estimating Programming

One formula approach that has been very successful for estimating the programming phase is a simplified function point approach. Let us detail this in order to understand how all formulas work. If you go through this exercise for the programming phase, you will have a much better understanding of all the other phases. Those who wish to skip technicalities may wish to go on to Section 13.3. The method is this.

There are basically only two factors that affect the duration of a task: the complexity of the task (C), and the productivity of the person performing it. The productivity of the person in turn depends on the number of years of general experience (G) and knowledge of the particular job (J). As a formula this can be expressed as:

$$D = C \times (G + J) \qquad \text{[formula 1]}$$

Where:

D is the task duration

C is the complexity factor

G is the general experience factor

J is the job knowledge factor

(You may be saying to yourself, "I hate formulas! Is this a math text? This is the reason I dropped out of math and went into computers!" Do not worry. This formula will be very simple and I promise that there will be no more formulas in the book.)

Let us discuss the factors in formula 1.

Complexity

To derive the complexity factor of a task you must break it down to the smallest possible repeatable functions within the task, and add up the complexity of each function. For a programming task, these are called *function points*. The function points could be *user input, user display, peripheral I/O, restructuring data, condition checking, calculation, branching and calling,* and so forth. (Sometimes the language constructs such as SEQUENCE, IF, WHILE, UNTIL, FOR, CASE, and ASSIGNMENT are counted.) The complexity of the program depends of course upon the language used and the complexity of each function point. Taking all this into consideration a table such as Figure 13.4 can be produced.

PROGRAMMING ESTIMATE COMPLEXITY FACTORS(C)

LANGUAGE	FUNCTION POINT	SIMPLE	CMPLX	VERY CMPLX
Interp'r	User Input	1	3	4
	User display	1	3	4
	Periph. Input	3	6	8
	Periph. Output	3	6	8
	Restructure Data	1	3	4
	Cond. Checking	1	3	4
	Calculation	1	2	3
	Branching	1	2	3
	Calling	2	3	4
High—Level	User Input	2	4	5
	User Display	2	4	5
	Periph. Input	4	7	9
	Periph. Output	4	7	9
	Restructure Data	2	4	5
	Cond. Checking	2	4	5
	Calculation	2	3	4
	Branching	1	2	3
	Calling	1	2	3
Assembly	User Input	4	5	8
	User Display	4	5	8
	Periph. Input	6	8	10
	Periph. Output	6	8	10
	Restructure Date	4	5	8
	Cond. Checking	4	7	9
	Calculation	3	5	8
	Branching	3	4	6
	Calling	4	5	8

LANGUAGE	FUNCTION POINT	SIMPLE	CMPLX	VERY CMPLX
Changing an	User Input	1		
Existing Pgm.	User Display	1		
	Periph. Input	1	2	
	Periph. Output	1	2	
	Restructure Data	1		
	Cond. Checking	1		
	Calculation	1	2	
	Branching	1		
	Calling	1		

Figure 13.4   Weighting factors for program complexity

These factors were derived by using actual measurement and then adjusted so that the formula $D = C \times (G + J)$ comes out in person-days. The factors in figures 13.4 through 13.6 are based on a paper by IBM (Reference 17), and is only an illustration of the method. You should define factors of your own. You may be thinking, "Boy, will I have to keep detailed time reports!" This is correct.

The total complexity (C) for a program will be the sum of all the factors for the function points.

Productivity

You need to establish factors for your staff's productivity. This is much more difficult to do than the task complexity factors, since people's productivity can change depending on their interest level, mood, and so forth. Recall that productivity is influenced by general years of experience and knowledge of the job. The following is a list of factors based on the general experience of the person:

PRODUCTIVITY FACTORS
BASED ON YEARS OF GENERAL EXPERIENCE(G)

Pgr.Type	Years of Experience	Factor Range
Senior	5 +	0.5 – 0.75
Average	1.5 – 5	1.0 – 1.5
Junior	0.5 – 1.5	2.0 – 3.0
Trainee	0.0 – 0.5	3.5 – 4.0

Figure 13.5 General experience factors (G)

Note that the productivity factors are presented as ranges to account for the variety in people. These figures are also based on IBM papers. (Reference 17). Develop your own factors by assigning '1' to your average person and fill in the data for the other people based on their history.

The speed at which a professional will produce a product depends not only upon the general experience (G) calculated above, but also on how much experience the person has at the particular job at hand and at related jobs. In addition, the amount of knowledge actually required should be factored in. The following table can be used to quantify this knowledge (J).

PRODUCTIVITY FACTORS
BASED ON   KNOWLEDGE OF THE PARTICULAR JOB(J)

JOB KNOWLEDGE	KNOWLEDGE REQUIRED		
	Much	Some	None
Detailed knowledge of this job and detailed knowledge of related jobs	0.75	0.25	0.00
Good knowledge of this job and fair knowledge of related jobs	1.25	0.50	0.00
Fair knowledge of this job and no knowledge of related jobs	1.50	0.75	0.00
No knowledge of this job and detailed knowledge of related jobs	1.75	1.00	0.25
No knowledge of this job and no knowledge of related jobs	2.00	1.25	0.25

Figure 13.6   Factors for job knowledge (J)

Again, you must develop your own job knowledge classifications and productivity factors.

Example of Using Formula 1, D = C x (G + J)

Let us estimate how long it would take to write a particular PASCAL program. The numbers in parenthesis are references to lines in the calculation below.

(1)The program prompts the user for something, (2)reads the user response, (3)validates it, (4)reads a record from disk, (5)calculates a number, (6)writes a record back to disk, (7)displays the result to the user, and (8)calls another module (returns). (9)The programmer has two years of experience, is a good but average programmer who has (10)fair knowledge of this particular application, but no knowledge of related applications. (11)Some job knowledge is needed to do this job.

Complexity (C) calculation. The factors are from Figure 13.4, for a HIGH LEVEL language.

Function	Factor
(1) USER DISPLAY(SIMPLE)	2
(2) USER INPUT(SIMPLE)	2
(3) CONDITION CHECKING(CMPLX)	4
(4) PERIPHERAL INPUT(SIMPLE)	4
(5) CALCULATION(SIMPLE)	2
(6) PERIPHERAL OUTPUT(SIMPLE)	4
(7) USER DISPLAY(SIMPLE)	2
(8) CALLING(SIMPLE)	3
TOTAL COMPLEXITY	C = 23

Productivity calculation

   General experience G. (Factor from Figure 13.5)

         (9)   Programmer is average (2yrs. exp) G = 1.00

   Job knowledge J. (Factor from Figure 13.6)

         (10)   Fair knowledge of application, no related knowledge, but

         (11)   some is required   J = 0.75

Plugging all this into Formula 1:

         Duration = 23 x (1.00 + 0.75) = 40.25

So it will take this particular person 40 days to design, document, code, and test this program.

   Conclusion to the formula method. This method will work *if you develop accurate factors.* The beauty of this approach is that it can be used for any task, be it programming or building a house. Note that this method, as any other estimating method, depends upon how well you granularize.

13.3 ESTIMATING THE ANALYSIS PHASE

Estimating analysis is very difficult because it is such a human oriented activity. Here is one method. Again, it depends upon breaking the task into its components. Figure 13.7 is the Level 2 WBS for analysis.

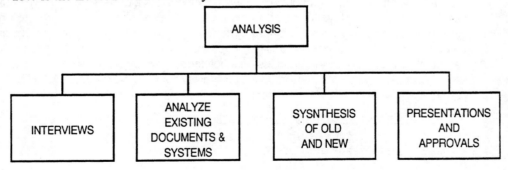

Figure 13.7   Analysis major components

The worksheet (Figure 13.8) is derived from level 3 of the WBS: each level 2 component is broken into appropriate sub-components and activites. A multiplication factor is then assigned to each activity such that the answer comes out in person-days.

ANALYSIS ESTIMATING WORKSHEET

INTERVIEWS

TYPE	NO.	FACTOR	DAYS	REF.	SUB	IPTS	TOT
Management		.5		1.2			
Supervisor		1.0		1.2			
Technical		1.5					
Clerical		.5					
TOT INTER.						1.25	

ANALYZE EXISTING DOC.'S, SYSTEMS

TYPE	NO.	FACTOR	TOT
Input forms		.5	
Output forms		.5	
Manual files		2.0	
Automated files		2.0	
Tables		2.0	
Systems		4.0	
TOTAL EXISTING SYSTEMS			

SYNTHESIS

TYPE	NO.	FACTOR	TOT
Interviews		2.5	
Documents		0.5	
Old system functions kept		1.0	
Old system functions changed		1.0	
New functions		1.5	
Alternatives presented		2.0	
TOTAL SYNTHESIS			

PREPARE FUNC. SPEC.

TYPE	NO.	FACTOR	TOT
Interviews		.25	
Documents and Systems		.5	
Synthesis		.5	
Other TOTAL PREPARE FUNC. SPEC.			

PRESENTATION (INCL. PREP)

TYPE	NO.	FACTOR	TOT
Attendees		.25	
Locations		.5	
Approvals		1.0	
Charts/slides		1.0	
TOTAL PRESENTATION			
GRAND TOTAL ANALYSIS			

Figure 13.8   Analysis estimating worksheet

The factors in Figure 13.8 come from DEC statistics and can be used as multiplication factors to calculate how long each activity should take.

An Example of Estimating Analysis

Figure 13.9 below is a filled in analysis estimate. The line numbers in parentheses were added to assist in the explanation. The items in bold were filled in by the estimator.

ANALYSIS ESTIMATE FOR ABC SYSTEM

INTERVIEWS

TYPE		NO.	FACTOR	DAYS	REF.	SUB	IPTS	TOT
(1)	Management	2	.5	1.0	1.2	1.2		
(2)	Supervisor	2	1.0	2.0	1.2	2.4		
(3)	Technical	1	1.5	1.5		1.5		
(4)	Clerical		.5					
(5)	TOT INTER.	5				5.1	1.25	6.4

ANALYZE EXISTING DOC.'S, SYSTEMS

TYPE		NO.	FACTOR	TOT
(6)	Input forms	10	.5	5
(7)	Output forms	20	.5	10
(8)	Manual files	2	2.0	4
(9)	Automated files		2.0	
(10)	Tables	2	2.0	4
(11)	Systems	1	4.0	4
(12)	TOTAL EXISTING SYSTEMS	35	2	5

SYNTHESIS

TYPE		NO.	FACTOR	TOT
(13)	Interviews	5	.5	12.5
(14)	Documents	35	.5	17
(15)	Old system functions kept	10	1.0	10
(16)	Old system functions changed	5	1.0	5
(17)	New functions	10	1.5	15
(18)	Alternatives presented		2.0	
(19)	TOTAL SYNTHESIS	64		59.5

PREPARE FUNC. SPEC.

TYPE		NO.	FACTOR	TOT
(20)	Interviews	5	.25	1
(21)	DocumentsandSystems	35	.25	9
(22)	Synthesis	64	.25	16
(23)	Other			
(24)	TOTAL PREPARE FUNC. SPEC.	104		26

PRESENTATION (INC

TYPE	NO.	FACTOR	TOT
(25) Attendees	10	.25	2.5
(26) Locations	2	.5	1
(27) Approvals	1	1.0	1
(28) Charts/slides	5	.5	2.5
(29) TOTAL PRESENTATION			7
(30) GRAND TOTAL ANALYSIS (PD)			125.9

Figure 13.9   Analysis estimate example

Explanation

Interviews. (1) 2 managers need to be interviewed, times factor of .5 is 1 (under DAYS). The REF is overhead for referral: you need to phone him or her, make an appointment, show up, and so forth. Multiply, and put the result under SUBtotal. Similarly the subtotals for interviewing 2 supervisors and 1 technician are calculated. The total of the SUBs is added, and multiplied by 1.25 for the interrupts during the interviews, to get the TOTAL INTERVIEWS of 6.4 days.

Analyze Existing Documents and Systems. (6) There are 10 existing manual input forms, (7) 20 reports, (8) 2 files in a filing cabinet (students and courses), (10) 2 tables (materials vs. courses, cost vs. courses), (11) and 1 system (warehouse). Result of these lines, when multiplied by the appropriate factors, gives TOTAL EXISTING SYSTEMS of 27 days.

Synthesis. This is the thinking, discussing, analyzing part. (13) For each of the 5 (NO. from (5)) interviews there is a synthesis factor of .5. (14) Similarly for the 35 (NO. from (12)) documents. Now comes the hard part. If there is an existing system, manual or automatic, count approximately how many of the functions in the old system are to be reproduced in the new system, and put under NO. in (15). Count the number of functions in the old system that are changed for the new system, and place in (16). NO. in (17) is the number of entirely new functions to be done in the new system. If several alternative approaches are to be analyzed, put down in (18). Multiply by the factors and total in TOTAL SYNTHESIS, in this example 59.5.

Prepare the Functional Specification. This section calculates the time that will be spent in the actual writing, word processing, proofreading, and correcting of the FS. In (20) we account for the preparation as a result of the 5 (from line (5)) interviews; in (21) for the 35 (from (12)) existing documents and systems, in (22) the total synthesis (from (19)). Put anything else you can think of in (23), multiply it all and add it, which comes to 26 on line (24).

Presentation. Each attendee is factored in (25) because they ask questions, each separate location (26), approvals required (27) (I would increase this one!) and factor in slides or charts that have to be produced for the presentations. Multiply and add on line (30). The GRAND TOTAL ANALYSIS is the sum of the subtotals on lines (5), (12), (19), (24), and (29).

Conclusions to using the analysis estimating chart. Obviously this chart will not give you an accurate estimate as it stands. It is very useful, however, if you develop factors that work for your applications. If anything, it serves as a checklist or WBS of all the activities that may be involved in analysis.

It is very important to be able to estimate analysis well. If you are using the two phase proposal process (See Section 4.2) the first step is the analysis alone. Even DEC, with all of its estimating expertise, prefers to do the analysis phase of a project on a Time and Materials (Cost Plus) basis.

13.4 RATIOS

If you tend to do similar types of projects you will find that your projects will consist of similar major activities, and that each major activity takes the same proportion of time from project to project. You should therefore calculate these proportions or ratios for your past projects. This is especially true if you find that the top levels of the WBS's for your projects tend to be similar. For example, if level 1 on the WBS of your projects always consists of the 7 phases (which it should!) you should have a good idea of the percentage of the total effort each phase will require. Figure 13.10 is a table of industry averages for a small to mid size *commercial* project:

PHASE	60% OF PROJECTS	90% OF PROJECTS
Definition	10%	
Analysis	20%	− 40%
Design	10%	
Programming	20%	− 20%
System Test	17%	
Acceptance	7%	− 40%
Operation	16%	

Figure 13.10   Ratio of effort in the 7 phases

Figure 13.10 shows that whereas only 60% of the projects fitted into the finer breakdown percentage, a very high percentage fitted into the 40% PLAN, 20% BUILD, 40% TEST ratio.

Brooks (Reference 3) found that for O/S 360 (huge project, first operating system in the world, written in assembler) it took 33% to PLAN it, 17% to CODE it, 25% to do MODULE TEST AND LOW LEVEL INTEGRATION, and 25% to do SYSTEM TEST. Establish common ratios at lower levels of the WBS as well. For example, Gildersleeve (Reference 2) found that:

> TIME TO DESIGN, DOCUMENT, AND CODE A MODULE
> EQUALS THE TIME TO DEBUG IT.

How to Use Ratios

You may be tempted to do an accurate estimate for one phase, and extrapolate this estimate to the remaining phases using past ratios. This is not very dependable, since projects are always different. Instead, estimate each phase as well as you can, then compare the new ratios to past ones to see if any item is out of the norm. Revisit the estimate for that item, taking a better look at the risks and contingencies.

13.5 DEC (AND OTHER LARGE CORPORATIONS) ESTIMATING RULE OF THUMB

Do large companies such as DEC use these approaches? Yes, they use formulas, but they keep to the following rules:

- *Never ask an inexperienced person to estimate.* Estimating is crucially dependent on experience. Here is how you teach a junior person to estimate: Either have him work with an experienced person as she is estimating, or have the experienced person work out all the formulas in detail and give it to the junior person to 'verify'.

- *Estimate in a group if you can afford the manpower.* A meeting of several minds follows the rule of squares: two minds are four times as effective as one; three minds nine times and so forth. When I teach Software Project Management to a class I always include a real case study to estimate in small groups. I find that a project that would take one person three to four days to estimate alone can be estimated by a group of three or four people in one to two hours! Group dynamics are fascinating. The members are motivated to be productive—peer pressure stops any slacking off. The group usually comes up with great ideas, identifies all the risks, and everyone on the team will be committed to the estimate.

- *Never force an estimate on a professional such as a programmer.* The supervisor should first ask the programmer how long he figures it will take. If the supervisor disagrees they must negotiate.

- *Never take an average of different estimates.* For a major product, have two or more separate groups or individuals estimate. If there is a significant difference between the estimates, get the people together and come to an agreement. The only reason two people with similar experience will estimate the same thing differently is that one has thought of something that the other has forgotten.

- *Granularize down to one week or less.* A software task of approximately one week seems to be the most a human being can conceptualize and estimate well.

- *Always add (multiply?) for contingency.* See Section 2.4 on risk management.

- *Always quote a range when giving estimates to managers or clients.* There is an interesting psychology to quoting estimates. If you tell a manager it will take 12 months, she thinks you have an accurate number; if you tell her it will take 10 to 14 months, she will know it is an estimate.
- *Use your 'gut feel'.* After you develop the estimate, sleep on it one night, then ask yourself, "Does this estimate feel right?" It is amazing how accurate feeling becomes *with experience.* At least it will warn you if the estimate is way out in left field.

13.6 THE ESTIMATING PROCESS

If you have a good project management software package available (see chapter 17) you can develop your WBS's on it and enter the estimates for all the appropriate tasks. The best packages will add up all the estimates and costs, and even roll them up to any level of the WBS. If you do not have such a package available, develop and use forms such as the following:

```
PROJECT ESTIMATE SUMMARY


Project _____          Date_____
Client_____          Author_____
Units_____


Definition                                        _____
Analysis                                          _____
System Design                                     _____
Prep. of the ATP                                  _____
Programming (DES, Doc, Code, Test)                _____
Prep. of User Manuals                             _____
System Test                                       _____
Acceptance                                        _____
Client Training                                   _____
Operation (Warranty)                              _____
Project Management                                _____
Project Meetings                                  _____
Contingency                                       _____
Other (_____)              _____


Total                                             _____
```

Figure 13.11   Project estimate summary

Note that figure 13.11 has an estimate for the seven phases of the project, as well as important and costly activities such as ATP preparation, user manuals, client training, project management and project meetings. This summary form, when completed, is what you end up with. You start with forms such as Figure 13.12, for granularizing each major item on the summary form. See Appendix A Project Plan for a completed set of summary and detail forms for a sample project.

Task Estimate Detail For Project_____

Item_____   Author_____

Date_____   WBS Reference_____

TASK	DESCRIPTION LX	CMP DYS	EST.	COMMENTS
.				
.				
.				
	TOTALS			

Figure 13.12   Task estimate detail

The field marked CMPLX is task complexity: enter Low, Medium or High. This will be used later to assign the task to a person with a low, medium ,or high level of experience. To estimate analysis, use the chart in Figure 13.9. For programming tasks, the major breakouts should always be DESIGN, DOCUMENT, CODE, and TEST, so a form such as Figure 13.13 can be used.

Programming Estimate Detail for Project_____

Item_____   Author_____

Date_____   WBS Reference _____

TASK	DESCRIPTION	CMP LX	DES	DOC	CODE	TEST	COMMENTS
			ESTIMATES				
.							
.							
.							
	TOTALS						

Figure 13.13   Programming task estimate detail

A detail sheet may be the rollup of other detail sheets. There is no limit, although you should not break down further than one half day. A long coffee break and there goes half a day!

13.7 CONCLUSION TO ESTIMATING

Estimating, as the subtitle of this chapter suggests, is our weakest talent. Yet all of our planning and control depends upon our estimating skills.

Estimating is iterative—expect estimates to change. That is why we must put milestones into the development of a product. Milestones allow us to stop, assess how long it took to get there, and re-estimate the dates of the remaining milestones based upon the experience so far. Do not allow anyone to hold you to an impossible date. (Point out to management the definition of the word 'estimate.')

Estimating is still an art. There are no foolproof software or manual tools available to help us at the moment. The key to estimating is granularization. Statistics help. If the tasks are broken into very fine pieces, and if you calculate a best estimate for each one, on some you will be over, but on others you will be under. It will average out in the end —and it is only the end point that matters.

QUESTIONS

1. When in the project life cycle must you estimate (and re-estimate), and how accurate are these estimates?

2. Describe the professional judgement estimating method. What are the advantages and disadvantages of this method?

3. Why is the historical method better than professional judgement?

4. Using the function point formula developed in section 13.2, estimate how long it will take to program the following:

   COBOL program, prompts the user for a key, ensures that the entry is correct length, gets a record from a DBMS, structures it into a displayable record, calls a subroutine to display the record as a screen form. The programmer has 3 years of experience, good knowledge of this application, fair knowledge of related jobs, some knowledge is needed.

5. Estimate the Analysis Phase of a project that involves the following:
   a. Interview 2 managers (referred), one supervisor, and one technician.
   b. The existing manual system has 10 input forms, 15 output forms, 2 manual files, and 1 table.
   c. 5 old functions are kept, 5 are changed, 10 new functions will be needed.
   d. One approval is needed, then a presentation to 3 attendees must be made. 10 charts will have to be prepared for the presentation.

6. What are the two ways to use ratios? Which one is better?

7. Why is estimating in a group worthwhile?

8. Group Exercise:

   Some of the estimates for the ABC project in Appendix A are purposefully inaccurate. Consider each of the estimates in Appendix A and revise any that you disagree with. Re-estimate the whole project.

14

Scheduling

Putting It All on the Calendar

14.1 INTRODUCTION

The estimate calculated in Chapter 13 is the number of person-days of effort that will be required to build the project. This is called *direct time*. Scheduling maps direct time onto a real calendar, to give *calendar duration* or *elapsed time*.

In Chapter 3 we saw that the actual steps in planning a project are:

1. The planners (usually the PM and the PL in a small to mid size project) details the Work Breakdown Structure (WBS). A person or group is allocated to be responsible for each lowest level activity.

2. The responsible party estimates the lowest level activities in person or direct days.

3. The reponsible party also indicates the precedent activities required for each task, and suggest the resources required for the task.

4. The planners draw the network of activities, usually in the form of a PERT chart.

5. The PM optimizes the network by allocating appropriate resources to each activity.

6. The PM produces the schedule of activities.

This chapter details steps 4, 5, and 6, the network and the schedule.

14.2 THE PERT CHART

PERT, which incidentally stands for Program Evaluation and Review Technique, was invented by the US Navy in 1958 when developing the Polaris missile—a project of over 300,000 activities! At first PERT was simply used to describe a sequence of activities using a set of arrows, such as Figure 14.1.

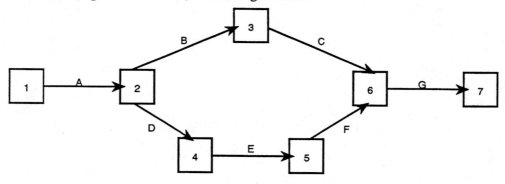

Figure 14.1   A PERT chart

Each arrow represents an activity and is labeled with the activity name, for example A, B, and so forth. If an activity cannot be begun before a preceding activity is completed, the tail of the arrow of the second *(successor)* activity is placed at the head of the *precedent*. In Figure 14.1, for example, E cannot be begun before D is done, G cannot be begun before both C and F is done. Starting and ending points are called *nodes* and are numbered. The chart in Figure 14.1 may seem trivial, but it is worthwhile to draw up a PERT for any size project, because it forces you to analyze the sequence of activities.

The PERT also shows which activities may be going on simultaneously. A sequence of activities, such as A-B-C-G is called a *path*. If there are paths or sections of paths running parallel, as path B-C and path D-E-F, then the activities B and C can be done simultaneously with activities D, E, and F.

The Critical Path

A vast improvement to the PERT chart above can be achieved by putting the duration of each task on the PERT, as in Figure 14.2. In Section 14.3 we will see how duration is determined when resources (people) are allocated to the task.

First, the *critical path* can be calculated. This is the longest path in the network, calculated by adding up all the durations along the path. For example, in Figure 14.2 the top path is 26 days, and the bottom is 25 days, making the top path the critical path (CP). The double line indicates the complete CP. Knowing the CP is essential to the PM. It shows the length of the total project: 26 days in our case. It also shows the activities to watch. If any activity on the CP slips (takes longer than planned) then the delivery date of the project slips.

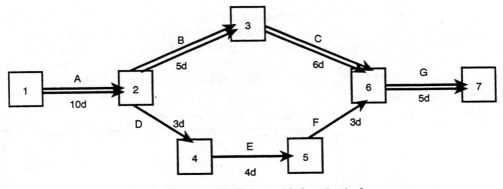

Figure 14.2   A PERT chart with duration in days

Float or Slack

Activities that are not on the CP have *float* or *slack*—a period of time that these activities can slip and still not affect the CP and therefore the delivery date. In Figure 14.2 , for example, activities D, E, and F have *among them* 1 day of float. (Calculation: CP activities B and C take 11 days; simultaneous non CP activities D, E, and F take 10 days together; 11-10 = 1 day of float.) Any one of activities D, E, or F, or all three together may take one day longer and still not affect the CP.

The Critical Path May Change!

What if activity D takes 5 days instead of 3? The CP has changed to the D-E-F path. This is why the PM must constantly update the network with any changes. Automation of all this is recommended of course, and Chapter 17 details the tools available to do this.

Free Float and Total Float

In the PERT chart in Figure 14.3 below the CP activities *Program Module A* and *Test Module A* are done by Programmer 1. Activities on the center path, *Program Module B* and *Test Module B*, done by Programmer 2 have 5 days of float. Activities on the bottom path, *Program Module C, Test Module C* and *Integrate* are done by Programmer 3 and the Project Leader. The bottom path has 5 days of float as well.

Let us say activities *Program Module A, Program Module B,* and *Program Module C* were all started at once and finish on time on April 1st. Programmer 2 comes to the PM and says, "I have 5 days of float, so I wish to take April 2 and 3 off." The PM, feeling benevolent, lets him take the days off. Seeing this, Programmer 3 comes to the PM and says, "I have 5 days of float as well, so I wish to take April 4 and 5 off." The PM looks at the schedule and says "No way. Programmer 2 has 5 days of *total float*, but you have 5 days of *free float*. Back to work!"

Total float is the float time that an activity has before it affects the CP. *Free float,* is the float time an activity has before it affects *any other* (non critical) activity. What if the Project Leader explicitly set aside April 4 to 6 to work on the *Integration and Test of C and D,* and she has some other activity planned for the subsequent days? Allowing Programmer 3 to be late with his activity will cause a major problem.

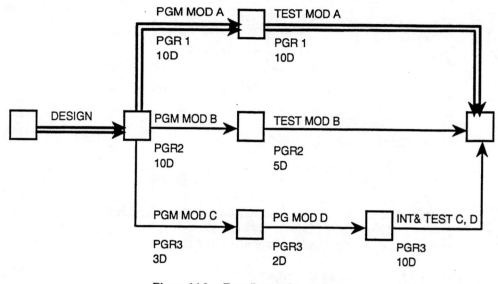

Figure 14.3   Free float and total float

Project float (any float on any activity) is an item owned by the Project Manager, to be used at his or her discretion. Some PM's even go so far so not informing individuals about the float on their own activities.

Dummy Activities

The PERT chart described so far is called *activity on arrow* format. The major drawback to this format of the PERT is the need for dummy activities. For example, in Figure 14.4A we have activities B, C, and D-F all starting at the same node and ending at the same node.

It would be better to have a unique starting and/or ending node for each activity. For example, if someone refers to the activity between nodes 2 and 3, it is not clear which activity he is referring to. This is especially true when the network is computerized. We all know how finicky computers are about unambiguous representation of things. Figure 14.4A is therefore usually redrawn as Figure 14.4B. Here all activities are represented by a unique start-end node pair. The activity between nodes 3 and 4 is a fudge, or dummy (that is, not real) of zero duration and drawn as a dotted line.

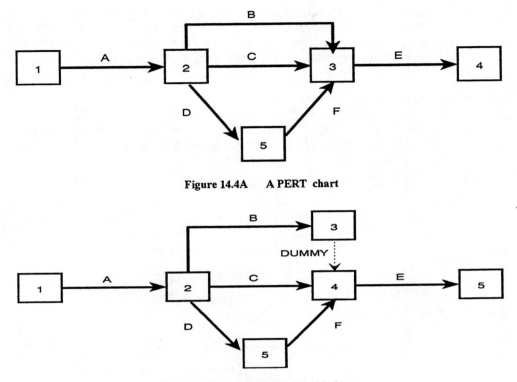

Figure 14.4A   A PERT chart

Figure 14.4B   A PERT chart with dummy

Activity on Node or Precedence Network

The *activity on node* or *precedence network* is another format of the PERT chart. Figure 14.5 is the same project as Figure 14.4, drawn as an activity on node PERT.

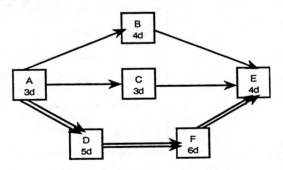

Figure 14.5   Activity on node PERT

The *nodes* are labeled with the task names, and optionally with task duration. The arrows indicate precedence only. Note that dummies never need to be used. Precedence networks are therefore better than activity on arrow networks, and are becoming more and more common, especially in the world of computer drawn PERT charts.

14.3 RESOURCE ALLOCATION

If you are doing the plan manually, the PERT chart is the best diagram to use for resource allocation. First draw the PERT ignoring all resources. The diagram for a software project may look like Figure 14.6.

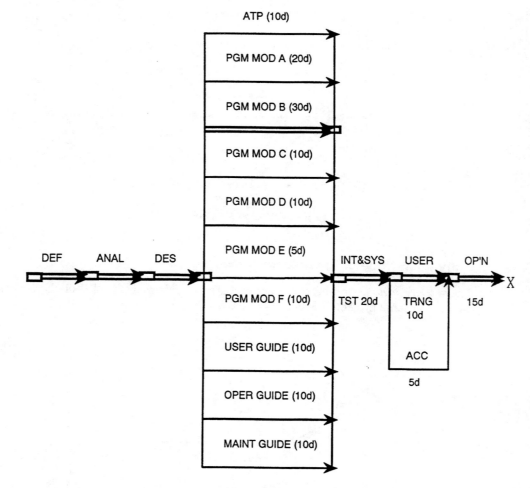

Figure 14.6   PERT ignoring resources

The next step is to redraw the PERT taking resources into account.

Allocating Human Resources

The network in Figure 14.6 has 10 simultaneous activities going on at one point in time, which may be an option if you have 10 programmers available. (Or one programmer who will spend one tenth of his time on each one!) Obviously there are better ways to use your people. Allocating human resources is very subjective and depends mainly on their availability, but the following are things to consider:

- Assign tasks to individuals whose skill level suits the task. Do not assign an expert an insignificant task, nor assign a very complex task to a junior person.

- Assign similar tasks to the same person. This will reduce learning time.

- Assign time critical tasks to your most reliable people. A reliable person is not one who *could* do the task in three days, but sometimes takes five or ten; a reliable person is one who says it will take five days and that is how long it takes.

- Assign tasks that communicate to the same individual to minimize people's interaction.

- Do not forget that the Project Leader will need to spend time supervising, especially at the start of the project.

Level your resources as much as possible. It is better to keep three programmers busy for five weeks running than to employ five for one week, no one for the next week, three for the following week and seven the next. The PERT in Figure 14.7 is Figure 14.6 redrawn with resources assigned. The direct time for each task is shortened if more than one resource is assigned.

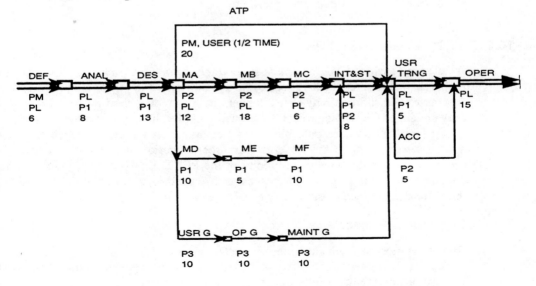

Figure 14.7   Resources allocated

Staff allocation decisions were made based on the following: P1 (Programmer 1) is available throughout the project, but P2 and P3 are only available for a shorter period. Modules A, B, and C are the most difficult but they are similar, so the Project Leader (PL) will help P2 code all of these together. Having the PL on the CP will also reduce the stress on the PM. P1 is a senior person capable of working on her own, P3 is junior so he is assigned the documentation (somewhat unfair!). Note that everyone works contiguous periods of time.

Reducing(?) Task Duration by Adding Manpower

As Brooks so aptly proved (Reference 3), adding people to a team does not *necessarily* reduce the task's duration. One industry rule of thumb that I have found useful is, "Add at least 10% to the direct time estimate for each additional member on a professional team." This implies that if a task takes 10 days for one person to do, with 2 people it will take 11 person-days, or at best 5 1/2 calendar days. Add 10% for each additional person cumulatively.

The task durations were translated from Figure 14.6 to Figure 14.7 taking the above rule of thumb into account, plus some professional judgement based on how well the subtasks can be divided, how well the individuals communicate, and so on.

Allocating 'Non-Human' Resources

Non-human resources needed for a software project may be computer hardware, software packages, operating systems, information, manuals, training, computer warranties, printing services, and so forth. These items were probably listed by the person responsible for the estimate. Usually we do not bother putting these items on the PERT, but ensure that they are listed somewhere.

14.4 THE TRIPLE CONSTRAINT

As we saw earlier, *"You can have it good, cheap or fast: pick two!"* Adding more resources will reduce the duration, but at a higher cost. Moving a reliable person from a complex but short activity onto a longer one may reduce the time taken overall, but may endanger the whole project if the quality on the short task is reduced.

Many options are possible when you assign resources. Always try several approaches, looking at the effect on resource utilization and cost, the length of the critical path and the general simplicity of the PERT. The PM must juggle the three constraints and come up with the best balance depending on the priorities placed on the three constraints *by the user or upper level management.*

Crashing a Project

One of the most difficult situations is when time is the highest priority among the three constraints. Take a scenario where your manager has asked you to estimate a project and you are presenting the results:

YOU: If all things go well, we can deliver this project on April 15th.

MGR: No way! Marketing promised it for April 1st. We have to pay a penalty of $1000 per day after April 1st. Can you do it faster?

YOU: Yes, but I'll have to crash—buy extra computer time, hire more people and do overtime. It will cost more to develop it.

MGR: Crash everything! Hang the cost!

YOU: (To yourself: sounds like there are political motivators here.) OK.

Should you indeed crash every task? Obviously not—why crash tasks that are not on the critical path? Figure 14.8 below is an example of calculating which tasks to crash and by how much:

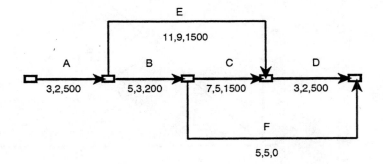

Figure 14.8A   PERT for a project

Step	Crash Task from Days to Days	Days Gained	Cost	Total Cost
1.	A, 3 → 2	1	500	500
2.	B, 5 → 4	1	200	200
3.	B, 4 → 3	1	200	
	E, 11 → 10		1500	1700
4.	C, 7 → 6	1	1500	
	E, 10 → 9		1500	3000
5.	D, 3 → 2	1	500	500

Figure 14.8B   Steps to crashing the project

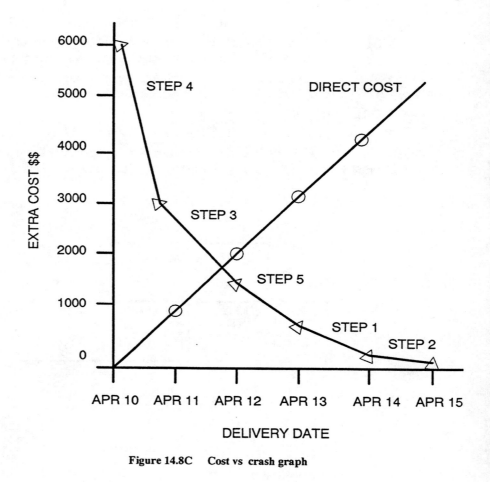

Figure 14.8C   Cost vs crash graph

First of all we must calculate three numbers for each task:

    1st number: The normal duration (days). This is the estimate you would present to your manager at first.

    2nd number: The minimum duration (days) into which you could crash (squeeze) the task.

    3rd number: The extra cost per day for the crash.

For example, task B (Figure 14.8A) would normally take 5 days. If the programmers work overtime it could be done in as little as 3 days (absolute minimum), but it would take $200 *per day* extra.

So let us crash the project. The algorithm to use is this: *Crash tasks on the CP, one day at a time as long as no other path becomes critical. If other paths become critical, crash those as well.*

Step 1:   (See Figure 14.8B.) Crash task A from 3 days to 2. There is 1 day gained at a cost of $500. No other path is impacted because there are no other parallel activities. Task A cannot be crashed further (3 is the minimum).

Step 2:   Crash B from 5 days to 4, cost is $200. E is on a parallel path, so check to see if it has become critical. E happens simultaneously with tasks B and C. With B crashed to 4 days, B and C together take 11 days. E is 11 days, it has just turned critical, but does not need to be crashed yet.

Step 3:   Crash B to 3 days at a cost of $200. Since E is parallel and critical, in order to gain the extra day, E also has to be crashed to 10 days at a cost of $1500, for a total cost of $1700.

Step 4:   Steps 4 and 5 are similar so the explanation is left to the reader.

Five days are the most that the project can be crashed. Note that not every task needed to be crashed, nor were all the crashed tasks squeezed to the minimum. And last, Figure 14.8C is a graph that is incredibly useful to management. It graphs the delivery date of the project (X-axis) versus the amount of extra dollars that will have to be spent to reach that date. The points were plotted backwards, from the lowest cost step to the highest: by taking Step 2 (lowest cost step), you could deliver on April 14, at an *extra* cost of $200. Then taking Step 1 (next lowest cost step), delivery can be April 13, but cost is $700 ($200 for Step 2 plus $500 for Step 1). Then Step 5 and so on until all the steps are plotted for a total cost of $5900.00. The straight line labelled 'Direct Cost' is a plot of the penalty charge of $1000 per day. Your manager will love you (perhaps you would prefer a raise) when you point out that it is only worth crashing to the date where the two lines intersect—April 12. After this date the crash cost is greater than the direct cost!

Conclusions to Crashing a Project

Several assumptions were made here: First, that tasks can be crashed. Adding manpower or overtime may not speed things up. Second, that tasks can be crashed in any order. Third, that tasks can be crashed independently. Crashing one task may affect others. The best computer packages will do all these calculations for you.

14.5 THE SCHEDULE OR GANTT CHART

A Gantt chart is just a time bar chart. It is called Gantt after its inventor Henry Gantt. The Gantt chart in Figure 14.9 is a schedule of the project PERT in Figure 14.8.

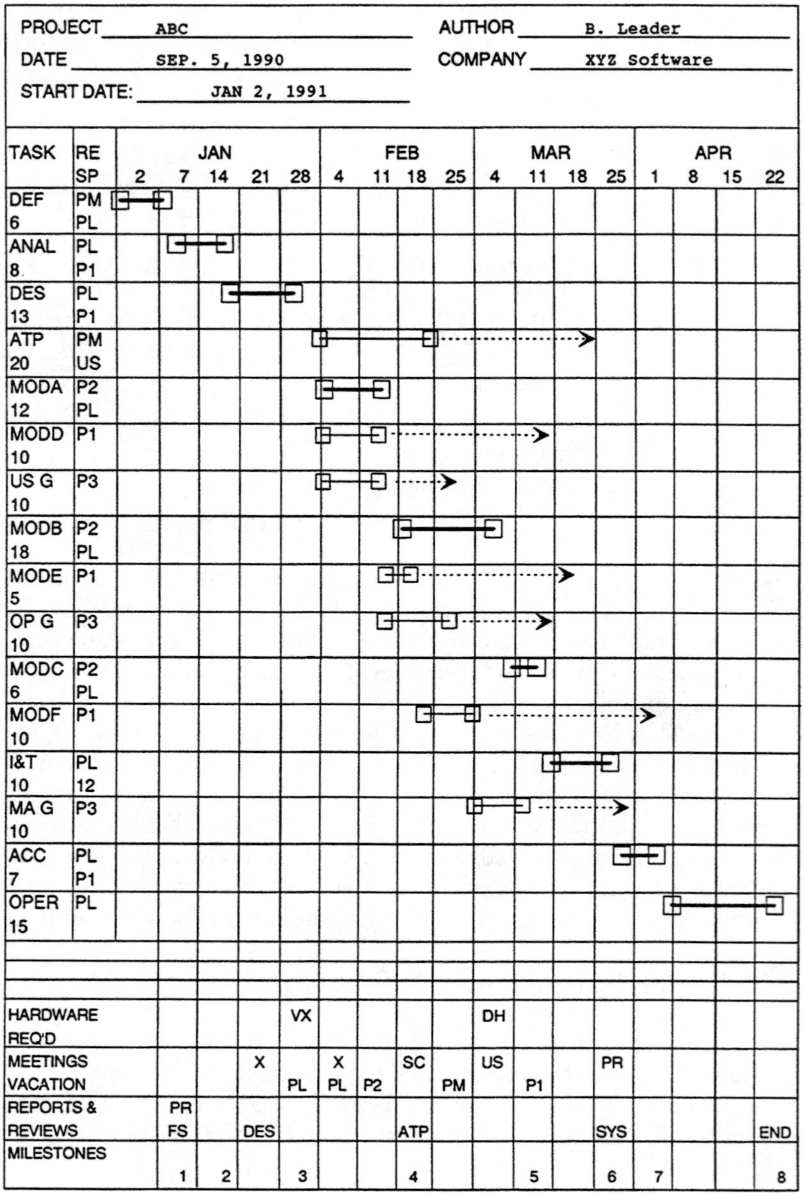

PROJECT_____ ABC _____   AUTHOR _____ B. Leader _____

DATE _____ SEP. 5, 1990 _____   COMPANY _____ XYZ software _____

START DATE: _____ JAN 2, 1991 _____

TASK	RE SP	JAN 2	7	14	21	28	FEB 4	11	18	25	MAR 4	11	18	25	APR 1	8	15	22
DEF 6	PM PL	▯━▯																
ANAL 8	PL P1		▯━━▯															
DES 13	PL P1			▯━━━▯														
ATP 20	PM US					▯━━━━▯┄┄┄┄┄➤												
MODA 12	P2 PL					▯━▯												
MODD 10	P1					▯━━▯┄┄┄┄┄┄➤												
US G 10	P3					▯━━▯┄┄➤												
MODB 18	P2 PL						▯━━━▯										
MODE 5	P1						▯▯┄┄┄┄┄➤										
OP G 10	P3						▯━━▯┄┄┄➤										
MODC 6	P2 PL								▯▯								
MODF 10	P1							▯━▯┄┄┄┄┄┄┄➤								
I&T 10 12	PL									▯━━▯						
MA G 10	P3								▯━▯┄┄┄➤							
ACC 7	PL P1										▯━▯				
OPER 15	PL											▯━━━▯		
HARDWARE REQ'D				VX					DH							
MEETINGS VACATION			X	PL	X PL	P2	SC	PM	US	P1	PR					
REPORTS & REVIEWS		PR FS		DES			ATP				SYS			END
MILESTONES		1	2		3			4			5		6	7		8

MILESTONES: 1 - Proposal   2 - Func. Spec.   3 - Design
              4 - ATP   5 - Mid. Pgm'g.   6 - Sys. Tst.
              7 - ALL   8 - END

Figure 14.9   Gantt chart of a project

The steps to drawing such a Gantt are:

Step 1:   Draw in the units of time at the top. Choose time units so that you will need no more than two such charts. You will see that the Gantt is the project manager's bible. All calendar dependent information can be put on the Gantt, and 99% of the PM's life is calendar dependent. Start dates of the weeks should be marked if space allows.

Step 2:   Mark all known calendar events at the bottom. These are the holidays, vacations, leaves, meetings, training, prior commitments, and so forth —all events that you have to schedule around.

Step 3:   From your PERT such as Figure 14.7, schedule each activity. Starting with the first activity, Definition, draw a bar equal in length to the calendar days on the PERT. Mark in the responsible people, and the percentage of time that you expect each one to work on the project if it is not 100%.

Step 4:   Schedule contingency task by task. For each activity ask yourself, "Is there anything that could extend the duration of this specific task?" For example, "What could make definition take longer than six calendar days?" Note that two days of contingency has been added to the definition phase, maybe because the user knew too little. Review the Risk Quiz (Section 2.4) to see if any of the items there apply. Figure 14.10 lists some common project risk items and the tasks that can be extended because of that risk.

Step 5:   Loop back to steps 3 and 4, scheduling all the tasks on the PERT, from left to right and from top to bottom for the parallel tasks. A task starts when the contingency for the last precedent task is finished. Add lots of contingency onto the last private task, the System Test, as a safety measure.

Step 6:   Mark in all other important events. Mark the major milestones indicated by the completion of important events and products. Be sure that milestones are frequent enough so that the time between each one is short enough that things can not get out of control. Every two to three months on a twelve month project is common. This implies that a 'fake' milestone may have to be invented, such as *Milestone 3, Mid-programming review in Figure 14.10*. Mark in important reviews and meetings. The participants at these events will appreciate being notified as far in advance as possible. Mark in dates when all the pieces of hardware are required. The longer the lead time that you give the manufacturer, the better are your chances of receiving the item on time.

RISK	TASK(S) IT EFFECTS
USER ORIENTED	
Poor relationship with user	definition, analysis everything user is involved in.
Delays of items (e.g. Approvals, provided by user)	definition,analysis,possibly ATP, documentation, test (data)
User knows too much	analysis, design, progamming, acceptance
User knows too little	definition,acceptance,operation
User unavailable (different city)	everything
NON USER ORIENTED	
Hardware down time, lack of system	programming, integration, computer time test, acceptance, operation
Interruptions, illness	everything
Major changes (Functional Spec. is weak)	everything between design and operation
Excessive acceptance requirement	ATP, acceptance
Inadequate development software	programming, system test
Hardware too small	design, programming, system test
Unstructured methods(full of bugs)	design, programming, system test, operation

Figure 14.10   Table of risks and tasks extended

14.6 FOCUS ON THE CRITICAL PATH

Calculating the Critical Path

If you are using a computer to draw the Gantt, the CP will be highlighted by special graphics or color (see Chapter 17 for examples). If you are drawing the Gantt manually you will have to highlight the CP using a character such as the '=' as used in Figure 14.9. To determine the CP, do the following: If you drew a PERT, calculate it there and highlight the corresponding critical items on the Gantt. It is simple to find the CP on the

Gantt as well. Take the last (rightmost) item and highlight it—it is always on the CP (*Operation* on Figure 14.9). Find its predecessor(s) (*Acceptance* and *Training)* and highlight the one with the latest end date (Acceptance). Find this last activity's predecessor(s) and so forth until the start date of the project is reached.

All the non highlighted or noncritical tasks have float. The float occurs from the end of the activity to the start of the next successor. If there are several successors, it goes to the start date of the earliest one. Float is shown as the dotted lines in Figure 14.9.

Reducing the Risk on the Critical Path Items

Although all of the tasks on the project need attention, you should always consider the CP items first. Look at the resources required for each CP item. Ask yourself, *"What is needed for the task, when, and what is the impact if it is late or not available at all?"* As discussed in Section 2.4, put contingency plans in place. Look especially at items provided by people outside of your control. See if you can exercise authority over those providing the resource. For internal staff, the best way to exercise authority is to provide input into their performance reviews. For external contractors try to negotiate milestones, walk-throughs and penalty clauses for late delivery. Get a second source for the item they provide.

The later the task, the higher the risk. The earlier tasks use up all the project float making the later tasks critical. Always add extra float to the latest tasks. The shorter the task, the higher the risk, since the chances of a short task exceeding its estimate is greater than that of a longer task. Add extra float to very short, critical tasks.

14.7 CONCLUSIONS TO SCHEDULING

As of this writing, the cost of a Personal Computer with excellent project management software is equal to the burdened salary of a project manager for *one week.* Cost is no excuse to avoid using a computer product to draw PERT's and Gantt's, to calculate the CP and so forth. The PC is also useful to redraw the project Gantt into individual *resource Gantt's:* for each person, the schedule of activities he or she is involved in. If you have never drawn a PERT or Gantt manually, do it on paper first to learn the concepts, then use the PC.

Consider keeping three sets of Gantt's: The first set is for yourself alone with all the float and contingency visible. The second set is for the individuals involved—it is their resource Gantt. On this one the length of each task does not include the float or the contingency you added. Hiding the individuals' float avoids slowdown due to Parkinson's Law, which states, "Work will expand to fill the time available." The third set is for distribution to upper level management. On this one the tasks are summarized; for example, there is one line per phase. Hide the contingency—the length of each task includes the contingency. This way they will not try to bargain you into a shortened schedule.

QUESTIONS

1. What is direct time? What is elapsed time? What is the relationship of one to the other?
2. Draw the PERT chart for the following plan:

ACTIVITY	DURATION(D)	PRECEDENT ACTIVITIES
A	3	-
B	5	A
C	3	A
D	11	B
E	7	B
F	4	C
G	9	E, F
H	2	D, G

   Highlight the Critical Path (CP). What is the length of the project?
3. What are the non CP activities in the plan? What is the float on each one? Why is the float on D free, but not on C?
4. What is the drawback of dummy activities?
5. What is the 'triple constraint' in a project?
6. Redraw Figure 14.7 with the constraint that there are only 2 programmers available. Discuss, in terms of the triple constraint, how this could effect the project.
7. Crash the project of Question 2, given the following likely, minimum, and extra cost per day to crash figures:

ACTIVITY	LIKELY	MINIMUM	COST/DAY
A	3	2	500
B	5	3	30
C	3	2	100
D	11	8	400
E	7	5	100
F	4	4	
G	9	7	100
H	2	2	

8. Draw the Gantt chart for the project in Question 2. Mark in the CP and float for each task.
9. What risk items can you think of that could stretch the analysis phase?

15

Prototyping

Working with a Model First

15.1 INTRODUCTION

Our Greatest Headache: Requirements

I overheard the following conversation during a recent analysis session. The analyst was interviewing the potential user, who was a course registrar with no computer experience. The analyst asked, "While you are registering a student, would you like to network from your PC into the department mini and see a window showing the student's current registration status, or would you rather network to the corporate mainframe and see a window of his company's credit rating, or both?" The user answered with a bewildered look, "I always wanted windows in my office!"

Anyone who has ever done a software project will agree that the first problem is getting proper requirements from the user. Our second problem is basing our agreement of what to build on the Functional Specification (FS). The FS attempts to describe the system using graphics and narrative. But a picture and an explanation cannot describe the way the system will feel, perform, behave, and affect the user's business. In addition, the FS is usually misunderstood (if it is read at all).

Misunderstandings between the user and the analyst result in expensive changes, or a system that is never completely implemented or one that is rejected outright. Prototyping can solve these problems for certain types of systems.

15.2 THE THEORY BEHIND PROTOTYPING

Would You Buy a Car from a Sales Brochure?

Just as you cannot judge a car without a test drive, the user cannot judge from the Functional Specification how the system will feel and behave. But if the user can see, touch, and *use* a 'model' or prototype of the proposed system, he can readily judge the system's usefulness. If changes are necessary the prototype can be modified, perhaps several times until the user states, "Yes, this type of system will solve my problem!" Then the developers have an excellent model on which to base the requirements for the final system.

Advantages of Prototyping

A prototyped system results in better requirements than those produced by the 'written specifications' method. Fewer changes should occur. Hopefully, the user has thought of most of the changes during the prototyping. The prototyping method will result in more accurate estimates than previously, because the required functions and their complexities are much better known.

Another benefit is a happy user. First of all, he gets a gentle introduction to computers. By playing with the protototype first (with the analyst holding his hand), he learns about computers and the application that will be built for him. Second, he will be involved right from the start and motivated to support the analyst for the duration of the project.

15.3 THE PROTOTYPING METHOD

The Steps of Prototyping

The following six steps must be done in order:

STEP 1   Request *initial* requirements from the user. With the old method at the Definition Phase you had to say to your user, "You must give us your requirements for the next 5 years by date X. If you don't, we must go ahead with what we assume you need and you will not be able to change anything (easily)." With the new (prototyped) method, you can say, "Give us what you *think* you need. And you can change your mind as much as you wish (almost)."

STEP 2   Build a prototype system to meet the initial requirements.

STEP 3   Let the user play with the prototype. The analyst must of course teach, assist, and sit with the user, especially at first. Encourage changes. The user must look at the functions and behavior of the prototype, see how it solves the business problems and suggest improvements.

STEP 4   Implement the suggested changes.

STEP 5   Cycle back to STEP 3 until the user is satisfied.

STEP 6   Design and build the final system as before.

15.4   SYSTEMS THAT BENEFIT FROM PROTOTYPING

Since requirements (read Functional Specifications) are mostly concerned with the user's view of the system, prototyping only the user interfaces is enough to check out the requirements. Menus, input screen forms, output screen or printed reports, queries, commands, and messages are ideal candidates for prototyping. On the other hand, complex calculations, batch updates and real-time and scientific systems are very difficult to model. (You can 'pretend' to do these activities; for example, you print, "Batch update of transaction file with 10 new transactions has been successfully completed" without any real processing.) The systems most suited to prototyping are the ones most dependent on user input/output—systems with on-line transaction handling via menus, screens, forms, reports, queries, and commands.

15.5   SOFTWARE FOR PROTOTYPING

What Must a Prototyping Software Package Provide?

A good product must provide the following seven things:

1. *Quick and easy menu creation*   The menus must be able to call sub-menus, forms, reports, prototype programs and provide on-line help for any menu selection and prompt. Figure 15.1 shows a menu construction program in action.

```
>   SCREEN PERSMENU MENU
>   DRAW "3,10 TO 7,55
>   TITLE "FUTURE INDUSTRIES INC" AT 4,15
>   TITLE "PERSONNEL SYSTEM  MENU" AT 6,24
>   SKIP 5
>   ALIGN (28,32)
>   SUBSCREEN STAFF
>   SUBSCREEN BRANCHES
>   SUBCREEN POSITION LABEL "POSITIONS"
>   BUILD
```

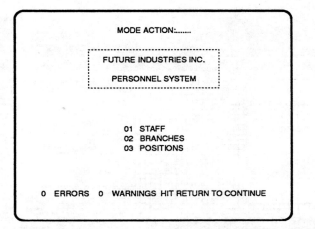

Figure 15.1   **Powerhouse menu designer (QDESIGN) (Reference 2.4)**

2. *Input and output screen form creation*   You should be able to 'paint' a screen form by placing the cursor at the desired field location (a mouse is best to do this), type the field name, and even specify edit rules such as field length, required alphanumerics, range of allowable values, error and help messages, and so on. Figure 15.2 shows a field definition program in action.

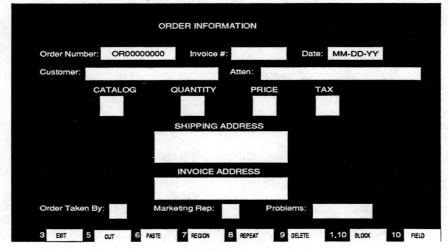

Figure 15.2   Excelerator form definition screen (Reference 2.2)

3. Similarly, you should be able to easily *describe the format of a printed report.*   The items to specify for report generation are titles, footnotes, which fields to put where (it is best if the program prompts with all the fields it knows), column headers, grouping, sorting and sub- and grand-totals. Naturally, one should be able to report on selected items only. Figure 15.3 shows the use of a report generator program.

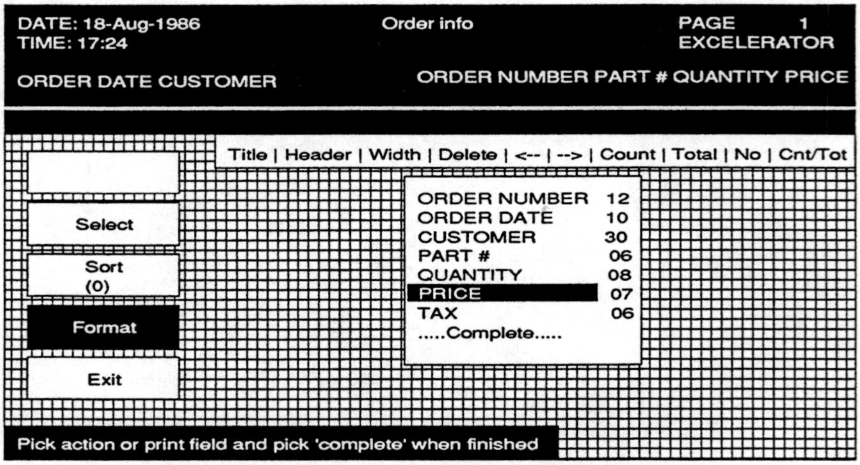

Figure 15.3   Excelerator report definition screen

4. The software should *automatically produce a data dictionary (DD)*   The DD keeps information on every known entity such as screens, reports or forms; but most important, it keeps information on every field, including length of the field, edits required, and on which reports and forms the field is used. The DD is the heart of the product, and implemented properly, the prototyping tool can use the DD to check that a field is used consistently on each screen, and can save repeated typing if the field appears more than once. In the same way, the software can keep track of all interrelationships among menus, screens, reports, and data. (See Chapter 6 on how such a tool can be used for Analysis as well as prototyping.)

5. The software *must be able to build a rudimentary database*   The input screen definitions such as the one used in Figure 15.2 tells the tool about the format of the record. The software must build the database and then allow the user to enter data using the input forms. The best products allow the user to optimize the data base by predefining the format and keys of the records.

6. Look for a product with *fast on-line query* to the data recorded on the data base. You should be able to do simple search, sort, select, and display of records.

7. What if the requirements include complex logic or calculations that need to be prototyped? Although not essential, the best programs have a *built-in simple structured programming language* to allow you to do special processing, timed events, automatic procedures, and so on.

Prototyping as Part of CASE

Prototyping is a method of automating the Definition and Analysis Phases, so it is part of CASE (Computer Aided Software Engineering). But prototyping feeds nicely into automating the subsequent phases as well. If the next step is to build the real system in a third generation programming language, the prototyping product should allow you to *print out all the items that it knows about*: all the menus (in the order of their logical tree structure), all the forms, reports, and commands. The best products allow the user to print a logically organized document, with chapter and section annotation that can be used as the Functional Specification document. Some even provide a word processor to insert explanatory text among the items. The product should also print out the Data Dictionary. This will save the designers many hours of labor.

If the design and programming are using Fourth Generation Language or an integrated CASE tool (see Section 6.6), you should be able to input the results of prototyping directly into the tool. The best of these CASE tools will automatically build the data bases and even the code for the final application.

How Fast Should You Be Able to Prototype?

The prototyping software should be able to let you *quickly* build the initial model of the system. Typically, you can build the first prototype of a small to mid sized project in only two to three weeks! You must be able to implement changes quickly as well. It should take a *few minutes* to make cosmetic changes such as moving a field on a form. It should take *less than an hour* to define a new menu or form, and at most a *few hours* to create a new file or restructure an existing file for a new field, key, or access. To achieve this speed it is essential to have a simple and logical user interface. In fact, if the prototyping software is simple enough, the developer can train the user to run it. The user will then develop the prototype and call the developer when it is ready to turn into the final system.

15.6 WHERE DOES PROTOTYPING FIT INTO THE SEVEN PHASES?

You may now feel that the prototyping method can completely replace the seven phased approach to project development (and may even feel annoyed that I made you read Section I of the book before telling you about prototyping!) Do not fear—prototyping replaces only portions of the Definition and Analysis Phases. Figure 15.4 shows the chronological events in the seven phases of the old method side-by-side with the corresponding events in the new (prototyped) method.

		OLD METHOD(7 PHASED)		NEW METHOD (PROTOTYPED)	
	PHASE	**ACTIVITY**	**COMMENT**	**ACTIVITY**	**COMMENT**
	Defini-tion	Req't Doc	Had to be final	Initial req'ts	Truly initial
TIME		Proposal is guess	Estimate	Proposal	Est. is accurate
	Analysis	Initial Func. Spc	Know it will change	Not needed	Changes to the prototype as required
		Negotiate the F.S.		Not needed	
		Final F.S.		Final F.S.	Prot. prints most of it. No negot'n needed
	Design	Des. Spec	Req'ts changes	Des Spec. fewer changes	Prot. prints DD, records, rest of design is same
	Prog'g	Programs	changes	Programs	Same-less change
	Sys Tst	Int.&Test	changes	Int. &Test	Same-less change
	Acceptnc	Acc. Test	changes	Acc. Test	No surprises-fast
	Operat'n	Cut-over, training		Cut-over, training	No surprises-fast less required

Figure 15.4 How prototyping fits into the seven phases

Opponents of the method argue that if you allow any number of iterations to the prototype, the requirements could take forever; that at least the old way of doing definition and analysis will take less time than the new way because a deadline can be set. This argument is not valid—if you like to set deadlines you can just as well set a limit to the number of prototypes. I have found that if the user and the developer agree to limit the cosmetic changes to one iteration, the prototype can be built in less than five versions, with three being the most common. Even if the new way takes longer up front, you will save time and money over the total life of the project because there will be fewer changes, the Design Phase will be shorter, the acceptance will be trivial, and the user documentation and training will be a piece of cake.

One last thought before you throw out the old life cycle. I feel that unless you do a few projects the old way first, you will not be able to fully understand and utilize the prototyping methods. Is there any truth to the saying, ''You must learn to ride a bicycle before you attempt to ride a motorcycle?''

15.7 SOME PRODUCTS TO LOOK AT

Excelerator as a Prototyping Tool

In Chapter 6 we saw a good analysis tool called Excelerator (Reference 2.2). But this tool has features that make it a good prototyping tool as well: It has menu, form, and report building facilities. It maintains an excellent data dictionary and it can create a data base using the defined input forms. Most important, it will allow you to print out a logically organized Functional Specification document consisting of all the items defined with word processed paragraphs inserted for good measure.

Fourth Generation Languages as Prototyping Tools

Sometimes we need complex screen handling logic, special calculations, automatic procedures or unique reporting features, and most prototyping tools do not have the power to do all this. There is a whole clan of products called *Fourth Generation Languages (4GL)* that do have this power. We will discuss these in the next chapter as tools for developing the whole system, but almost all the 4GL's *can be used as prototyping tools as well.*

15.8 CONCLUSIONS

Prototyping has been used very successfully to enhance the implementation of many software systems that involve heavy user interfacing via menus, screens, reports, and on-line transactions. Business oriented systems typically fit into this mold. Real-time systems and scientific systems fare less well when using this method.

The question that is probably uppermost in your mind at this point is, ''Why go to all this trouble to build an empty shell? Why could I not have software that allows me to build all these menus, screens, and forms and *end up with a real, working system?*'' Indeed you do have that software. Read the next chapter on Fourth Generation Languages!

QUESTIONS

1. What is the greatest problem with the old (specified) method of getting requirements?
2. Why is the Functional Specification not the best tool to describe a system?
3. Why is prototyping better than specifying the system requirements?
4. Draw a flowchart of the steps of prototyping.
5. What types of systems benefit from prototyping? What types do not?
6. What items should a prototyping tool provide to assist in describing the user interfaces?
7. What internal functions must a prototyping tool provide?
8. Why is prototyping part of CASE? What other tools would you expect from an integrated CASE product?
9. Would you expect the prototyped definition and analysis to take longer or shorter than the equivalent specified method. Would the total development be longer or shorter?

16

Fourth Generation Languages

Developing Applications Five Times Faster

16.1 INTRODUCTION

A new set of tools, called Fourth Generation Languages (4GL), can be used to develop *certain types* of applications much faster than third generation languages (3GL) such as COBOL, BASIC, or FORTRAN. As with any tool that provides more automation, the benefit comes at a price.

This chapter goes hand-in-hand with the last one on prototyping: you must read Chapter 15 to understand this one. On the surface, A 4GL provides essentially the same features as a prototyping tool (see Section 15.4), but with more power and detail. The best way to understand the 4GL approach to development is to imagine building a prototype as described in Chapter 15, but instead of building a throw-away model, you are building the basis of the final working system. In fact, developing an application using a 4GL usually involves a prototyping approach: a core system is first developed as a prototype that lets the user see the interfaces of the system and use the basic functions. The user is encouraged to run the system and suggest changes. These changes are *incorporated into the prototype (next iteration of the prototype), and in a few iterations the prototype itself becomes the final system.*

I am assuming that you are familiar with 3GL project development discussed earlier. This chapter will emphasize only the differences between the third and fourth generation approaches.

End-user and Developer 4GLs

There are two major kinds of 4GLs: end-user oriented and developer oriented. The end-user oriented 4GL emphasizes ease of use; it is intended to be programmed by the end user. This user friendliness is usually traded for fewer functions and loss in performance. The developer oriented 4GL emphasizes function and performance, at the cost of user friendliness. Most of the examples in this chapter use a 4GL called Powerhouse from Cognos Inc. (Reference 2.4). Powerhouse does not do any one thing significantly better than other 4GLs, but (in my opinion) it does everything well. It is a developer oriented tool as opposed to an end-user oriented tool since it does require knowledge of the Powerhouse (PH) language syntax. PH is completely integrated into the host operating systems (uses RMS and RDB on VMS directly) and therefore provides good performance. It is also reasonably priced.

16.2 FEATURES OF A GOOD 4GL, OR HOW TO EVALUATE A 4GL

Following is a list of functions that you should look for in a 4GL.

1. *Menu Setup*   The programmer of a 4GL (called developer) must be able to set up a tree of menus. Menus must be able to call sub-menus, input screen forms, output screen forms, reports, processes or functions. One level must be able to pass parameters to other levels and provide security such as password prompting between levels. The 4GL should provide automatic entry numbering and the user should be able to make a selection, deletion or correction using the cursor and/or mouse. The best products provide two levels of help at any entry: a short message at the bottom of the screen or a full screen. Look for a fast method of accessing sub-menus and automatic return to any menu level after something is completed. Fancy cosmetics such as headers, footers, and highlight (color, shade, inverse video, bold, letter size, blink, framed box) are nice to have. Figure 16.1 is an example of what a developer would type to set up a menu in QUICK, the Powerhouse screen design program. Items in square brackets are my comments.

```
    SCREEN REGISTRAR MENU                              [Name the screen.]
TITLE ``Registrar's Functions'' AT 2,40               [Will appear second
line,                                                       col 40]
TITLE ``Please enter the number of your choice.'' AT 22,10
TITLE ``To exit type `^'.'' AT 23,10
DRAW THIN FROM 4,2 TO 20,79             [Draws a thin line box.]
SKIP TO 6                               [Skip to line 6.]
SUBSCREEN REGISTER CLEAR ALL REFRESH ALL MODE E LABEL
``Register a Student''                  [First choice, clears the
                            screen and calls Register a student'
                                entry form, in    ENTER (input) mode.]
SUBSCREEN CANCEL CLEAR ALL REFRESH ALL PASSING STUD-NO LABEL
``Cancel a Student''                [Second choice, passes to
                        the form previously entered student no.]
```

```
BUILD                          [Command to Powerhouse to
                               'compile' this menu.]
GO                             [Command to Powerhouse to
                               actually run this menu to see what it
                               looks like.
```

Figure 16.1A   Building the menu screen

And the result is:

```
MODE:E ACTION:__                      [Cursor is here.]


                   Registrar's Functions


          01 Register a Student
          02 Cancel a Student

          Please enter the number of your choice.
          To  exit type "E".
```

Figure 16.1B   Resultant menu screen

2. *Input Forms*   You should be able to point to any position on the screen and specify that a field will be entered there. You should be able to specify the name of the field, its format, edits (range of values, lookup valid values, automatic re-format) and help messages. Complex functions such as storing data from one screen into different files, ensuring that there are no duplicates on keys, providing default values, calculations and conditional input logic should be allowed. Look for the ability to enter repeating fields in a scrolled region. How about moving a field by pointing to it with a mouse and dragging it to the new position? The best software can even provide an audit trail of the input data automatically. Figure 16.2A shows an example of building an input screen in Powerhouse and the result is shown in Figure 16.2B.

```
SCREEN REGISTER
FILE STUDENTS PRIMARY    [Where the data will go.]
TITLE "Student Registration Form." CENTERED AT 2,40
TITLE "Use arrow keys to get to a field. Enter // to
       get to ACTION prompt. At ACTION you can enter the
       field number to jump to a specific field, or type
       U to update the file with this student record.''
AT 17,5
DRAW THIN FROM 4,2 TO 15,79
ALIGN (ID 5, LABEL 9, DATA 35) [Format the output at specific
                               columns.]
```

```
FIELD STUDENT-NO OF STUDENTS REQUIRED LOOKUP NOTON
STUDENTS LABEL ''Student Number''      [First field to display.
                               Must enter, it must be
                               unique, and the label to
                               prompt with.]
FIELD LAST-NAME OF STUDENTS REQUIRED   [Next field as above. Prompt
                               label defaults to name of
                               the field, ''Last Name''.]
FIELD FIRST-NAME OF STUDENTS ID SAME   [Do not assign new ID number
                               (see below).]
FIELD STREET OF STUDENTS FIELD CITY OF STUDENTS
FIELD PROVINCE OF STUDENTS LABEL       ''Province/State'' .
                               [Other fields desired. There
                               is also a command to auto-
                               matically generate FIELD
                               statements for every field
                               in the file.]
```

Figure 16.2A   Generating an input form

```
        Student Registration Form.

01        Student Number         44
02        Last Name              Perry
          First Name             Kelly
03        Street                 944 Red Street
          City                   Ottawa
          Province/State         Ont.

Use arrow keys to get to a field. Enter // to
get to ACTION prompt. At ACTION you can enter the
field number to jump to a specific field, or type
U to update the file with this student record.
```

Figure 16.2B Resultant input screen

3. *Output Forms*   Output forms display records given a key or other field contents. Some people design systems of many files that are interrelated by key fields. Some of us even write down the names of the fields, and the keen ones even spell the names correctly. When access is to multiple files the 4GL should *automatically* match the records by a common key field. When the output form is displayed, update of the fields should be allowed (with security restrictions) using the same format and logic as was on the input screen. Tools such as Powerhouse can be programmed to use the same screen for input and output. At the top of a screen an ACTION is prompted. If the user types 'E' then Entry mode is assumed and all the fields are prompted. If the user types 'F' then Find mode is assumed. The user is prompted for a key or other fields, and the record is found and displayed.

4. *Report Generation*   The 4GL should allow the developer to format reports with headers, footers, and columns of data. Grouping, paginating, sorting, and record selection logic must be available. Complex requirements such as multi-file access, calculations, totals, and counts must be supported. Report formatting can be a complex task so look for a simple report generating language.

Some of the 4GLs allow ad-hoc report generation. The user can specify in a very simple fashion the content and format of the report. Some 4GLs such as Focus (Reference 2.3) have a question and answer method of specifying the report format. Cognos' product Powerplay uses mouse and icon graphics under MS Windows to set up cross tabulated or columnar reports (Figure 16.3). Powerplay takes this feature one step further by allowing a 'drill down' capability to isolate lower and lower levels of information. The reports can be displayed in text or graphics format.

Report of Students by Geography by Year				⇧ ⇩
File	Data Compute Display Format Window			
Years	Change Rows	al	West	Total
1985	Change Columns	07	412	1502
1986	Change Pages	10	499	1612
1987	Change Domain	13	518	1730
1988	Swap Rows & Columns	21	612	1809
1989	Swap Rows & Ranges	82	701	1962
1990	Swap Columns & Ranges	91	852	2010
	Show Total Row			
	Show Total Column			
	Show Total Page			
All Years	1849	4024	2742	8615

Figure 16.3   Icon driven graphic report generator for Cagnos Powerplay

5. *Data Dictionary (DD) and File Definition*   A 4GL must have a data dictionary to keep track of menus, screens, reports, records, and the interrelationships among them. Most important, the DD must be able to store all field related information such as format, edit, security, and error/help messages. As opposed to prototyping software, a 4GL should not automatically create files and record definitions. (At the least the developer should be able to override the defaults.) This is because the performance of an application written in a 4GL is crucially dependent upon the design of the files. An automatic system cannot possibly foresee the optimal key relationships, access rates, and future needs of the user. The developer must be able to enter all the file, record and field definitions, and then optimize the files for the host operating system.

6. *On-line Query*   For pre-defined queries, the 4GL should allow you to specify multiple files to be accessed, the keys to use for access (the 4GL should be able to detect the common keys and automatically access secondary files by those) and the format of the output. For unforseen queries, some 4GLs insist that a special processing language be used. For example, using DEC's DATATRIEVE product, the user would first have to set up links to all the files required using "DEFINE DICTIONARY," "DEFINE DOMAIN," "READY" the domain(s), set up the interrelated fields, then issue a command such as "FIND STUDENTS WITH AMOUNT-PAID EQ 0," Needless to say, this is difficult. This complexity may force the user to ask the developer to write a program, which is one way to achieve some security and performance since the query applications are controlled by the developers.

The more user-friendly products allow a request in freeform English. Using rudimentary Artificial Intelligence, the program searches the request for keywords, and asks questions for clarification until a meaningful request can be determined. The most powerful products can even 'learn' this type of request and will not ask the same questions again.

7. *Built-in Programming Language for Special Processing and Calls to 3GL Subroutines*   This seems redundant, but why a built-in language in addition to a 4GL one? This language is used to do complex menu or screen handling logic. The developer must be able to handle special security requirements (hide fields from certain users,) take special action depending on input to certain fields, do a special task at a certain time of the day, evaluate a complex formula and so on. Look for a structured language that gives you blocks of code that can be accessed at each screen and field. For example, if a Powerhouse input screen has a field 'AMOUNT-PAID,' there is a procedure called 'PROCESS AMOUNT-PAID' automatically created. If the developer needs to do something unique when the user enters a value for this field, he or she merely adds some statements to this procedure. For example,

```
IF AMOUNT-PAID < AMOUNT-OWING/10
     THEN DISPLAY ''Pay up or we will get angry!''
     ELSE...
```

Since some things are more easily done in a 3GL (due to the nature of the problem or the experience of the developer) the 4GL should also allow calls to 3GL subroutines.

8. *Structured Printout* As with prototyping software, the 4GL should allow you to print out all the defined menus, screens, reports, relationships. This helps in producing the Functional Specifications, and the user/training documentation. You also need a detailed report on all the fields, including the screens and reports that use each field.

9. *Documentation, Consulting and Training* A large amount of documentation will discourage most people. Yet the opposite should be true. In most cases, the more manuals the better. Consulting and training should also be provided.

10. *Good Performance* And most important, look for a product that performs. No one will publish that their product performs poorly, so here are some *clues* that may indicate that the product will not give you the performance that you require:

- 90% of the installed base is on large mainframe computers.

- Too much emphasis on user friendliness. If the 4GL is so end-user oriented that 'even an idiot can program it', there is usually too much overhead spent on supporting idiots.

- The menus, screens, reports are not compiled. ('Compile' can mean different things to different vendors: threaded code is not as fast as object code.)

- No direct interface (read and write) to the host operating system files.

The only way to evaluate the performance of a 4GL is to look at working applications that are similar to yours. Ask the vendor for a list of contacts at installed sites in your area and talk to those who use them.

16.3 DEVELOPING AN APPLICATION USING A 4GL—A CASE STUDY

The Phases in a 4GL

Let us see how the ABC system (developed in Appendix A using a 3GL method) would be developed using the Powerhouse product. The following sections can also provide a framework for the phases in the development of a 4GL project.

Developing the Requirements Definition

The approach to analyzing the user's problems in a 4GL environment is much the same as in a 3GL environment. First a Requirements Document is written to define the user's problem. The RD for the 4GL development is not as detailed as that of the 3GL one because the user's problems may be hazy until a first prototype is built. Drawing a data-flow diagram is the best way to begin, and the result would be the same as before (see Figure 6.1). As with a 3GL, the next step is to detail each bubble. Figure 16.4 details the Registrar bubble.

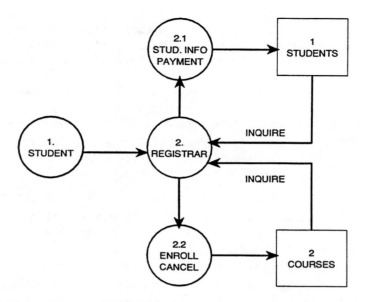

Figure 16.4   Data flow diagram of registrar functions using Excelerator

Define What—Analysis

There are three major differences between 3GL and 4GL analysis. First, with the 4GL the user must be familiar with the approach: he or she must realize that only a basic system of core functions will be built first, detailed functions and cosmetic changes will be added later, and after a *limited number* of iterations the final system will be ready. The second difference is that the user will have to be a lot more active in a 4GL environment than in the 3GL, spend a lot of time with the developers, perhaps even become familiar with the language. The user should also be aware that the system may not provide every function exactly as requested—the developer may suggest alternative functions (even changes in the business) so that the 4GL may be used most efficiently. Third, the analyst required for a 4GL needs to be *very familiar* with the language. In fact, the analyst should be a developer as well.

In the 3GL SDLC the estimates at this stage were 50%-100% erroneous. With a 4GL the estimate should be only +/- 20% in error. Why this improvement? Because you will have a much better handle on what needs to be done. The 4GL methodology is based on standard building blocks, plus limits can be put on the first prototype and the number of iterations. After the estimates are done, a formal proposal should be written to define project scope, cost and duration and to provide a milestone for this phase.

Define How—Design

The first item to define in a 4GL development is the top level design or basic structure of the system. It is usually easiest to use the business functions of the application as the basis of the top level design. The TLD in Figure 16.5 follows the function bubbles defined in the data flow diagram in Figure 6.1 and others such as Figure 16.4.

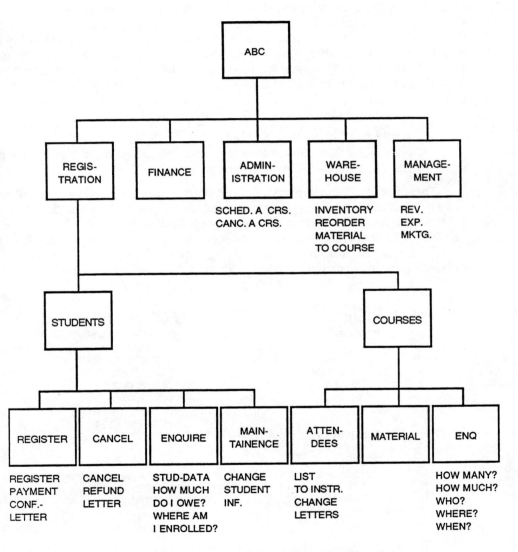

Figure 16.5   Top level design with business functions

The next step is to list the system requirements under each function box, shown in Figure 16.5 as the lower case items. Read through the requirements document item by item and ensure that all the features are listed. Revise the TLD if necessary.

Design the File Structure

Files are designed at the same time as the structure of the system. Design the files the same way as before: First, determine the data entities and relationships, then define the fields in such a way that all the accesses are as efficient as possible and the fields are repeated as little as possible. (For more information on data base design see references 19 and 23.) However, there are a few more rules to be followed when designing files for a 4GL, especially if an indexed file structure such as DEC's RMS or IBM CICS is used.

1. Avoid variable length records.
2. Avoid variable content records.
3. Avoid records that are too long. It is preferable to have more files with shorter records than fewer files with very long records.

These rules are more important with a 4GL than with a 3GL because a 3GL such as COBOL handles variable length records with clauses such as the 'OCCURS n TIMES.' But most 4GLs do not have an easy (default) way of processing records of variable length or content, forcing the developer to write procedures (which is no fun).

Look at the file structures defined earlier for the ABC system (Section 7.8). We can redesign these files to remove the variable length records as shown in Figure 16.6.

PK = Primary Key, SK= Secondary Key

STUDENT
(One rec per student)

STUDENT-NO(PK)
LAST-NAME(SK)
FIRST-NAME
STREET
CITY
PROV/STATE
POSTAL-CODE

COURSES
(One rec. per course type)
COURSE-NO(PK)
COURSE-NAME(SK)
DESCRIPTION

STUDENT-COURSES
(One rec per student per
registration)
COURSE-CODE(PK)
COURSE-NO(SK)
COURSE-DATE
LOCATION
STUDENT-NO(SK)
AMOUNT-PAYED

COURSES-SCHED
(One rec. per run of a crs.)
COURSE-CODE(PK)
COURSE-NO
COURSE-DATE
   LOCATION
   PRICE
INSTRUCTOR

Figure 16.6   File structure for ABC

COURSE-MATERIAL   MATERIAL
(One record per course   (One record per material)
per material)   Material-No(PK)
COURSE-NO(PK)   MIN-INV
MATERIAL-NO   SUPPLIER-INFO
                                   WAREHOUSE-INFO
                                   DESCRIPTION

HISTORY
(Records from STUDENT-COURSES copied here
after a course is run)

Figure 16.6   File structure for ABC (continued)

At first glance this figure appears to be more complex than before because there are more files, but this structure is more straight-forward and allows more flexibility. This is just a first crack at the design. As we will see later the structure will have to be modified because of a new user requirement.

A good test of the data structure is to run through all of the known requirements and see if the files can accommodate them. For example, the requirement, "List all courses that use material 'MATERIAL-NO'" can only be done using a sequential search of the COURSE-MATERIAL file. If this is an often needed request, making MATERIAL-NO a secondary key will speed up the search. The analyst must determine the frequency and performance required of each function and alter the file structure accordingly.

Design the User Interfaces (UI)

In the 3GL we designed the user interfaces (UI) up front in the Analysis Phase. In the 4GL approach we may prototype the UI up front but it is not final until the major system structures are defined. This is because the system design determines in part the appearance of the UI. The TLD and the list of system functions (Figure 16.5) are used to define the required menus, screens, and reports. The main menu for this system prompts for the major functions and can appear as Figure 16.7A.

```
ACTION:_
   ABC System Main Menu
01 Registrar
02 Finance
03 Administration
04 Warehouse
05 Management
06 Other


Type the number of your choice.   To EXIT type 'E',
type '?' for HELP
```

Figure 16.7A   ABC main menu

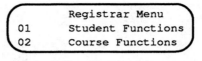

```
                   Registrar Menu
        01         Student Functions
        02         Course Functions
```

Figure 16.7B   Registrar sub-menu

The '01 Registrar' choice on the main menu can result in the Registrar Menu (Figure 16.7B), and the '01 Student Functions' choice on the Registrar Menu can result in a screen such as Figure 16.8.

```
STUDENT FUNCTIONS
    01 Student No.
    02 Last Name
    03 First Name
       04 Street
       05 City
       06 Province/State
       07 Postal-Code
       10 Courses for this Student
To Find (enquire) a student recond type 'F'
To Enter a new student record type 'E'
To Delete a student record type 'D'
To   Update any information on the file first
           Find the student, then type the number of the
           field you wish to update, change the field,
           and type 'U' to updaqte the file.
To change any course information for this student
           (as well as ENROLL or CANCEL) type '10'
```

Figure 16.8   Student function sub-menu

```
Course Entry
        Student: John Smith        Student Number: 123456
Course Data for this Student       [following is a scrolled region]


          Course No.    Date            Location   Amount Paid
01        101           1988/Jan/01     TOR        900.00
02        403           1988/Jun/01     NYC        900.00
03
04
05
06
To    ENROLL use E (Enter) and enter the course information on the
  first empty line
To    CANCEL use D (Delete)
To    change any information simply  type new information and then
  U   (Update)
```

Figure 16.9   Course entry screen

The screen in Figure 16.9 was accomplished by accessing from the STUDENT-COURSES file all the records that match the STUDENT-NO key. Note that the 4GL to be used (Powerhouse) and the previously defined file structure affected the format of the user interfaces. The user may have preferred a separate menu for Enquiry on a student, Delete a student, Enroll a student and so forth. But Powerhouse provides record enquire-find-enter-delete-update by default on any screen, so we combined all these functions on one screen. Similarly, we provide one screen to do all course registration. We have altered the requirements somewhat to use the language efficiently. The user gets the functions he requested but not exactly the way he requested them. This is where a compromise has to be reached.

When the user sees the interfaces that the developer defines he or she will immediately request many 'cosmetic' changes. The developer must ensure that all the basic functions are accomplished by this first design, and politely defer all low priority changes by promising to do them later.

A formal Functional Specification (FS) can be now be written and signed off to provide a clean milestone. Remember that the FS contains the project team's commitment to provide a system with documentation, training, and warranties as well as adequate performance. The FS will still be the formal mechanism to ensure acceptance. In fact, the only difference between a 3GL FS and a 4GL one is that the format of the UI in the 4GL is not final (but the functions are)!

Build the First Prototype (Programming, System Test, Acceptance of First Prototype)

There are seven steps to programming the prototype:

Step 1. Build the Files. The developer begins by building the Data Dictionary (DD). Figure 16.10 shows how one would use the Powerhouse DD maintenance screen to enter information about all files, records and fields (type, size, key type, edits, ranges, look-ups, help and error messages, etc.). The CREATE command can then be used to create the empty file.

```
                          RECORD SCREEN
_____

  01  Record      STUDENTS
  02  File        STUDENTS        Organization: INDEXED    Type: RMS
      Open        STUDENTS

  Mode:E ACTION: E    Element Attr          Item Attributes
_____
      Element    Usage Type Size Dec    Datatype Size Occ Key Seq.No

  01  STUDENT-NO  ID   C    5            CHARACTER 5   1  U      1.0
  02
  03
  .
  .
  .
```

Figure 16.10   Creating the data dictionary

Step 2. Build the Menus. Menus are built as shown in Figure 16.1. All submenus are built similarly.

Step 3. Build the Input forms. Figure 16.2A shows how to construct an input form. All the screen input and output forms are built in a similar way. As we saw, it is very simple to access information from more than one file. The developer can indicate a primary file and several secondary files. As each secondary file is accessed the program looks up which keys match with keys on the primary file and sets up the link via the key. Optionally, it can show the developer all the fields in the secondary files for display on the input form.

Step 4. Build the Reports. Figure 16.11 shows a PH program that prompts the user for the STUDENT-NO and generates a confirmation letter to be printed for that student.

```
Quiz Confirm.Letter [QUIZ is the PH report generator]
Access Students Link to Student Courses [Specifies primary
                            and corresponding secondary file]
Choose  Student-no Parm Prompt  [Prompt for Student-no and
                            access Students record with that key
Page Heading Skip 2
        Tab 50 SysDate                          [Date]
        Skip 2 Tab 10 First-Name Last-Name Skip 2 [From Students
        Tab 20 ''Dear  '' First-Name '','' Skip2 [From Students
        TAB 25 ''You lucky duck! You get to go on course ''
            Description '' on date '' Date  [From Student-COURSES
Set  Report  Device  Disc Name Confirmlet [This file will
                                    be queued for printout.]
```

Figure 16.11   Report generated to print confirmation letters

Step 5. Build the Other Functions. Add in all the required special processing, logic, extra programming, timed events, batch runs, and 3GL calls if necessary.

Step 6. Show the User and Solicit Improvements. The user is now encouraged to try all the functions in the system, use all the menus and screens, enter test data, and run sample reports. All change requests are written down, their cost is evaluated and (hopefully) most of them are accepted for the next iteration. Keep up the enthusiasm —show your user *something working* within 2 to 3 weeks even if it is just a part of the prototype.

Step 7. Build the Next Iteration. The next iteration will include all the changes suggested in step 6 and go through the steps again. Hopefully, you will only need to cycle back to step 2, although a major change may force you as far back as step 1.

Here is a real-life story about how easy it is to change a 4GL. After the first prototype of the ABC system was delivered, the user requested a major change: He wanted the confirmation letters produced *automatically* when a student enrolled in a course.

The first suggestion of the developer was, "We'll generate the letter whenever a new record is entered into the STUDENT-COURSES file." But a design reviewer asked, "What if the course DATE or course LOCATION is updated? A new record would not be entered, but a letter would still have to be sent!" The developer, being a compromising sort, changed the suggestion to "Generate a letter at all updates to the STUDENT-COURSES file." Again the reviewer found a problem. "What if *we* change a field that does not affect the student, such as the COURSE-NO, or the AMOUNT-PAID? No letter should be sent in these cases!"

Sometimes the best solution to such a complex problem is to dump the whole thing into the user's lap. They gave the user the ability to indicate when to send a letter. The STUDENT-COURSES record size was increased to hold a "Y" or "N" (yes/no) flag, with "Y" meaning that the student has to be sent a letter. Figure 16.12 shows how the new course entry screen displayed this flag in a new 'Conf.Let' column (bold items are new).

```
Course Entry

Student: John Smith          Student Number: 123456
Course Data for this Student    [following is a scrolled region]

       Course No.     Date      Location Amount Paid Conf. Let
01       101       1988/Jan/01   TOR       900.00      N
02       403       1988/Jun/01   NYC       900.00      N
03       707       1989/Feb/03   ONT      1000.00      Y
04
05
06
07
99   Print Confirmation Letters Now
To ENROLL use E (Enter) and enter the course information on the
first empty line
To CANCEL use D (Delete)

To change any information simply type new information and then U
(Update)
Choosing  item  99  will Print Confirmation Letters for those
records that have ''Y'' under Conf. Let.    You   may   set   any
record  to  ''Y''  or  ''N''
```

Figure 16.12   New course entry screen

The Conf.Let flag is set to "Y" by default for any record update. It can be set to "N" by the user. If item 99 is chosen on the form screen, the system runs a report generation program which prints a confirmation letter for each student whose flag is "Y," When the print successfully executes, the flag is set to "N." Just in case the user forgets to ask for the letters, a batch job can be run daily to search the file for any records with the flag set to "Y" and print a letter. This way all contingencies are handled.

It would have been very difficult to add this feature using a 3GL program. But with a 4GL, the complete modification (restructure the STUDENT-COURSES file, change the Course Entry screen, display the ''Y'' after an update, produce the new reports, queue them to print and then change the ''Y'' to ''N'') *took less than one day* to implement. After all the functional (not cosmetic!) user requested changes are made, any functions that may have been left out of the first prototype are added. These may include operation functions such as automatic start-up, shut-down, backup/restore, and default log in or accounting routines. The operating system may provide many of these functions. Set up any required networks and interfaces to existing software. When all the required functional changes and features are added, then the cosmetic changes can be applied. Lastly, do not forget to finalize the user documentation—hopefully this has been progressing all along.

It may take a great deal of effort to make all these improvements. Remember that there may be several iterations so break up the work. Usually three to four iterations are needed before Version 1 of the system can be released. (I suggest that the maximum number of iterations be limited and agreed upon in the Proposal.) Subsequent enhancements can go into Version 2. As with the first prototype, keep up the momentum by showing the user some progress every two to three weeks even if the results are incomplete.

Acceptance and Operation

Despite the fact that the user has been involved in the production of the first prototype all along, a formal demonstration of the whole system must take place to show that it functions as promised. As in the 3GL method, an Acceptance Test Plan must be drawn up and agreed upon to avoid hassles. The FS is the basis for acceptance. Acceptance will be simpler and faster in a 4GL environment than in a 3GL since the user is familiar with the system.

Operation is exactly the same as with a 3GL system. You can do a parallel run or cutover to the new system after acceptance. Warranty and support must be provided. There will definitely be an opportunity to sell a new system (Version 2) since many changes may have been left out of Version 1 due to the limited number of iterations. User training will not be difficult because some of the users are already 'experts.' Try to get the 'expert' users to train the others in the company.

16.4 TEAM ORGANIZATION AND RESPONSIBILITIES IN A 4GL ENVIRONMENT

In Section 18.8 we will detail the roles of the project team members of a 4GL project, but a summary can be provided here. The PT will be smaller when a 4GL is used. There must still be a Project Manager to handle all the administration, but this person will have to know the language. The Project Leader will be the chief developer. There will no longer be any 'programmers.' They will be called 'developers,' since they will have to wear a suit and tie and talk to the users.

16.5 TIME DURATION OF THE PHASES WHEN USING A 4GL

Figure 16.13 shows typical 4GL activities and the time it takes to do each item. The ABC project would fit into the 'SMALL TO MID SIZE APPLICATION' column. The numbers in the 'COMPLEX APPLICATION' come from a large field service maintenance system, distributed across the country, that handles approximately 500 items and over 10000 parts. The system has over 50 menus, 150 reports, 18 complex batch runs and 25 major functions. In the simple application case I would have expected the equivalent 3GL development to take three times as long, for the complex one twice as long.

	Simple Application (Person-days)	Complex Application (Person-days)		Average Small To Mid Size App. (Person-days)	
Initial Requirements	3	15		10	
File design	3	25		15	
Each menu	0.5	1.0	(x50)	.5	(x15)
Each screen/form	0.7	1.0	(x50)	.5	(x25)
Each report	0.8	1.5	(x150)	1.	(x20)
Each batch run	1	2.0	(x18)	1.	(x4)
Create data dict.	1	5		3	
(incl help/err msgs)	5	15		10	
Up to first prot.					
(Sum of above)	20	421		82	
For each iteration:					
Use & gather					
Changes	5	15		10	
Impl. changes	2	15		10	
No. of iterations	3	3		3	
Total iterations	21	90		60	
Total for Project	41	511		142	

Figure 16.13   Typical durations for 4GL activities

I suggest that you try to break a project into parts so that the timing is approximately this: initial requirements done in one month, and first prototype ready one month later. This keeps the user interested. Then plan for three to four iterations at about one month each, with Version 1 to be implemented in six to eight months.

16.6 CONVERTING A 3GL ORIENTED COMPANY TO A 4GL

Use the following five steps in this order:

Step 1   Start with the upper levels of management. Always use a cost/benefit argument. Show them the statistics in the previous section to prove that many more applications can be developed in the same time for the same money. Show the possibility of turning a normally hostile user

department into friends. Invite the 4GL vendors to make a presentation to management.

Step 2   Get permission to do a quick, one or two person application (the
software vendor may give you the 4GL for an evaluation period).
Advertise the success.

Step 3   If you are not the Manager of MIS, convince the MIS department.
Starting with the top management, prove that a 4GL will leave the
organization unchanged (that MIS will still be in charge). Prove that
the backlog of applications will go down, the programmers will be
happier because they will not be as isolated as before, and the users
will be happier because they will be more involved. The technical
people will be easy to convince—they are motivated to learn new
things.

Step 4   Get the Project Team trained. Two aspects of the product must be
learned: the language itself and how to develop applications in the
language. My experience has shown that a developer needs approximately six months of training. This consists of one to two weeks of
language training, followed by one to three months of practice. Then
one to two weeks of advance language and application development
training is needed, followed by one to three months of practice.

Step 5   Educate the users. Before starting the first project the user must be
shown the new approach. Point out that specification will no longer be
formal (this should be a welcome step), but in return the user may have
to compromise more—mainly in cosmetics and somewhat in function.
Everyone will have to understand that there will be more of the ''wait
until the next version'' syndrome, but that the versions will happen
more frequently.

16.7 COMPUTER AIDED SOFTWARE ENGINEERING

CASE from Start to Finish

The ideal CASE tool is one that will take you from analysis to operation, do everything
you want it to, and do it more simply than with the non CASE method. Let us describe
this ideal tool and then see where the technology stands.

The tool to do this should allow you to Define the business processes and data
flows with a DFD or other logic drawing tool. You should then be able to describe the
user interfaces (Analyze) with a screen formatting tool. The data elements from the
DFDs should be reconciled with those on the screens, then fed into a DBMS for
automatic creation of records and fields. At the same time the application to manipulate
all these processes should be built underneath. The result is 3GL code or a 4GL
application with a wealth of features that handles all your requirements. We have
already seen tools that accomplish all this: prototyping tools automate the definition and
analysis, and 4GLs automate design and programming. All that is needed is a
combination and we have a start to finish CASE tool.

How a CASE Tool Works

On the front end, a CASE toolkit provides the DFD and the menu, report and form design graphics. A structured language may be used to define some processing. In the middle, CASE creates a data dictionary to ensure consistency, and automatically creates a data base, usually using a relational data base management system. (The developer may have to enhance this data base schema by providing record and field relationships.) At the end, out pops the application in a 3 GL such as COBOL or C, or in a 4GL.

For simple applications, this is all that is needed. We have seen that prototyping tools and 4GLs automate parts of this development. Why can't the two be combined? All we need is for the prototyper to automatically feed its output into the 4GL. In fact, there is a product from Cognos called Flex, which is Excelerator combined with Powerhouse.

The Miracle of a 4GL Integrated
with a Relational Data Base Management System

We have seen how the 4GL automates the life of an applications developer. A 4 GL that incorporates the power of an RDBMS can drastically improve the productivity of the system maintainer and user as well. For the system maintainer, a good DBMS provides automatic backup/restore, audit trails, and clean up of the data base if there was a crash during a transaction. If a new application has to be added on to existing data, it may simply need to add a few new relations. The tool may even provide a facility to simply draw the relationship.

The real benefit is the power provided to the user. Unforseen forms, reports, and ad-hoc queries will be accommodated without a rebuild of the data. Depending on the power of the 4GL, complex requests can be handled. For example, you could do a query of the ABC system such as, "CITY=SELECT CITY FROM COURSES WHERE AVERAGE NUMBER OF STUDENTS>10." Imagine all the programming this would require in a 3GL.

Choosing a CASE Tool

But what if the application is very complex? Following is a list of items that are most difficult to accomplish with CASE:

    a. Secure, multi-user access to the application and data.

    b. Audit trail, data backup and recovery.

    c. High volume transaction handling.

    d. Flexible data access, needed to service ad-hoc requests and add new features without reprogramming.

    e. Network access to application and data.

    f. Change management (tracking, control, releases).

    g. Data sharing among different applications.

Figure 16.14   Things hardest to do with CASE

h. Transportability of the application between operating systems and hardwares.

i. Decision support, graphics, statistical analysis, complex calculations and logic.

j. Real-time, process control.

Figure 16.14   Things hardest to do with CASE (continued)

The key to solving items **a** through **d** in Figure 16.14 is a good RDBMS. All of these features are built in so that the application need not worry about them. That is why most CASE tools are based upon a relational data base. Evaluate your needs and make sure that the product will do what you want.

Solving items **e** through **i** in Figure 16.14 depends upon the specific CASE tool. There are dozens, and each one does different things depending on the application that it was built to suit. You must analyze your needs and choose one that suits you. If the CASE tool does not automatically provide the feature, you should be able to manipulate the resulting application to have it do what you need. As a last resort you should be able to access a 3GL to do what the CASE will not. This is what you would need to do for item **j** in Figure 16.14.

16.8 CONCLUSIONS

Let us summarize the pros and cons of using a 4GL.
First the bad news:

- New products must be bought and learned. Old systems may have to be converted. All this takes time and costs money.

- A 4GL in the hands of many users opens more security leaks. Strong data administration and security measures have to be devised.

- A 4GL invites many new users and applications, causing a drop in system performance.

- Real-time, scientific, complex, non transaction oriented systems are not suited to be developed in a 4GL.

- More talent is needed to develop in a 4GL than in a 3GL. The simple programmer (my apologies to all you programmers—surely you are not 'simple') will not suffice when user interfacing, negotiating, and explaining is required. Retraining will be needed. (Is this really a 'con'?)

- Most important, at this time, a well designed application in a 3GL will outperform the same application in a 4GL. To prove the cost/benefit of a 4GL you must show that the cost of the additional hardware required to run the 4GL is worth the productivity gained and the increased number of applications that can be developed.

The good news far outweighs the bad news:

- It is easier to manage a smaller project than a larger one, it is easier to divide a large project into small projects using a 4GL. With a 3GL the usual way to divide and conquer is to develop one function out of many. But one function is usually meaningless until all the other functions are done. With a 4GL you can produce a *meaningful small system* by developing the core of every function. The next iteration is another small project and so on.

- With the 4GL approach the user is involved, the relationship is friendly, and all companies benefit from interdepartmental communication.

- Most important, the productivity gained when using a 4GL can increase by three to five fold the number of applications developed in a period of time.

QUESTIONS

1. What are the two kinds of 4GLs and what are the differences?
2. What does a 4GL provide that a prototyping tool does not? Can a 4GL be used to prototype? How about vice-versa?
3. Which features of a 4GL are usually not found in a prototyper?
4. Compare the activities and products in the Definition and Analysis Phases of the 3GL and 4GL development methods.
5. What items must be designed when using a 4GL?
6. Why is the DFD analysis method especially useful when using a 4GL?
7. In a 4GL, why is the user interface not final until the design is complete? Give an example of a case where the design may dictate the user interface.
8. Outline the steps of building the first prototype. Which of these should be done together with the user?
9. What makes the Acceptance and Operation Phases faster in a 4GL than in a 3GL?
10. Who are the people in a typical company that may have to be 'converted' from a 3GL to a 4GL? List arguments that you would use to convince each one.
11. You are the accountant for the MIS department. You have to calculate the cost of converting completely from a 3GL to a 4GL. List the items that may cost you (indicate with -) or profit you (indicate with +) when converting from a 3GL shop to a 4GL one. Begin like this:

ITEM	COST
Have to buy the 4GL	-
Save on development costs	+

12. Show how a CASE tool automates each phase of the development process.
13. What in your opinion are the three most difficult items to program with CASE?
14. Discussion topic: CASE and 4GLs will never replace 3GLs and traditional system development methods.

17

Project Management Software

Planning and Controlling With a Computer

17.1 INTRODUCTION

At this time, there are over 500 project management software packages written for mainframe, mini and microcomputers. In fact, there are companies whose only business is to evaluate these products and publish their findings (Reference Section 3). Chances are that there is a product out there that will do the job for you.

I recommend these products wholeheartedly. There is no reason why a highly paid project manager has to spend hours drawing and constantly redrawing PERT and Gantt charts, calculating budgets and evaluating resource allocation strategies when a $1000.00 micro with a $500.00 software product can produce these items in minutes.

But beware: a software package *will not manage the project for you*. It is simply a *tool* to speed up some of the mechanical activities of the job.

17.2 PLANNING TOOLS

Data Input

The best products allow you to input on one screen the headers with their sub-tasks, the resources for each, durations, start dates, stop dates—in fact everything to do with the project. Most people find that this is the screen they will use to plan most of their projects.

190

| Outline | SuperProject Expert | | | | | SOFTWARE.PJ |
| View | Edit | Select | File | Output | Help | |

Heading/Task	Resource	Dur	Schd Start	Schd Finish	Total Hours	Total Cost	
SOFTWARE.PJ		20	11-27-89←	12-22-89	680	15500.00	
DEFINITION		17	11-27-89	12-19-89	216	5400.00	
REQUIREMENTS	DOC	5	11-27-89	12-01-89	80	2000.00	
	PM	5	11-27-89	12-01-89	40	1000.00	
	USER	5	11-27-89	12-01-89	40	1000.00	
PROPOSAL		12	12-04-89	12-19-89	136	3400.00	
PRELIMINARY	PLN	5	12-04-89	12-08-89	80	2000.00	
	PM	5	12-04-89	12-08-89	40	1000.00	
	PL	5	12-04-89	12-08-89	40	1000.00	
WRITING		7	12-11-89	12-19-89	56	1400.00	
	PM	7	12-11-89	12-19-89	56	1400.00	
ANALYSIS		5	12-11-89	12-15-89	64	1600.00	
FUNCTIONAL SPEC		5	12-11-89	12-15-89	64	1600.00	
TECH SECTIONS		3	12-11-89	12-13-89	24	600.00	
	PL	3	12-11-89	12-13-89	24	600.00	
MGT SECTIONS		5	12-11-89	12-15-89	40	1000.00	

TASK SLCT: tst

Name of heading/task or resource.

Figure 17.1   Outline view of Superproject

Work Breakdown Structure (WBS)

Some products allow you to interactively draw a WBS such as Figure 17.2.

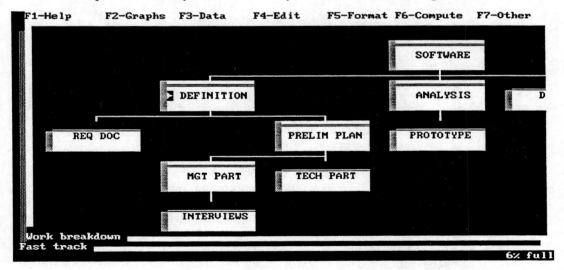
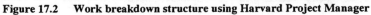

Figure 17.2   Work breakdown structure using Harvard Project Manager

This is helpful if you like to plan on line using a WBS. The best products can even build the PERT by connecting the lowest level WBS boxes which usually represent activities. Look for a product that also gives you the option to omit making this connection. Sometimes you want to detail the network yourself.

PERT

Most of the project management products give you some form of PERT. It is easiest to work with the 'activity on node' type of PERT as shown in Figure 17.3.

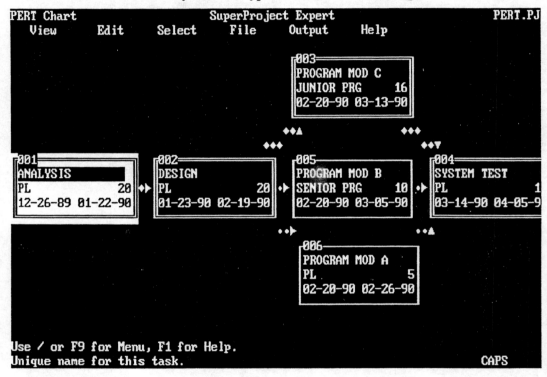

Figure 17.3   PERT created using Superproject

Some people find that the PERT chart is the best graph to use to enter a plan into the computer. This is fine for a project of 25 tasks or less, but over this number even the best PERTs appear cluttered. The PERT is best to see the 'network' of activities. The software should allow you to enter the precedents and successors of a task and immediately display the PERT network. The program should also allow you to move the activity boxes to any location on the screen. Some products use the ASCII characters to produce the PERT. This means that the connecting lines must be vertical or horizontal (done using the vertical and horizontal bar characters,) or on a diagonal (done using dots or diamonds) as in Figure 17.3. Some products (Project Scheduler 5000 for example) uses bit mapped graphics. This results in very low resolution on a CGA PC, but quite acceptable for EGA or VGA. Apple Macintosh products such as Macproject and Microplanner use bit mapped graphics most effectively. Printout in all cases should have straight connecting lines.

Gantt

You will use the Gantt more than any other screen. You should be able to add, delete, link, and modify tasks on the Gantt. The Gantt should clearly indicate the critical path, the noncritical tasks, floats, and milestones. Some products encourage you to plan your project using the Gantt (by not giving you a PERT at all) but the best allow you to enter activities on either one. As a control tool, the Gantt should show progress against a baseline plan, and portions of tasks actually completed.

Resource Planning Tools

All of the project management products allow you to allocate resources to tasks. As you enter each task (or perhaps afterwards) you can enter who will be working on it as well as any non human resources required for the task. The better products allow fractions of people (preferably the upper parts) to be allocated to several tasks in one project or *across several projects.* (I highly discourage putting people on several projects simultaneously. It takes a person about one half hour to 'switch context' when moving from one project to another.) Some products even give you a resource usage histogram such as Figure 17.4.

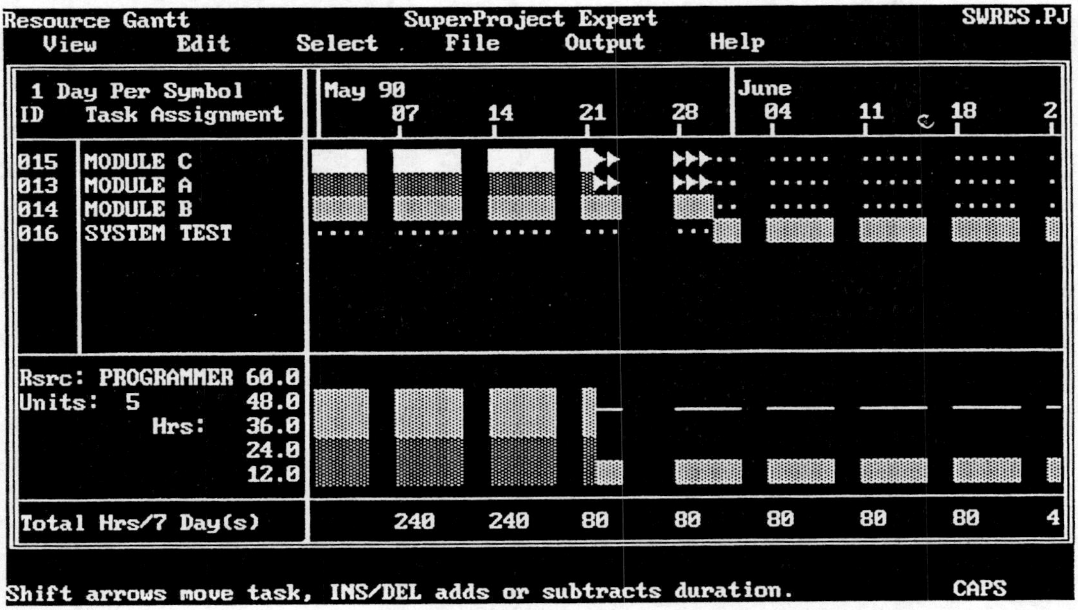

Figure 17.4   Resource histogram created using Superproject

Look for a product that can indicate when a resource has reached its limit.   For example, in Figure 17.4 Superproject uses a horizontal line to show that the maximum of five programmers is exceeded in May. The best products will (optionally please) reschedule activities and projects so that no resource exceeds its limit (see Section 17.4).

Cost Planning Tools

Costs go hand-in-hand with resources. As resources are entered for each task, the cost of the resource can be entered. You should be able to specify that the cost of the resource depends upon the duration of the task (variable cost,) or on a fixed price independent of duration. The program calculates costs by task and resource and rolls it up as the total project cost. The products that support a WBS should be able to roll up the costs to any level of the WBS. This can give you an indication of the costs by project phase. Costs can be incurred at the start or the end of a task, or pro-rated as the task progresses. Several packages produce line graphs such as Figure 17.5 showing costs, by week and/ or cumulatively, for the length of the project. Others allow easy export of the figures to graphics packages such as Lotus 1-2-3.

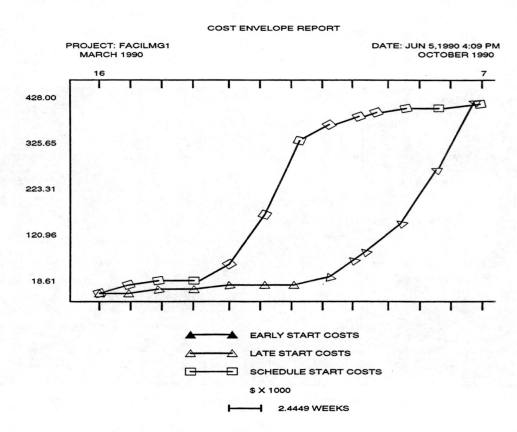

Figure 17.5   Cost line graph created using Microsoft Project

Gaming (What If?)

You will really appreciate a project management product when you try your hand at gaming: playing 'what if' with the multitude of factors that the product will allow you to manipulate. As you alter a factor the product will instantly show you the results of the alteration. You can reallocate some or all of a task's resources; alter task cost or duration; move tasks around the network for optimal sequence; reschedule one or more activities. There is no better way to study the effect on the three constraints of quality, duration, and cost. At planning time you can fine tune a project to the best of your knowledge, and as the project unfolds you can constantly readjust to take the most efficient course of action. The best products can show two or three scenarios on one screen.

Reports for Planning

When you finish entering your original plan you may wish to produce several paper documents for your own records or for inclusion in a proposal. The software should allow easy printing of the graphic reports such as the PERT and Gantt charts. Make sure your brand of printer is supported (there is a printer driver provided for it), otherwise the printed graphics may not look like the screen display. You may wish to print resource Gantts—a Gantt chart for each resource (person or thing) showing only the activities the resource is involved in. These must be shown to the resource providers to obtain their commitment.

   You should be able to print text reports of all the useful facts about the project. Figure 17.6 shows a task detail report for the budget planners, and 17.7 shows one without cost but with float figures for the resource planners.

Task No.	Desc.	January Fixed Cost	Var Cost	February Fixed Cost	Var Cost	March Fixed Cost
1.	Definition	10000	11000			
2.	Analysis			20000	25000	20000
3.	Design					50000
.						
.						
Totals		100000	50000	150000	....	

Figure 17.6   Task detail report – any good package

No.	Task	Start	Stop	Float Days	Float Type
1.	Definition	01/01	01/15	0	Critical
2.	Analysis	01/17	02/10	0	Critical
.					
.					
7.	ATP	05/12	06/17	23	Total
.					

Figure 17.7   Task critical /float report - any good package

Look for a product that can list any field (entered or calculated) in any column, and provide selection criteria, sort, subtotals, and totals. The best products allow you to customize your own report formats. This is usually done by specifying that the report be broken down by three or more fields; for example, the report in Figure 17.6 was a request in Superproject to report on all tasks, by month, FIXED COST vs. VARIABLE COST.

17.3 CONTROLLING TOOLS

The key to control is measuring progress against plan and reporting to everyone affected if things are not on track. A project management software product should allow you to enter the actual start and stop dates for each activity, actual duration and cost, time spent on the activity by resource, and expenses incurred by resource. Charts and reports can then be produced to show how the project is tracking against plan in terms of time and cost. The most powerful packages can track earned value, extrapolate the trend, and forecast the delivery date and cost.

Gantt Chart as a Control Tool

The best tool to show how the project is tracking against the time plan is the 'double' Gantt chart such as Figure 17.8.

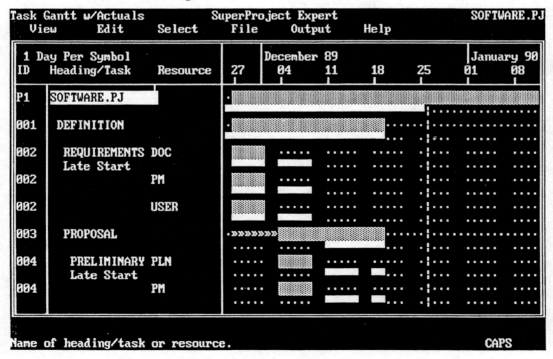

Figure 17.8 Double Gantt created using Superproject

The software must be able to show:

1. LOB (Line of Balance)—a vertical line at today's date.
2. Actual start of any activity that has started (and original planned start).
3. Actual completion of any activity that has ended (and original planned completion).
4. The portion of any activity that is completed.
5. Planned start of any activity not yet started (and original planned start).
6. Planned completion (and original planned completion) of any activity not yet completed. The most important item is the planned completion of the *last* activity in the project.

The double Gantt in Figure 17.8 shows two lines for each activity. The top line shows the plan, and the bottom line shows the actuals. LOB and partial completion of tasks is indicated by shading.

Cost Control and Earned Value (EV) Reporting Tools

Look for a program that can store and report earned value (EV). This can be either a true EV in dollars or as percent completed for each task. In both cases you will have to calculate the true earned value. The software should be able to report earned value versus budget, and actual expense via text reports and line graphs. For example, Figure 17.9 plots earned value, budget, and actual expenditure.

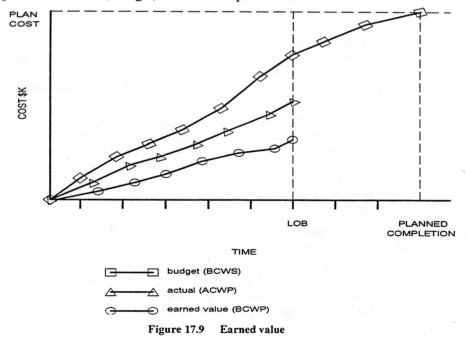

Figure 17.9 Earned value

See Section 20.2 (Budget Problems) for interpreting this kind of graph. Most microcomputer software products do not have this kind of graph built in, but some of the products allow you to create customized plots, and most of them will allow you to easily export the figures to a graphing tool such as Lotus 1-2-3 or Harvard Graphics.

Other Reports for Control

In Chapter 21 on Meetings, Reviews and Reports we discuss the content of the Status Report. It should contain a double Gantt such as Figure 17.8, an expense plot such as Figure 17.9, and for those who wish more details than what the graphs provide (such as accountants), a report such as Figure 17.6 or 17.7 can be produced. Some companies require a breakout by resource cost or account codes. The key is to have the flexibility to enter all of this data and to print it out on reports.

17.4 HOW TO EVALUATE/BUY PROJECT MANAGEMENT SOFTWARE

Sections 17.2 and 17.3 detailed the basic features required of a Project Manager program to run a project. The following features distinguish a good product from a mediocre one:

User Interface and Documentation

I prefer a pull-down menu to the in-line type. The menu choices should be logically organized into groups under main headings that are visible at all times. If you find that you are asking yourself, "Where did I see that menu choice?" the organization is inferior. The most common functions should be accessible by a one or two keystroke 'fast track' method. Some of the products can be set up to run in 'beginner,' 'intermediate' and 'expert' modes. The menus and features become more complex only in the advanced modes. The screen graphics should be clean, simple, attractive, and the use of color should help, not overwhelm the user. Look for clear, context-sensitive on-line help.

The product must come with a high quality, clearly written, well organized user guide. Look for one section of this guide where all the menus and commands are organized in the order that you would use the commands, and a reference section where all the commands are listed alphabetically. There should be an index of all the important words in the document. An on-line tutorial or learning guide should be provided as well.

Necessary Features

The basic features that these products have are listed in Sections 17.2 and 17.3. The following are optional extras that you may wish to have:

Full Project and Resource Calendars. All the products allow you to set up working and nonworking days for the whole project. The best allow you to set up a nonstandard work week down to a specific hour or minute of the 24 hour day. Look for products that allow this detail to be set up on an individual calendar for each resource as well.

Cost Charging Flexibility.   The best products support overtime rates that can be different for the same resource from task to task. They provide the flexibility to charge for a fixed price resource at the beginning or the end of a task, or to be prorated throughout the task. Every company has its own accounting system. Make sure that yours will be supported.

Resource Allocation and Scheduling Flexibility.   The good products allow you to define the duration of each task, and assign resources to work on a task for its total duration. The schedule that comes out of this calculation is time based. The best products calculate the duration of each task depending on the availability of the resources assigned to the task. This is resource based scheduling.

Resource Leveling.   The best project management tools allow one resource (or part of one resource) to be scheduled on several activities of one project or across several projects. If this is the case the software should be able to warn you if the resource exceeds its limits, and *optionally* reschedule the tasks or even the projects so that the resource limit is not exceeded. Some softwares allow you to control the algorithm used for leveling; for example, moving tasks within their float period only, or moving the lowest priority tasks first. The product must indicate where rescheduling took place.

Large Limits.   The less powerful products limit the number of resources per task or the number of tasks per project. The more powerful ones have no limits, as long as the main memory (RAM) of your computer is large enough. I find that most of the micro products will hold approximately four to six tasks per kilobyte of free RAM. If you have over 640K of RAM, make sure that the product you purchase will support extended memory.

Flexible Reporting.   The reporting capability makes or breaks a product. Look at how many useful built-in reports the program provides, as well as the ability to customize these reports or to create new ones of your own format. You should be able to ask that any known field appear on a report. Look for easy sort, search, and select capability. For example, you should be able to select a specified date range (used to report only for the past period,) a specific WBS code range (used to report on a certain level or phase), or a specific float (used to report on CP items only—float is zero). You should be able to preview all the reports on the screen.

Sub-projects.   Many projects involve thousands of activities, but one cannot plan and control a project that has over one hundred activities. It is therefore necessary to break a large project (*the superproject*) into many smaller projects (*sub-projects*), which can be managed more easily. To support this the software should allow one task in the super-project to represent a sub-project of many tasks. You should be able to zoom from a task in the superproject into the appropriate sub-project and vice versa. Several levels of sub-projects should be supported. If a change is made at one level that affects another, all the appropriate items affected should be automatically updated by the software.

Multi Project Merge.   If the product allows scheduling of resources (or fractions of resources) across several projects, it should allow a view of all the ongoing projects together. The best view is a Gantt that includes the activities of all the merged projects.

In addition, look for a product that can give you schedules and costs for the resources across all the projects, warn you if a resource is overloaded, and do resource leveling across many projects.

Data Import/Export. A spreadsheet program such as Lotus 1-2-3(TM) is much better than a project management program for manipulating numbers. Similarly, a database program such as dBase III(TM) can do search, select and report formatting better. You may therefore wish to transfer the information created on your PC project management program to other PC products, or even to a mini or mainframe computer. Look for easy data interchange in *both directions* with the software you wish to use.

Networking. If you have a LAN, you will want a product that will share the program among users. You may desire sharing resources such as printers or disks, as well as data files. Make sure the data can be secured.

The Icing on the Cake. The following features are not absolutely necessary but are nice to have:

- Full featured report formatting, such as control of column headers, column location, field size and format, page breaks, and multi level sort.

- Gantt chart that shows more than one baseline, percent complete, and a link to precedent activities. PERT chart automatically arranged so that the lines do not cross and have arrows on the ends time scaled PERT chart.

- Mouse input, particularly if most of your work involves choosing items from pull down menus or manipulating graphics. This is less useful when a lot of text needs to be entered. Some people find that switching back and forth between the mouse and the keyboard is bothersome.

- Estimating and statistical tools. Several products have a software estimating tool such as COCOMO built in. Other products use CPM to calculate project estimates. You enter a pessimistic, a probable, and an optimistic estimate for each task, and the program calculates three project estimate ranges: one with 99%, one with 95% and one with 68% probability.

- Outlining that allows you to indent sub tasks and sub-sub tasks to indicate work breakdown. You should be able to collapse the outline to any level, move major or minor sections at once, and expand only selected sections.

17.5 SOME PRODUCTS TO LOOK AT

Personal Computer Products

At this time, the following are the four most popular IBM compatible PC project management products (and indeed the four best ones in my opinion). Although they are listed in descending order of my own preference, every one of them is a full—featured, friendly product. In fact, if I were to grade the best as 100, the other three would be graded 99, 98, and 97 respectively.

1. *Superproject Expert* (Computer Associates, 2195 Fortune Drive, San Jose, CA 95131; also Vancouver, Canada)

Pros: Excellent user interface (pull down menus), best graphics, just about all the features listed above including a word processor that allows you to make notes. Every feature that is supported is done well and logically. Computer Associates is very helpful in support and training.

Cons: Weak on documenting the use of reporting, PERT chart connecting lines not graphic, no line graphs.

2. Timeline ® Symantec, 10201 Torre Ave., Cupertine, CA 95014

Pros: Best user interface, with '/' type menu tree structure, good on-line help and tutorial, and a quick pick feature that lists all the possible choices for an entry. Typing the first few letters of the desired choice reduces the list until only the selection is visible. Activities can be scheduled down to one minute, making TL useful as a 'Things to do Today' notepad.

TL allows you to display and print any column of information in front of the Gantt. Figure 17.10 shows a 'notes' column that may show dates when action needs to be taken. This column can be sorted and the display used as a reminder list.

```
Tuesday          26-Dec-89   9:00am               Press [/] for Main Menu
SOFTWARE                        Resource:
SUMMARY, 97 days, 26-Dec-89  9:00am thru 14-May-90  5:00pm.  Future.
                                            Dec Jan Feb    Mar    Apr      May
Task Name                   Resource Notes  26  16  29    20 5    26   16  7
   SOFTWARE
      DEFINITON                      90/01/15
         REQUIREMENTS DOC            90/01/25
         PRELIMINARY PLAN  PM, PL
         PROPOSAL          PM, PL
      ANALYSIS                       90/02/01
         FUNCTIONAL SPECIF PM, PL
            TECHNICAL ASPE PL        90/02/12
            MANAGEMENT ASP PM
         PRESENT           PM, PL    90/02/28
         APPROVAL          PM, USER
      DESIGN
         TOP LEVEL         PL, AN1
            OBJECT ORIENTE PL        90/03/01
            HIPO           PGR1
         MEDIUM LEVEL      PL
         REVIEW            PL, AN1    90/03/15
      PROGRAMMING
         MODULE 1          PGR1
Caps                       SOFTWARE End: 14-May-90  5:00pm
```

Figure 17.10   TL Reminder list with Gantt

Cons: Lack of resource calendars. Weak PERT—all the activities appear in a straight line. You must buy an extra package for good graphics printout.

3. *Harvard Project Manager* (Software Publishing, P.O. Box 7210, 1901 Landings Drive, Mountain View, CA 94039)

Pros: Window on two forms at once, good bar and line graphs. Good graphics including activity on arrow type of PERT.

Harvard has a 'Fast Track' approach to building a single line of activities for a particular resource. (See Figure 17.11). You can cursor to the spot where the activity is to appear and simply type in the name of the activity.

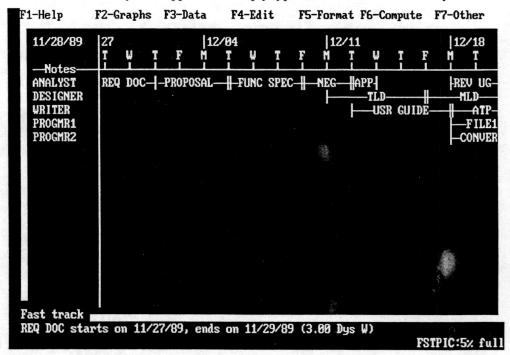

Figure 17.11   Harvard Fast Track screen

Cons: Automatic creation of PERT from WBS is more of a hindrance than a help; PERT easily gets cluttered due to restrictions; it is also difficult to manipulate the PERT. Not enough activities visible on the Gantt screen. Harvard is the slowest of the four products listed, especially when doing graphic printout.

4. Microsoft Project ®(Microsoft Corporation,16011 NE 36 Way, Box 97200, Redmond, WA 98073)

Pros: Good line and bar graphs, excellent reporting, great import/export and networking, least costly of the four products. Microsoft Corporation is also very helpful and supportive.

Cons: Not easy to use unless you are familiar with other MS products.*Microsoft* delivers fewer features, such as a limit of sixteen resources per task and no resource leveling. Also, the PERT is weak.

The above products are all in the $300-600 (US) price range, so price should not be a deciding factor.

Evaluate more than the products above, because new and better ones are appearing constantly. Personal computer magazines are the best sources for the most recent product evaluations.

Minicomputer and Mainframe Products

The following products all work on DEC VAX (VMS) and IBM (MVS or VM) hardware and software. Some of them work on the HP and DG families as well. The following products have everything a project of any size would require, so it is difficult to differentiate based on features. Look rather at the company behind the product. Since you may need answers to questions, consulting, and installation, look for a vendor that has experience in your type of application, and a good reputation for service. Look for an active user group in your area. These products are so complex that having someone with experience on the product, preferably in a similar field as your own, is a godsend.

The cost of these products is a major deciding factor: they range from approximately $2,000 to $500,000, depending on your computer and the number of modules and features you buy.

The following are listed in my order of preference. Value for the money has been considered:

1. *Artemis* (Metier Management Systems, every major US city; Toronto, Canada; and worldwide. ($27K-$95K)

   Metier's only business is project management, and it shows. *Artemis* features a thorough cost tracking and reporting system. Cost levels can be imported from other data bases; costs can be allocated to tasks depending on early and late start, at the beginning or the end of the task, or using a distribution throughout the duration defined by the user. Earned value can be tracked and reported using several algorithms.

   Artemis is a flexible system with built in menus, reports and commands, as well as the power to modify any menu, report, calculation or graphic chart. You can build/edit graphics such as a logo, or overlay charts; preview portions and print them out.

   The user interface is reasonable for a such a sophisticated system, with input via menus, mouse, or a structured English-like command language. Interface to other mainframe applications is excellent. You can transfer information to and from accounting systems, payroll, inventory, time-card reporting, budget datasets, and so on. It even has a configuration management system built in to help track changes to items like drawings and purchase orders. *Artemis* uses its own relational database to store all this information and its performance is second to none.

In the past, large customers have asked Metier to implement certain features required for projects such as plant shutdown, construction, petroleum processing and such, and these features are now available in *Artemis*. It may therefore be to your benefit to approach Metier with your project and see if they have the experience and software for it.

Nit-picks: One of my clients phoned *Artemis* recently for technical help. After the fourth phone call he finally got someone who started that day and was learning the system by answering questions. There is a PC version of *Artemis* that is a subset of the full blown one, but *Artemis* has not expended the same effort on the PC product as on the Mini. It is very weak in comparison to the others.

2. *DECSPM* (Digital Equipment Corporation, Maynard MA., and everywhere else) ($1K-$54K)

This product is the weakest of all in terms of features. For example Version 1 supports only one project. It is slow and unwieldly in manipulating graphics. But for the price and if you like the DEC 'feel' it is a good value. *DECSPM* (they call it DEC Software Project Manager) is especially suited to the software project since the COCOMO software estimating algorithm is built in. Simply call the ESTIMATE menu option and all the pertinent COCOMO parameters will be prompted. The product produces effort in person-months, a schedule and the cost for each phase. (see Figure 17.12)

```
                    Estimation Mode Form


Name:Test
Mode:   Simple (Intermediate Complex)
Outputs:
PDCOST:    5500      (Prel. Des. = Analysis Phase)
DDCOST:    5500      (Detail Des.= Design Phase)
CUTCOST:   5500      (Code&Unit Test)
ITCOST:    4800      (Int. & Test)
Inputs:
Line of Source Code: 10000
Factors (1 - low through to 5 - extra high)
Relability:       3   Exec time const:  1   Analyst cap.    1
Data base size: 2     RAM constrained:  3   Applicat'n exp  3
SW complexity:  3     VM volatility     1   Progrm'r cap    2
                      Turnaround        2   VM experience   3
                                            Lang exp        4

Modern programming practices:          3
Software tools:                        4
Schedule constrained:                  3
```

Figure 17.12   COCOMO parameter prompting screen (adapted)

The graphics, mostly line drawings, are adequate if not glorious. PERT, Gantt, line graphs, and histograms are available. Input is oriented to graphics using icons and mouse.

All of the *DECPM* graphic manipulations can be done in a command mode but there are over 200 commands. The product can automatically create the commands from graphic input, and the user can alter and run the file commands in batch mode. Keep your eye on this product; knowing DEC (and the developer) subsequent versions will be much more competitive.

3. Project/2 ® (Project Software and Development Inc., 20 University Road, Cambridge, MA 02138) ($50K-$500K)

PSDI has been in the project business for over two decades, and has the client base to prove it. *Project/2* is the most powerful of any product, with a price to match.

The best feature of *Project/2* is that it has the Oracle data base management system built into it. This gives *Project/2* a relational data base that integrates all the data on the project (scheduling, cost, and resource,) supports an ad hoc reporting system, a structured query language (true SQL) and a menu system. The menu system comes with a full tree of predefined menus, plus gives flexibility to create your own. The data base also provides configuration management and audit trail tools.

Special features of *Project/2* include: Discontinuous activity scheduling. An activity can stop (due to network logic, reported progress or resource leveling) and restart anytime. Activities can be segmented and resources assigned to a segment only. Consumable resources, as well as created resources (for example, one activity creates funding for another to use are supported.)

Project/2 has the best costing system of all the products. Cost can be input and viewed as spreadsheets. Input and reporting can be by account codes, organization codes, work breakdown structure levels and so on. Cost rates can be determined using 'rating factors' such as unit cost, escalation rates, exchange rates, overhead rates, time-varying rates, rates by account, organization in the company, and quantity. Risk factors can be built in and cost trends and forecasts varied accordingly. The costing system can be integrated with existing systems on your computer.

Project/2 has a menu driven graphics editor to customize the graphic outputs.

PSDI has sold *Project/2* for large projects such as plant certification, contract management, equipment maintenance and so on, and they can of course be hired for training and consulting.

Project/2 comes in modules (Schedule Manager, Cost Manager, Graphics Manager, Relational Database Manager, and Screen Application Manager) and the price varies accordingly.

PSDI's PC product is called Qwiknet. It is more powerful than the products evaluated above, especially in tracking costs, but again the price puts it out of the range of those products.

4. *Primavera* (Primavera Systems Inc., Two Bala Plaza, Bala Cynwid, PA 19004) ($4K-30K)

Primavera will do almost everything that the above products will. It has a menu interface that is somewhat cumbersome, but probably necessary to get all the different data input. It has the most sophisticated built in reporting system of all the products, with excellent support for graphics output to dot matrix printers.

Primavera also comes on the PC, and is fully compatible with Microsoft Project. This gives a good growth path from a $400.00 micro product (Microsoft Project) to a $2000.00+ PC product (Primavera PC) to a sophisticated VAX product without major data modification.

5. PAC I,® II® and III ® (AGS Management Systems, 880 First Avenue, King of Prussia, PA 19406) ($33K for *PAC III* and *WINGS*)

The low end product, *Pac I* is a single user, single project system typically used on small to medium sized engineering, construction, manufacturing, and publishing projects.

Pac II is a widely used multi-project management system that is flexible and easy to use. It has full scheduling, resource utilization, and cost processing capabilities.

The top-of-the-line *Pac III* and *WINGS* products are sophisticated systems with most of the capabilities of the products mentioned above. Mainly used on IBM mainframes with 3278 type terminals, special features include: Automatic resource matching and allocation so that the task gets done as soon as possible, progress reporting on a Gantt containing original plan, revised plan, actual and projected bar for each activity. Costs may be reported by cost center, report center, company department, WBS level or box, responsible person, purchase order, contract, change order, and so on.

When to Use a Mini or Mainframe Rather than a PC

Following is a list of items that may urge you to use the mini or mainframe for project management:

- You need multi user access. If several people must input data, receive unique reports and supply updates, it is a burden to run on even a networked micro.
- You have a large or complex project. The micro products run out of steam if there are over several hundred activites. The larger products usually allow you to specify complex costing, accounting or scheduling calculations.
- You need unique or changing reports and calculations. Most of the larger products allow full customization of reports and costing formulas, usually in

- You need to interface to existing data bases and systems. These products allow full access and conversion to and from the usual IBM and DEC data bases for cost, resource, accounting, materials, suppliers and so on.

- You need to interface the project management system to company wide accounting, job costing, time-card, or inventory control systems.

- You need sophisticated project management tools such as complex resource leveling, hammocking, work breakdown and cost reporting by accounting codes or company departments.

- You need automatic backup (you are too lazy to back up the PC and you know the mini will be backed up).

- You have a VAX; you are already familiar with it; it has room on it for PM; you can afford it.

- You have found a mainframe product and a user group targeted specifically to your industry.

- You want to stay with one vendor (training, tech support).

- You need a huge plotter which is only supported on the VAX. Personal opinion: At a 1 to 10 price ratio, I suffer and live with the PC products.

17.6 CONCLUSIONS

There is no question ''if'' you should use a computer project manager: the question is ''Which one?'' Most vendors provide a 'demonstration' version of the product that will show you the features and let you play with the program. Be sure to evaluate three or four, read the appropriate literature and visit companies that have bought the products that you are considering. Choose the one that has the features that you need and that you can learn to use and like most quickly.

QUESTIONS

1. List, in chronological order, the automated project planning tools that you would use to plan a project.
2. What two items contribute to the cost of the project? Why are automated tools useful for tracking cost?
3. What is gaming? Why is this useful for managing a project?
4. What reports would you send the following people when the first plan for the project is complete?
   a. Department head who provides you with a programmer for several tasks.
   b. Accountant for the company.
   c. President of the company.
   d. Yourself.

5. What reports would you send the same people as the project progresses?

6. One of your users asks you to recommend a project manager PC product. The user is naive, he does not share his resources across tasks, his projects are approximately 200 tasks, he wishes to use data already on dBASE, and he has to report only to his boss who is interested in costs. Which product features would you look for in choosing a product?

7. Your manager asks you to recommend a project manager. He wishes all five programmers to input their own time, there are 500 tasks in the project, and the existing accounting system on the VAX has to provide the cost rates. Which product would you recommend?

PART 3
People

18

Organization

Who Does What and When

18.1 INTRODUCTION

We have all attended meetings where many action items are discussed but no one is assigned these tasks. These items never get done-everyone thinks someone else will do it. A major project milestone is reached when everyone knows exactly what they are responsible for.

18.2 ORGANIZING THE PROJECT TEAM

The Small to Medium Sized Project Team

As mentioned in Chapter 3 (PLANNING), a good team organization for a small to medium sized project is the one shown in Figure 18.1.

Each person on the team has a specific job. The programmers program. All technical people need close technical supervision, so the Project Leader (PL) provides this by leading the technical activities and solving any system problems. The major responsibility of the PL is product quality. The Project Manager (PM) is there to provide management leadership and handle all communication between the Project Team and the outside world. The major responsibility of the PM is to plan and to control.

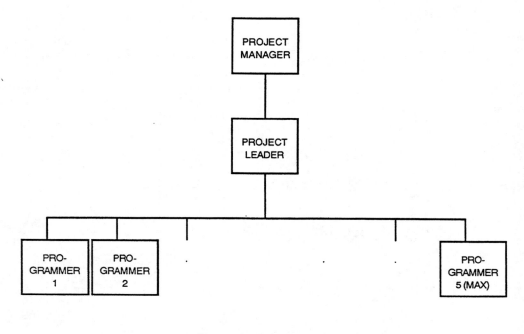

Figure 18.1   Project team

The Larger Project Team

Since a technical leader (PL) cannot effectively supervise more than five programmers, consider organizing larger project teams as shown in Figure 18.2 (on page 210.)

If you attempt this form of organization, divide the large project up in such a way that the individual teams can treat their portion as a stand-alone project. One of the most interesting conclusions made by Tom Peters in the book *In Search of Excellence* (Reference 4) is that the best products in the world were produced by teams of less than seven people.

The Functional Project Organization

Most companies are organized functionally. For example, if a software constructing organization is responsible for several different types of software, there may be a function or group dedicated to producing each type. The banking software would always be done by the bank applications group, the process control application by the process control group and so on. The manager of the banking applications group, called the functional manager, is automatically the Project Manager for the bank software project, and the functional manager of the process group is PM for the process control applications.

Organizing this way has advantages and disadvantages. On the plus side, you can easily find a home and a manager for a familiar project. On the negative side, projects usually require experts from outside the group, and problems may occur if people have to be borrowed from another group. These experts are ususally lent 'part time' to the project, and we saw what happens when people have to devote portions of their time to different projects—they spend more time switching than producing. It is also boring to always work with the same people, for the same manager, on the same type of project.

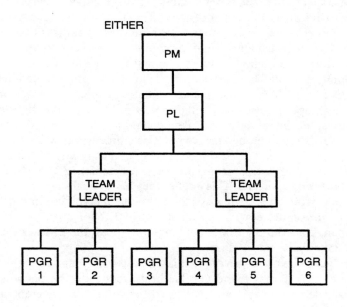

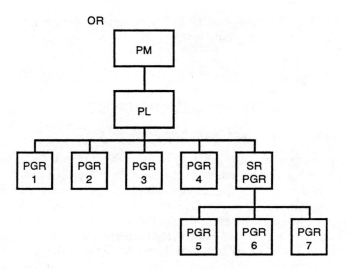

Figure 18.2   Larger project teams

The Matrix Project Organization

DEC and other large software producing companies sometimes use the following method of organizing project teams: Groups of programmers report to a function or Line Manager (LM). The programmers are in their specific groups only because they happen to live near a particular office or a job slot was available when they were hired. When a project is begun, someone with the necessary skills is first found to manage the project. This PM is usually a senior programmer who has experience with the client and the application and who knows how to manage people. The PM then decides which programmers would be best suited to build the project, and negotiates with the respective Line Managers for the use of these people.

The people are assigned to the project *full time* for the duration of their specific task, and at the end of the project the people go back to the LM. The PM pays the LM for the use of the people, and the payment is commensurate with the profit of the project. Thus both the PM and the LM have a stake in the success of the project.

This form of matrix management works best if the *PM and the LM have equal responsibility and authority*. This implies they have equal say in project decisions as well as in the performance reviews of the individuals involved. In most companies, some managers are more equal than others. In DEC for example, since the LM is the permanent boss and the PM is the temporary boss, the LM has the final say over the people involved.

Nevertheless, the idea of organizing the team dynamically to solve the problem is excellent. Tom Peters found that the best products come out of small, dynamically organized teams. People are motivated to work with different team members, for different managers, on different problems, as long as they do not have to reorganize too often.

> Reorganization gives the illusion of progress. In reality, it creates
> demoralization and insecurity.
>
> *Petronius (Roman General) 66 A.D.*

18.3 THE ROLE OF THE PROJECT MANAGER

Selling the Project Manager Job

If you organize a project team as shown in Figure 18.1, you will have no trouble convincing anyone that there is a need for a Project Leader (all technical teams need supervision) but you may have trouble selling the need for a Project Manager. Since the PM's major role is to interface with the user, your user will argue, ''Why put a person in place to communicate with me? I will 'manage' your project!'' This may be possible on an internal project. But there is a lot more to project management than interfacing to the user. Will the user know how to handle people, interface to upper level management, obtain resources, and control the milestones? Will this user be impartial when a major change is requested from the user side and the project team does not want to implement it?

Your upper level manager may also argue against the PM position. Showing you an organization chart, he says, '' We have lots of managers around—make one of them the PM!'' This is fine if these managers have the specific skills required to manage a software project (see Section 19.2). The skills are not the same as those required for a personnel or general business management job.

All multi-person efforts require organization, communication, and firm leadership. Sell project management as a necessary job, advertise successes from your own experience, and from your industry. (Or tell the manager to read this book!)

General Responsibilities of the Project Manager

The major role of the PM is to interface the project team to the outside world. They are responsible for reporting on plans and progress to the client, to upper level management and to all those concerned. All information from the outside regarding changes, budgets, schedules, people, and company issues—anything that affects the PT—is communicated to the PM who informs the appropriate team members. The PM obtains all the resources required to get the job done.

Another responsibility is to manage the project people. The PM is the leader, motivator and solver of any people problems as necessary.

And, last but by no means least, the PM protects the team from the politics and bureaucratic baloney showered on it from the outside (and generates any baloney required to get the job done). ''The project manager is the buffer or screen for the administrivia.'' Metzger (Reference 5).

Specific Responsibilities of the PM in Each Phase

1. *Definition*   The PM may be the one to make the go/no-go decision. This may involve interviewing the user and helping in the writing of the Requirements Document. The PM will probably be the author of the proposal. The PL will help by providing technical assistance with items such as the preliminary project plan. The PM will plan the higher levels of the work breakdown structure, then give the WBS to the technical people to break the work down and do the estimates. When the detail is done the PM will calculate the total cost, draw up the schedule, and get tentative commitment for resources.

The PM will chair any internal or client reviews and approvals, negotiate the proposal, ensure that the technical team approves all proposal changes, and obtain the client signoff.

After the proposal is signed, the PM formally initiates the project by establishing the Project File (PF). The PF will be the central repository for all the *latest versions* of project documents, including status reports, minutes of meetings, nasty memos concerning the project and so on. She calls a project kickoff meeting (see Section 21.5) to set the objectives, establish the rules, and set an enthusiastic mood.

2. *Analysis*   The PM should write the following sections of the Functional Specifications (see Section 6.3): Deliverables, Specification Changes, Acceptance, User and Project Team Interfaces, User's Responsibilities (input from PL on details), Terms and Conditions, Warranties, and anything about the effects of the new system on the user's environment.

The PM will ensure that the FS (or prototype system) gets done on time (mainly that the user's input is received in time), negotiates the FS with the client and obtains the client sign off. The hard part is to ensure that the user understands the FS, that changes do not go on forever and that any changes are approved by the technical team.

At this point the PM is heavily loaded down with the planning tasks of the project. He gets firm commitment from the functional managers for all the resources, especially for designers and programmers. Courses are set up for anyone who needs training.

Control starts in this phase as well. The PM monitors progress by running all necessary status and review meetings, writing status reports to all concerned and handling any problems that crop up. If staff has been borrowed from other departments, the performance of the individuals must be fed back to the appropriate managers.

Control is very important when using a prototype or 4GL. The PM ensures that the model is improving, that there are not too many iterations, and that the developers are providing the appropriate support, and he may even do some of the hand-holding! The PM makes sure that the user is involved and motivated.

3. *Design*   Since this is a highly technical phase, the job of the PM is less demanding. Formal control procedures are established now, and used for the remainder of the project. The PM sets up regular status meetings, and publishes a regular status report. Weekly he or she checks time and budget progress against the plan, forecasts final cost and delivery date and resets expectations if necessary. The PM must detect any problems, solve them if possible, replan if not. If there are any management meetings such as steering committee or milestone review meetings, the PM will preside. Most important, the PM will ensure that the client is satisfied with the progress of the product.

The issue of changes to the requirements will first rear its ugly head at design time. The PM must establish and maintain the change control procedure to ensure that the impact of changes is reflected in the project price.

4. *Programming*   This phase involves the most people and therefore the most people problems. The PM will have to monitor the happiness of the team and react *immediately* if something is amiss. The line manager will be looking for input into the performance appraisals, so the PM must be aware of each individual's performance.

This phase can be the longest stretch of time without a clear milestone. The PM will have to be most perceptive to ensure that progress is being made. The PM must walk around a lot now, talk to programmers, and use his or her intuition to detect any problems (see Section 20.2 for detail on how to 'walk around').

5. *System Integration and Test*   The best thing the PM can do in this phase is to keep out of the integrators' hair. The outside world (client, upper level management) is probably getting anxious by now, phoning the PM, calling endless meetings and asking for daily progress reports. This is when the PM is really needed to keep all this flack away from the PT.

And at last when the PL reports that the system is all integrated and working, the PM first ensures that the ATP is run through and corrected, and then calls a major milestone meeting (pizza and beer) to announce to the world that "We have a system!"

6. *Acceptance*   The PM schedules the time, facility, and the resources required for the acceptance run, and ensures that the user signs off as agreed.

7. *Operation*   The PM must ensure that the technical support promised earlier is available and that the user is satisfied with the operational system. If she wants to sell a new project, this is the opportune time.

And finally, the PM calls the post project review meeting to evaluate the project, and writes a post project report to close the book.

18.4   THE ROLE OF THE PROJECT LEADER

General Responsibilities of the Project Leader

The major goal of the PL is to produce a high-quality product. Whereas the PM is oriented toward the outside world, the project leader is oriented inside the project. If you are the PL you will have to make sure that the product is built according to the specifications and it will not be full of bugs. You will lead most of the technical activities, chair any technical reviews, assign tasks to designers and programmers, solve major problems, and perhaps do the most complex tasks yourself.

Specific Responsibilities of the PL in Each Phase

1. *Definition*   The PL will do most of the Preliminary Project Plan, such as the lower levels of the WBS and the estimates (or at least supervise the estimators). If the user must provide technical details at this point or if there is a prototype involved, the PL will be the main interface.

2. *Analysis*   In a small to mid size project the PL is the chief analyst and writes all the technical sections of the Functional Specification such as the Overview, Objectives, System Requirements, and Component Descriptions (see Section 6.3). If the PM needs technical assistance with the negotiation of the FS or needs to know the cost of a change, the chief technician is standing at the sidelines ready to help. The PL should also help choose the remaining members of the project team.

3. *Design*   The PL is the head of the design team. They will conduct all the design reviews and walk-throughs, assign tasks to designers, and probably do most of the design, especially at the higher levels.

In this phase, as well as in the Programming and System Test phases when the PM remains in the background, the PL will meet with the PM (weekly is best) to report project status. Since it is the PL who is in direct contact with the workers, he must provide formal feedback to the PM about the performance of the individuals.

4. *Programming*   This is when the PL wears the T-shirt with the big "S" on the chest. The PL will make all the programming assignments, and solve any problems that the programmers cannot solve. She must approve (walk-through) program designs, test plans, codes and user documentation, and ensure that the programmers interact if necessary. A very long or complex program can be assigned to a programmer who will be assisted by the PL. This allows the PL to code the complex sections while the programmer fills in the detail. The PL may also write entire programs, but not those on the critical path.

5. *System Test*   Integration and final test of the product is completely the responsibility of the PL. He plans the integration, controls it, keeps track of the results and keeps the PM informed of progress—perhaps daily.

6. *Acceptance*   The PL will run the technical aspects of the acceptance. She will probably write the ATP, do a dry run of it at the end of system test, and execute it for the user.

7. *Operation*   Although a senior programmer may be adequate, the PL may be the resident warranty person, or the person who is available by phone to answer questions, or even to do most of the user training.

18.5 WEARING SEVERAL HATS AT ONE TIME

If yours is a five person company or department, the same person may be PM, PL and even the programmer on a small project. You may have little choice here, but I suggest that you try to separate the administrative job (PM) from the technical job (PL). There are several good reasons for this: First, if the PL is supervising 4 or 5 programmers (and doing analysis, design, programming and problem solving on the side,) he will find his time 100% occupied. Project management of a small project is not 100% (industry standards state that managing a project takes 15% of everything else,) but it is an event driven job. You are constantly interrupted to attend meetings, answer the phone, and fight fires. Doing a full time job (PL) along with an interruption driven job (PM) makes you *ineffective on both jobs*. It is therefore good to put a 'fire-chief' in place (the PM) to handle the administration and the interruptions.

The second reason to separate the PM and the PL jobs is psychological. During definition and analysis the user and the PL are together interviewing, talking, prototyping and becoming good friends. User changes are encouraged. But beginning with the Design Phase user changes are discouraged or rejected outright. If it is the PL who has to say "NO" to these changes, the user will feel that the former friend has suddenly turned into an enemy, and this may spoil the rapport needed throughout the whole project. If there is a separate PM and a change control process is in place, the user changes need not be refused. The PL can simply remind the user that all changes must go through the proper channels and everyone can remain good friends.

18.6 RUNNING SEVERAL PROJECTS AT ONCE

If a Project Manager is supposed to spend only 15% of his time on a project, how can one possibly justify hiring an expensive full time person to manage the project? The solution is to give the PM several projects to manage at once. Watch out, though: each phase of a project places a different load on the PM. As shown at the bottom of Figure 1.1, the first two phases and the last two phases of a project will take most of the PM's time. The center three phases (Design, Programming, System Test) will take the least, but these three usually take the longest elapsed time. A good PM can in fact manage as many as five or six small projects at one time, as long as not too many of the time-consuming phases of the projects occur together.

18.7 THE ROLE OF THE PROGRAMMER

The programmer receives the medium level design for a module, designs the lowest levels, plans how to test the module, codes it, documents it and then tests it. A programmer may also be responsible for user documentation and training, although a good case can be made for hiring professional writers and trainers to do this. A good programmer is not necessarily a good author or teacher. The programmer must report progress to the PL, and assist at System Test time with integrating and testing those aspects of the system that involve his or her programs. Watch out for friendships between the the user and the programmer. The following scenario is very common, especially in an internal project:

ACT I, SCENE 1   **(Programming Phase, user talking with PM)**
USER: I wish an additional field F on Report Y.
PM: Looks difficult, but I will submit it to the PT.

ACT I, SCENE 2   **(Next change meeting. PM did not submit change to PT because everybody was running around like chickens with heads cut off, project is already late and over budget, and PM will have to take the blame.)**
PM: That change will cost you 25% overrun in budget and a 6 month slip in schedule. Do you still want it?
USER: I guess not.

ACT II, SCENE 1   **(Discouraged by the formal change procedure, User invites Programmer out to a bar. After several drinks...)**
USER: How long would it take you to add field X to Report Y?
PGR: (hiccup) No sweat. Couple of hours. Consider it done.

ACT II, SCENE 2   **(User meets with PM)**
USER: I want field X added to Report Y.
PM: You saw the last time how difficult it is to add fields to Report Y.
USER: Oh yeah! Your programmer said it would only take a few hours!

Alternative ACT II, SCENE 2 (Acceptance time)

> PM: Where did this field X on Report Y come from?
>
> USER+PROGRAMMER: Oh, did we not tell you about that?
>
> PL: Do you realize this puts everything on form Z out of synch?

Comment: The programmer is welcome to fraternize with the user as long as *no commitments are made.*

18.8 RESPONSIBILITIES OF THE PM, PL AND PROGRAMMER IN A 4GL ENVIRONMENT

The team structure suggested in Figure 18.1 will work just as well in a 4GL environment with one major change—the teams will be smaller. Three or four people are enough to program a small application. The roles will change a little as well.

The Role of the Project Manager

The PM is still responsible for project administration: there will always be meetings, reviews, status reports, and sign offs to handle. The PM will have to become a bit more technical than before. Since the team is smaller, the PM is more involved. They will have to be familiar with the 4GL approach as well as the language used. This knowledge is needed because the PM, in the role of chief negotiator, will at times have to convince the user to compromise on certain requirements in order to reap the benefits of using the 4GL. The PM will have to teach the user about the 4GL and set the expectations: what can be expected of the first prototype, how many iterations there will be, what the time frames will be and so forth.

The Role of the Project Leader

The PL will be the chief developer of the 4GL. As well as doing the requirements and the data analysis, they will be the one working most closely with the user to develop the prototype and the iterations. The PL will need new skills: communication to explain the product, to help draw out the requirements, and to help the PM convince the user to compromise.

The Role of the Developer

The classical 'hacker' (coding alone in a corner, talking to no one, wearing a dirty T-shirt,) for the longest time on the endangered species list, is now nearing extinction. Today's 4GL developer is a competent communicator who looks presentable, because they must interface with the user.

18.9 THE ROLE OF THE LINE OR FUNCTIONAL MANAGER

The Functional or Line Manager lends their staff out for projects, and will get them back when the project is over. Since the FM is responsible for the happiness, growth, and motivation of his people, he must keep tabs on the projects in which his people are involved. The FM must make sure that the people are treated fairly, are enjoying the project and are not burning out. The FM will therefore attend some project meetings, meet with his people occasionally, and receive the status reports.

As in most matrix organizations, the FM's goals may at times conflict with the PM's goals. For the FM one project is just part of the overall business, but for the PM that one project may be the only responsibility. Upper levels of management must make sure that the responsibilities and authorities of the FM and PM are clearly communicated and agreed upon by both parties.

18.10 THE ROLE OF THE USER

The user may have explicit responsibilities, such as writing documents or providing test data. In all cases the user must appoint a user project co-ordinator to interface with the project team on management matters. The client should also ensure that there is at least one knowledgeable person available to answer the PT's technical questions.

The user should take the effort to learn about project management so that they know where user reviews and sign offs fit in. When there is a document to be approved, the user must read it and return it in time. If users stay out of the technical phases, use the PM as the sole contact, and abide by the rules such as the change procedures, they will find that the PT will deliver a fine product.

18.11 CONCLUSIONS

You will find that assigning responsibility for each known task is the only way to get things done. But what about unforseen tasks? Who does those? I suggest that you define the following *general* responsibilities as well: The PM is responsible for any activity involving contact with the outside world, as well as for people oriented issues. The PL is responsible for all technical isssues. This way, if a new responsibility pops up it will be automatically adopted by someone without any hassles.

QUESTIONS

1. Why shouldn't the PL supervise more than five programmers?

2. Group Exercise:
   Company A, with 25 professional employees, has the following organization chart.(Expertise in brackets)

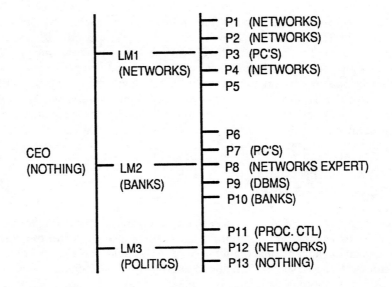

```
                                              ┌─ P1  (NETWORKS)
                                              ├─ P2  (NETWORKS)
                        ┌─ LM1 ───────────────┼─ P3  (PC'S)
                        │  (NETWORKS)          ├─ P4  (NETWORKS)
                        │                     └─ P5
                        │
                        │                      ┌─ P6
                        │                      ├─ P7  (PC'S)
     CEO                ├─ LM2 ───────────────┼─ P8  (NETWORKS EXPERT)
     (NOTHING)          │  (BANKS)             ├─ P9  (DBMS)
                        │                     └─ P10 (BANKS)
                        │
                        │                      ┌─ P11 (PROC. CTL)
                        └─ LM3 ───────────────┼─ P12 (NETWORKS)
                           (POLITICS)          └─ P13 (NOTHING)
```

A new project on networks is accepted. It will require a PM, a PL and four programmers. On the diagram above, mark with an X the people involved if you would organize the project functionally. Mark with a Y the people involved if you would organize the project as a matrix.
List the possible advantages and disadvantages of each organization.

3. Why is it difficult to 'sell' the project manager job? How would you convince upper level management to hire a PM?

4. What are the three major roles of the PM? Which is the most important?

5. List the seven project phases in descending order of load on the PM. Explain why you chose the first three.

6. What are the major roles of the project leader?

7. List the seven project phases in descending order of load on the PL.

8. Is it possible to have one person do both the PM and PL job?

9. What are the reponsibilities of a programmer?

10. How has the role of a programmer changed with the advent of 4GLs?

11. Can the PL and the programmer job be combined?

12. Why must the line manager know how the project is faring?

13. List the roles of the user in each phase of the project.

19

Staffing

The Right People for the Right Task

19.1 INTRODUCTION

Staffing is having the right person do the right job. This chapter will be particularly useful to those of you who must choose individuals from existing staff or who must hire a project team. If you have a five person company or department there will be little choice as to who gets to do what, but one day you may have to make that choice, so read on.

19.2 CHOOSING THE PROJECT TEAM MEMBERS

If you organize the project team as shown in Figure 18.1, the slots to be filled are the Project Manager, the Project Leader and the programmers. Let us look at how you do this.

The Project Manager

The PM is the first position to fill. This job is filled when the project is still a gleam in someone's eye, since it is the PM that may first have to establish whether or not the project is worth building.

Upper level managers appoint the PM. They are looking for someone with excellent communication skills. Other skills they look for are knowledge of project management, the ability to organize, and lastly they consider technical expertise. It helps if you know what the techies are talking about—but this is *not as essential as people oriented skills.*

At times the PM job requires unpopular actions such as saying ''NO'' to a divergent change request, announcing a slip, or disciplining people. The PM must know the people involved as well as the politics and procedures of the user and project companies. The skills required for such a job are in large leadership, negotiating ability, and diplomacy.

The politics of the organization may limit who can be chosen as PM. A large city government data processing department called me once to help choose a program manager (the person to whom all the project managers would report). Due to the political nature of this department I felt that the only person who could get anything done would be someone who had organization chart authority over every project manager. I recommended that the City Auditor be appointed. He was the only person at a high enough level that had any project experience—even though he had no computer expertise. He made an excellent PM because he could enforce the project rules by his position of authority.

Be especially careful in a matrix organization where the functional manager has greater authority than the PM. Here the PM must have leadership qualities that will motivate the workers even though they do not have the final say in their performance reviews.

The Project Leader

This is the second position to be filled. It is best if the PM picks this person. The PM must first negotiate with the appropriate functional manager for the PL's services, then convince the PL to join the team. The PL is signed on at proposal time since a lot of the proposal detail is done by the PL. This job is highly technical, so choose the best expert. Do not look for a 'bits-and-bytes' person, rather look for someone who can keep in mind the *general details of the whole project.*

The PL must have good communication skills as well. She will conduct the major user interviews and be the day-to-day supervisor of the programmers. Choose someone who can organize tasks, make assignments, and track progress. This person's reputation should be such that the programmers will do as asked due to their respect for the PL's technical knowledge.

The Programmer

Even before the go-ahead is obtained for the project, the PM and the PL should start thinking about who could make up the programming team and ask the appropriate functional managers (if necessary) about the availability of these people. (Add some contingency to their availability dates, as *other people*'s projects are always late.) Later, when contracts are signed, start assembling your programmer team. If you are lucky you will get everyone promised to you but more often than not, you will have to scramble for resources.

Choose programmers first by their programming ability. In addition, look for experience with the particular application, but not someone who has done the same thing five times recently—this person will be bored! If the candidate has no experience with the particular application, background on the operating system or related applications is the next best thing.

The Guru Programmer

A new life form has evolved since computers were invented. It is the programmer guru, or 'hacker.' This person works in mysterious ways, at strange hours; is argumentative and unruly, wants it always their way (we will not mention appearances). But darn it, the guru can program those complex tasks ten times as fast as anyone else. My suggestion is that if you have gurus, organize a team with *one* guru surrounded by juniors. This will be especially successful if the guru likes to explain things to others (which they usually do)—the juniors will learn from this person.

The Junior Programmer

Whenever I ran a project at a fast-growing company such as DEC, I was rarely able to get very experienced project team members—the experienced people were always managing or leading projects themselves. Most of the time I got people who were fresh from school with little or no experience on a programming project. But I was never let down by junior programmers!

Junior programmers are usually talented and eager to prove themselves. There are two skills, however, that are not always taught in school: team and management communication. There is always competition in school (only the top *n* people will be accepted in next year's class). Even on a team project students may not assist each other. They may not be taught to share the work and the knowledge, and to communicate the vital issues and problems to the other team members. In a company a team member wins only if the whole team wins.

Along the same lines, students may not be taught that their managers must at all times know what each one is doing and how their task is progressing. This may not be required for a school assignment. But if you teach your juniors to communicate, you will have invaluable team members.

19.3 PERSONALITIES

Personalities can impact the project. Here is a list of desirable personality traits for project staff. (Be careful, because no one will suit this description to a "T." Use your judgement carefully.)

1. You want a *communicative* person who is part of a team and who can share valuable knowledge and ideas. Not only should this person express ideas well, but should also be willing to fight for them.

2. You want a good *listener,* someone who will hear other people's opinions and be willing to concede if these opinions are better. (There once was a sign on the office door of a software designer that said, "This is *not* Burger King: you may *not* have it your way." Mind you, he was in charge of standards.)

3. You want an *organized* person. There will be many tasks to perform, each one at its appropriate time. Beware of the person who keeps dropping tasks part way through to start another. Soon there will be a dozen tasks partly done.

4. You do *not* want a *perfectionist.* Choose a person who can meet a deadline. There is always a better way, but if it works now, get it out in time and save the improvements for the next version.

5. You want the best *technical* person, one who is analytical and logical, with appropriate experience.

19.4　ASSIGNING TASKS TO INDIVIDUALS

In the book *The Psychology of Computer Programming* (Reference 14), G. Weinberg states that the greatest motivator of a programmer is learning new things. Always assign a task that is just a bit more challenging than the previous one. But do not assign a very complex task to a junior person— it may never get done; and interestingly a paltry task in the hands of your expert may never get done either.

　　If there are related tasks, assign them to the same person. Take advantage of the learning curve. Similarly, if there are programs that communicate with each other, give them to the same person (or to two that talk to each other).

　　Assign critical tasks and the most complex tasks to your most reliable person. A reliable person is not the 'expert' who is capable of completing the task in two days, but who sometimes takes four, or ten depending on his or her mood! A reliable person says, "It will take five days," and that is how long it takes.

　　Never assign tasks so that one person becomes indispensable. IBM has found that a chief programmer team (CPT) organization is very productive. With the CPT method an expert chief programmer does all the complex code (80%,) assisted by 'juniors' for the easier code (20%). But if the chief were to leave, the tribe would be sunk. To prevent this, IBM usually uses a buddy system, where one programmer is assigned to work very closely with the chief programmer, assist and share the load when possible, and learn everything that the CP knows.

19.5　MOTIVATING PEOPLE AND FURTHER READING

The PM is the coach of the team; the PL is the captain. The PM leads, motivates, teaches, and uses the carrots and sticks to get the job done. The PL plays on the team and motivates by example. The project leadership (PM, PL) must be available and approachable. Use MBWA (coined in the book *In Search of Excellence*, Reference 4) *M*anagement *B*y *W*alking *A*round.

　　When a person approaches you with a personal or technical problem, do them a favour: be quiet and listen. Usually the presenter will solve the problem while explaining it. Never forget the three basic tenets in the book *The One Minute Manager* (Reference 21): If deserved, praise (one minute), if necessary, criticize (one minute), and always set objectives (one minute) to communicate exactly what is expected of each person and how they will be measured for success.

　　Involve your people in all the important project decisions and they will be committed. For example, always have each person re-estimate their work and reach a concensus if your estimate and theirs do not agree. Read *The Soul of a New Machine*

(Reference 22) to learn how to get people (hackers!) to 'sign on' to a project.

Send your people to courses (see Reference 3.2 for my Project Management course)—it is amazing how much can be learned even by the most experienced person. A period away from the office will foster renewed enthusiasm and productivity.

19.6 CONCLUSION

After all the discussion on how to choose the right people, keep in mind that the availability of the people will be the first deciding factor.

QUESTIONS

1. Who selects the PM? When?
2. What are the skills, in order of importance, of a good PM?
3. Who selects the PL? When?
4. What are the skills of a good PL?
5. Who selects the programmers? When?
6. What are the skills of a good programmer?
7. Would you rather have five gurus or five juniors on your project team? Explain.
8. List, in the order of importance, the personality traits of a good project team member.
9. Group Exercise:
   The following five modules need to be coded:

MODULE NAME	DESCRIPTION	DURATION (avg pgr)	PRECE-DENTS	CALLED BY
MAIN	Control of whole system	12	–	–
TA	Tests hardware A	4	–	MAIN
TB	Tests hardware B	4	–	MAIN
TC	Tests hardware C	4	–	MAIN
REPS	Generate a report on tests	6	–	MAIN, after TA, TB, TC done

You can have the following five programmers:

Joe   -   guru, wrote control systems before, but has trouble communicating.

Henry -   junior, likes to learn, has done well on a small report generation program before.

Sue   -   average, does not like anything to do with hardware.

Jane   -   average, slow but reliable.

John   -   new hire, junior, no past history.

Who would you assign to program the modules?

20

Controlling the Project by Monitoring

Management by Exception

20.1 INTRODUCTION

Management by exception is leaving alone anything and anyone that is doing well, and reacting only to problems.

Controlling a project involves only three activities: constant monitoring of project progress against plan, solving any problems that crop up, and, if the problem cannot be solved, replanning and warning everyone affected by the new plan.

20.2 PROJECT MONITORING

Monitoring by the Project Leadership (PM and PL)

The PL supervises the day to day progress of the Design, Programming, and System Test phases. Unless the PL watches over the shoulders of the professionals involved, it is very difficult to measure progress. Reports by programmers stating, "I am 90% done," are meaningless. It may take as much time to complete the remaining 10% as it took to do the first 90%. The only percentages that can be measured in the progress of a programming task are 0% and 100%. The PL can ensure progress by being close to the workers and reacting to any major problem that could cause a delay.

How much monitoring should a PL do? The amount of monitoring will depend on the expertise of the programmers: junior programmers will have to be watched more closely. More monitoring will have to be done if there is communication among the

226

programs (and therefore among the programmers). Most of the monitoring will have to be done at the beginning of each phase or major task.

How can the PL watch the programmers and not be a pain in the neck? Monitoring can be informal—walking around, talking to programmers, participating in social activities such as having coffee with them. There should be formal monitoring as well —that is why there are weekly status meetings.
Here are the issues the PL should watch out for:

1. The programmers are building the *promised product.* Each task is done on time, functions according to specs and has no bugs or unsolicited bells and whistles.

2. The programmers are keeping to the prescribed *standards* for the module designs, for structured programming and for the user manuals.

3. The work is *progressing* according to plan. Any problems that may cause delays are solved.

4. People are generally *happy.* They are learning on the job, not much overtime is needed, no one is burning out, people problems are reported to the PM and solved.

The PM supervises as well, but from the sidelines. The PM must monitor project progress, time spent, money spent, quality, and people's happiness. They may also walk around and get informal input from the PL and the programmers, but receive most of the project status from the team in formal meetings and written reports. (See Chapter 21 on Meetings, Reports and Reviews.) The PM watches for the following problems:

1. Project *progress is less* than the amount scheduled.

2. Project *expenditure exceeds the budget.* This may not be a problem if the accomplishment exceeds the budget as well. See section 20.3 on Budget Problems.

3. *People problems.* Even though the PL is the one in constant contact with the team members, they may not be the best person to notice people problems the PL is too close to the action and probably suffers from the same problems. The PM must therefore keep in touch, using intuition to detect these problems.

4. User and upper level management *communication problems.* The PM watches out for phone calls and memos that begin with, ''Why was I not told about...''

In the next section we will discuss how the PM solves these problems.

Monitoring by the Upper Level Management

The PT's umbrella management has a right to know what is going on in the project. Their theme is, ''No surprises please!'' They will monitor the following issues:

1. *'Bottom line'* issues such as ''Will the project be done on time?'' and ''Will the project make the budgeted profit?''

2. Overall *user happiness.* There may be several projects under construction for

the user department or company. There should be interfaces between the highest levels of the user organization and the PT's upper levels of management to monitor overall satisfaction.

3. Project team and PM *morale problems*. Upper levels must help the PM if there is a problem that they cannot handle. What if the PM is having personal problems?

Upper level management must monitor the project formally: attend meetings and reviews, be on the Steering Committee, get copies of the status report, and meet with the PM. They should not hang around the project team.

Monitoring by the User

The theme of "No surprises!" holds true for the client as well. Although the PT may disagree, the user also has a right to know how the project is going, since the user is the one most affected by project failure. He will be anxiously checking whether or not the product will be on time, if the final price will be as quoted and if the product will perform as promised.

The user should also monitor the project formally by obtaining the status reports to see project progress, trends, and forecasts. She can attend the steering committee and milestone meetings. There are specific user reviews and signoffs throughout the development that indicate project progress. The user project coordinator will also meet with the PM regularly.

20.3 DETECTING AND SOLVING PROBLEMS

Schedule Problems

The most common problem you will encounter as PM is a slip in the schedule. It is not difficult to detect when a task slips: either the person doing the task will report that it will be late, or the task will simply not be done by the scheduled date. First, check whether or not the task is on the critical path (CP). If it is not a CP task, and the slip is less than the float there is no problem. If the slip is greater than the float, or if it is a CP task, the whole project will slip. The first reaction to this is usually, "We will catch up later (somehow)." *Never bury a slip—you will not be able to catch up.* React like this:

1. If it is an ongoing task that is slipping, you may be able to get it back on track by *management* focus. If it is a technical problem that is slowing things down, get help from an expert (maybe you or the PL can help the programmer in trouble.) If it is an individual's performance that is causing the slip, see if it is a personal problem. Communicate, motivate, and use carrots or sticks as necessary.

2. If management focus does not work, see if additional resources can be put on the task to speed it up. You may be lucky and find that one task does not need all the resources assigned to it, in which case the excess resource can be

and crash the task by using overtime or hiring more resources. Be careful! Not many programming tasks can be sped up by adding manpower.

3. Look at the CP of future tasks. Are there tasks that could be done in parallel but are scheduled in sequence because of resource constraints? Re-visit the resource providers. Maybe their requirements have changed and they can now spare an extra resource.

4. If it is a future task that is predicted to slip, (and it is not caused by a slip in an ongoing task) it usually means that a required resource will not materialize in time. Focus management, pull strings, threaten or cajole as necessary.

5. If all of the above fails, be brave and announce a slip. This is the most common and in some ways the best solution because it is the least risky.

How to announce slips.   There is an interesting reaction when people hear about a slip. To an uninitiated person (read user), weekly reports that the project 'keeps slipping' implies that the PT is out of control. Yet the opposite is true: the PT is monitoring the project very closely. Since you get into just as much trouble for announcing a big slip as for announcing a little one, consider hoarding the weekly slips and announcing a big slip at the end of the month.

Caution: do not hoard if you are nearing the end of the project. If you are 10 months down the road on a 12 month project, tell your user about every slip—even the slightest delay will affect her at this point. To your internal management you must announce each slip as you notice it.

Try this approach the next time you have to announce a slip:

> There is bad news and good news. Bad news is that we will slip. Good news is that *we are telling you now*.

Budget Problems

The second most common problem that you will encounter is that actual expenses to date exceed the budget. To see if this is really a problem, and to be able to forecast final project price as well as delivery date, you must track Earned Value or accomplishment.

Forecasting Completion Date and Final Cost by Tracking Earned Value

Consider the Budget and Expense figures in Figure 20.1 (as shown on page 229.) Figure 20.1 shows that the plan was to complete one module a month, at a cost of $100 per module, so the budget was to spend $100 per month. As of today (April 30) $450 was spent instead of the budgeted $400. At first glance this may look bad—but we have completed five modules instead of the budget of four. We have also spent only $450 on the five modules. How can we report all this good news?

Since we must report accomplishment in dollars, we report that the Earned Value, (which is defined as the budgeted amount for the five completed modules) is $500. This is usually reported graphically as shown in Figure 20.2.

Today's date: April 30

TASK	PLANNED COMP. DATE	ACTUAL COMP. DATE	BUDGET COST	ACTUAL COST COST TO DATE	ACT. CUMUL
1	Jan 30	Jan 30	100	100	100
2	Feb 28	Feb 15	100	100	200
3	Mar 31	Feb 28	100	100	300
4	Apr 30	Mar 31	100	75	375
5	May 31	Apr 30	100	75	450
.					
8	Aug 31				

Figure 20.1   **Task budget vs. actual**

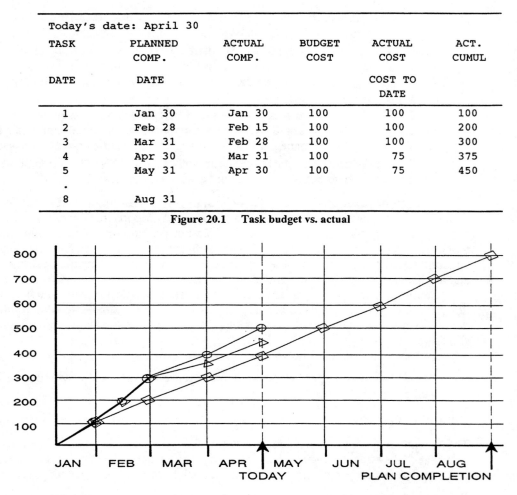

LEGEND:

    ▱━━━▱   BUDGET

    △━━━△   ACTUAL

    ⊝━━━⊝   EARNED VALUE

CONSTRUCTION OF GRAPH:

```
JAN: BUD  =   ACT =  100; EV IS VALUE OF 1 MODULE =   100
FEB: BUD  = 200, ACT =  300; EV IS VALUE OF 3 MODULES =  300
MAR: BUD  = 300, ACT =  375; EV IS VALUE OF 4 MODULES =  400
APR: BUD  = 400, ACT =  450; EV IS VALUE OF 5 MODULES =  500
(BUD CAN BE GRAPHED UNTIL AUG)
```

Figure 20.2   **Earned value graph**

This figure shows that although the actual expenditures are tracking above the budget, the earned value is even higher than the actual expense. The PM can use such a graph to evaluate project trend and forecast completion date as well as final price. Assuming that the actual and the EV line remains straight, the PM can extrapolate these lines. Use the following steps (See Figure 20.3):

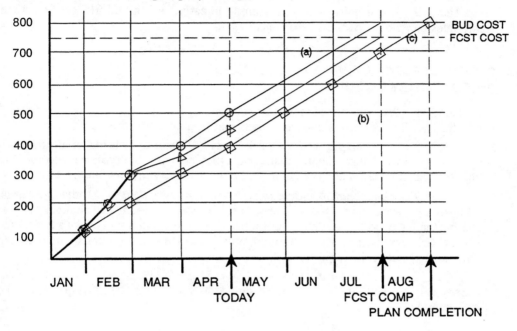

Figure 20.3 Forecast graph

1. The project ends when all eight tasks are completed, or the earned value is equal to the budget of $800. So extrapolate the EV line (a) until it reaches $800 on the Y axis. At the end of the EV line, draw vertical line (b). Where this line meets the TIME axis is when the project is forecasted to finish, in our case, July.

2. We stop spending when the project ends, so extrapolate the ACTUAL line until it meets line (b) at point (c). Draw a horizontal line at point (c). Where

this line meets the EXPENSE axis defines the forecasted cost of the project, in our case $750.

Crashing and uncrashing.   If the actual expenses are under budget, but the EV is also under the amount planned to date, crash spend more to get back on track. If the actual expenses are higher than planned, and the EV is also ahead, uncrash: spend less furiously. It is usually not worth coming in early, as you will just get your time estimates bargained down the next time.

20.4   DETECTING AND SOLVING PROBLEMS UP FRONT (BEFORE THEY OCCUR!)

Remembering that an ounce of prevention is worth a pound of cure (substitute gram and kilo for Canada,) here are some early signs that trouble is brewing.

1.   *There are no plans*   If someone says, "The project is too small to plan," or, "The plan will happen later," insist that a plan be made. No project is too small to plan (see Section 22.3), and the PT will be much too busy to draw one up later.

2.   *The Functional Specifications are bad or non-existent*   If someone claims, "The user does not know what he wants," or "The specifications will change," or you see that there are too many assumptions made about the requirements, take a look at the FS. Get the user involved and commited, prototype the interfaces, or use the two-step proposal to finalize the requirements.

3.   *The estimates are by edict*   If you hear, "We'll never do it in that time-frame or for that amount." someone is forcing an estimate on the PT. Do a good estimate and defend it.

20.5   DETECTING AND SOLVING PROBLEMS DURING DEVELOPMENT

Here are typical problems you will encounter during the development phases:

1.   Watch out for *requests to change the specifications*   Try to say "NO" and defer user requested (major) changes to the next release. Someone on the PT may request to change the specs, after realizing that the product will never be delivered on time. Scissors are snipping at your specs! This is not allowed unless the user agrees. Bite the bullet and take the slip.

2.   *Documentation is not getting done*   The first items that fall through the cracks in a crunch are the project documents, followed closely by the user documents. These documents are the most important items in the project! Ensure that the documentation gets done well, even if it means delaying some of the other tasks.

3.   *Programming or testing before the design is completed*   As we saw earlier, programs written before the design will always have to be rewritten. If you need to do something with idle programmers send them on training.

4. *Problems are implied in status reports*   If the status reports arrive later and later every week (or stop arriving altogether), or if progress is lacking, the project may be stuck. Walk around, find the problem. Try the solutions suggested in Section 20.3 (Schedule Problems).

Look for schedule changes in the status reports. No one can plan to the day all the activities in a major project. A status report containing statements such as ''We predict Task X will be 1 week late, and since it affects Task Y making it 1 week later as well, we are announcing a 2 week project slip,'' actually means that the PT is controlling the schedule well.

5. *The Project Team is disappearing*   If project members do not return phone calls, refuse to attend meetings, or avoid you in the corridors—there is trouble. Corner them, insist on communication, see what the problem is.

6. *The user is dissatisfied*   If someone on the project team (or on the user side) claims, ''There is no love lost between the project team and the user,'' there is a major problem. The PT may have alienated the user by condescension, rejecting changes outright, not involving the user in reviews or not reporting (true) progress. Since the PM is supposed to be the major interface to the user, this is a failing on your part. Do whatever it takes to satisfy the user.

20.6 DETECTING AND SOLVING PROBLEMS TOWARDS THE END

The end of the project is a crucial stage because all the slack has been used up and *everything is on the critical path.* Look out for the following:

1. *Lack of computer time*   If someone claims, ''We are not getting enough machine time,'' the testing is taking longer than anticipated due to bugs. It is too late to fix this problem. Take a slip rather than release a low quality product.

2. *Too much overtime*   A sure sign of impending burn-out is constant overtime. Programmers are willing—even eager—to work after hours. Some overtime can be productive, but after a point you will find that overtime buys no extra productivity at all. Do not let people work regularly more than two extra evenings per week.

3. *Upper level management 'concern'*   Toward the end of the project (especially if it is late) upper levels of management will become apprehensive. You will notice them hanging around more, asking for more progress reports, calling you more and asking you to meet with them endlessly. You will just have to spend extra time convincing them that everything is under control—but this is exactly what the PM's job is all about.

20.7 CONCLUSION

Keep your finger on the pulse of your project, react immediately to any problems that you detect, and most important, stay cool. After all, if there were no problems, you would not have a job.

QUESTIONS

1. What does controlling a project involve?
2. How does the project leadership monitor the project?
3. What issues does the PL monitor?
4. What issues does the PM monitor?
5. Why does upper level management have the right to monitor the project? What problems must they watch out for?
6. How can upper level management monitor a project?
7. Why does the user have the right to monitor the project? What problems must they watch out for?
8. How can the user monitor a project?
9. List three ways you may be able to fix the problem causing a slip.
10. What is the most common solution to a slip? How do you announce a slip to a person who is not familiar with project management?
11. Draw the earned value graph for the following project report:

TASK NO	PLANNED COMP. DATE	ACTUAL COMP. DATE	BUDGET COST	ACTUAL COST
1	JAN 30	JAN 30	100	100
2	FEB 28	MAR 31	100	150
3	MAR 31	APR 30	100	150
4	APR 30	JUN 30	100	200
.				
.				
8	AUG 31			
.				

Forecast the completion date and cost.

12. What BUDGET-ACTUAL-EARNED VALUE relationship would tell you to crash? What relationship would tell you to uncrash?
13. Many project problems are easily fixed with knowledge learned from this book. Discuss one such problem that occurs up front, one that occurs during development, and one that occurs at the end of the project.

21

Control Using Meetings, Reviews and Reports

Communication with the Outside World

21.1 INTRODUCTION

The project team must communicate with each other as well as with the outside world. This communication will be done using meetings and reports.

There are three kinds of meetings in a project. First, there are regular status meetings to assess project progress. Second, there are product review or walk-through meetings to detect and correct technical problems. And last, there are management meetings to report progress to management. The management meetings may occur regularly, such as the steering committee meetings, or at major events such as project milestone reviews.

The second form of project communication is via reports. To reach those people who cannot meet with the team the project issues the status report.

21.2 THE STATUS MEETING

Purpose and Attendees

On a small-to-mid-size project there should be a weekly status meeting, attended by the whole project team. This meeting provides an opportunity for the project members to report progress and problems to the project leadership. On a larger project, especially if there are several teams involved, I suggest that the status meeting be divided into two sessions. First, the whole group, including the PM meet for a short time (30 minutes) to discuss issues common to everyone. Then each team meets with their individual leader. This meeting is also short (30-60 minutes, depending on how close the team leader is to the project members during the week) and the team members report *verbally* to their own team leader. A third meeting between the PM and the team leaders or project leaders may take place later. At this meeting they discuss progress, trends, and problems that need the PM's attention, and they calculate total project status. If the PM is in charge of many projects he or she may request a written report, otherwise input may be verbal.

Interestingly, the least popular meeting will be the one where the whole group meets. Some people will claim, "Why should I meet with them? My work has nothing to with theirs!" It is amazing how many issues effect everyone, from machine time and resusable code to parking and the cafeteria. Always hold group meetings, perhaps less frequently than the other status meetings.

When to Hold a Status Meeting

Always hold the weekly status meetings at the end of the week—Friday afternoon is best. If members must report progress by Friday afternoon, they will get busy by the middle of the week at the latest, shut out non-project interruptions and make progress by Friday. If you hold the status meeting Monday morning people will only begin to worry toward the end of the week and work through the weekend to make progress by Monday. Everyone needs their weekend to rest or they will burn out.

21.3 THE STATUS REPORT

Purpose and Size

The main form of communication from the project team to the outside world is a short, *standard* project status report published regularly by the PM. There is a major problem with status reports, and it is a problem not only in the software industry but in most project areas as well: The reports are too long and they take too long to prepare. It is common knowledge that people will read the first paragraph of any document. If it is an interesting paragraph, they may read one page and skip to the last paragraph. A status report should contain only *one page of narrative*, followed by one or two pages of computer generated reports. It should take the PM *no longer than 30 minutes* to prepare it. You do not need to rehash past problems, make long-winded excuses or theorize about future events in a status report. Do this at informal discussions.

Frequency of the Status Report (SR)

Since it is rewarding to report measurable progress, the frequency of the status reports is determined by the average length of the work packages in the project. Weekly is most common for small to mid size projects, which fits in with the suggestion that your work be broken down to tasks that take a week or less. If most of the activities take one month, the SR should only be published monthly. You could still consider publishing more frequently if there are individuals who will get ulcers if they do not see signs of progress, or if the project is very dependent on outside resources (the status report can serve as a weekly reminder that their deadline is approaching).

Contents of the Status Report (SR)

Here are the topics that a status report should contain:

1. *Activities and accomplishments during the reporting period.*
   List each activity that was worked on, progress on each one, and the completion of any.
2. *Problems encountered.*
   Explain any new stumbling block, who or what caused it, who is responsible for fixing it, and what you are doing about it. Most important, state how it impacts the project.
3. *Problems solved.*
   Explain the problem (or refer to a past SR), how it was solved, who solved it, and how this impacts the project.
4. *Problems still outstanding.*
   Remind past offenders that you have not forgotten about an unsolved problem. Only a phrase or two is needed. Reference earlier SRs for a description.
5. *Schedule progress versus plan.*
   Page 2 of the SR (see Figure 21.2, top) should be a computer produced Gantt chart showing two lines for each activity: the plan and the actual duration for past activities, the plan and rescheduled duration for future activities. Explain all changes from last week's Gantt, especially if the project delivery date has changed. Underline the announcement of a slip.
6. *Expenses versus budget.*
   Reference the attached computer generated numerical reports such as the one in Figure 21.3, or if you are clever, the line graph of budget aligned with the Gantt as in Figure 21.2, bottom. Summarize the actual expenditures that occurred and the earned value versus the budget.
7. *Plan for next week.*
   List the planned activities and milestones for the next period.

Figures 21.1 and 21.2 show an example of a status report. Figure 21.3 is an optional third page of budget reports that may only be required for the accountants. This status report is from the PM. A copy goes to functional manager X, from whom the project leader of this project was borrowed, and to the head of department A, who is the boss of functional manager X. This report does not go to the client. (An edited version does, in which our personal problems are deleted.)

To: Project Team,   project File,   From: Project Manager
          Functional Manager   X   Date: June 20, 1990
          Head of Dept. A

Subject: Status Report for Project ABC, week ending June 16
Page 1 of 3

1. *Activities and accomplishments.*

   The User's Guide and System Programmers Guide were completed this
   week, ahead of schedule. Programs B and C are being programmed and
   are on schedule. Program A was completed but was not walked-through
   by Project Leader, so it is one week behind.

2. *Problems encountered.*

   Jane Doe, my Project Leader, was pulled off my project last week
   by Functional Manager X. Apparently a major problem was found in
   a program she wrote on a past project, and she has to fix it. This
   may take as long as two weeks. I will meet with functional manager
   X next week to try and resolve this. If J. Doe is not returned to
   this project by next week, each week of delay will *slip project by
   one week.*

3. *Problems solved.*

   None.

4. *Unsolved past problems.*

   None.

5. *Schedule progress versus plan.*

   As shown on Page 2 we are one week behind schedule. The only change
   from last week is a delay of one week in walk-through of Pgm. C.
   We are forecasting delivery date of Oct. 6, 1990.

6. *Expenses versus budget.*

   Expenditures this week were $2200 on labor and $500 on word
   processing supplies (see page 3). We are under budget by $50K to
   date, and as shown on page 2 bottom, our earned value is also ahead
   of plan by $50K. We are forecasting a total cost of $950K.

7. *Next period.*

   We will go on to programming of modules D and E, but unless J. Doe
   is returned, we will be idle by the end of the following week.

Figure 21.1 Status report page 1 (narrative)

Status Report Page 2 of 3

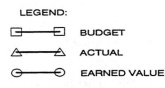

Activities	JAN	FEB	MAR	APR	MAY	JUN LOB	JUL	AUG	SEP	OCT
REQ. DOC.										
FUNC. SPC										
TL DES										
ML DES										
PGM MOD A										
PGM MOD B										
PGM MOD C										
PGM MOD D										
PGM MOD E										
SYS TEST										
ACCEPT										
OPERATION										

EXPENSE DOLLARS (K)

1000
900
800
700
600
500
400
300
200
100

JAN FEB MAR APR MAY JUN LOB JUL AUG SEP OCT |--SLIP!--|

LEGEND:

⊟——⊟ BUDGET

△——△ ACTUAL

⊖——⊖ EARNED VALUE

Figure 21.2 Gantt and budget chart (computerized)

```
Status Report Page 3 of 3 (Accounting Dept. Only)
Expense  and  Budget Report as of June 20, 1990
All Numbers are $K
```

Task WBS Ref	Planned Comp. Date	Actual Comp. Date	Budget Cost	Actual Cost	Planned Cumul. Cost To Date	Act. Cumul. Cost To Date
1.1	Jan 30	Jan 30	100	100	100	100
2.1	Feb 28	Feb 15	100	100	150	200
3.1	Mar 31	Mar 15	100	100	250	300
4.1	Apr 30	Apr 1	100	75	300	375
4.2	May 31	May 1	100	75	500	450
4.3	Jun 30	May 15	100	100	600	550
4.4	Jul 20	Jun 30	100	100	700	
4.5						
.						
.						
10.1	Oct 5		75		950,000	

Figure 21.3   **Budget report (computerized)**

21.4 REVIEW MEETINGS

Some of the review meetings (for example, the system design reviews and the management reviews) are very expensive because of the people's time. Run these meetings efficiently:

- Set an agenda with time allocated to the discussion of each item.
- Distribute this agenda well in advance, as well as any material that attendees must review before the meeting.
- Schedule a location where there will be no interruptions. Have a good moderator, keep to the agenda and to the time allotments. (Do not overkill this one —sometimes it is worthwhile to digress a little or take a little longer on an important topic.)
- Keep good minutes with action items assigned; follow up the progress of the action items.

Technical (Plan, Design, Code, Test, Documentation) Reviews

These reviews were detailed in the appropriate project phases, so here we need only discuss why we have these reviews and who is involved. To review a program, a design, a document or a test plan you walk through the appropriate product looking for errors and suggesting improvements. Only the author of the product under review, one or two peers (from the same project or from another team) and the PL need to attend. The only exception is the system design review where 3 to 4 outside experts are invited.

Management Reviews

The steering committee review.   Behind every successful project there is a steering committee (SC). The SC consists of the PM, the user project coordinator, one or more functional managers who provided staff to the project, and at least one upper level manager who has authority over all of the departments that will be supplying resources to the project. The SC meets at a set frequency—usually every 6 to 8 weeks on a 6 to 24 month project. The purpose of the meeting is to receive information on project status and to focus on problems. It is amazing what strings a group of high level managers can pull to get a floundering project back on track. This meeting also gives the PT some management visibility which motivates everyone.

Milestone Reviews.   Reaching a major milestone calls for a party. Most milestone meetings should have two sessions: One for the technical team to discuss accomplishments and problems of the last phase and to plan the activities for the next phase. The second session is for everyone on the project including the user, management, and the PT. The PM chairs this meeting and provides pizza and beer. Before the beer arrives be sure to discuss general project accomplishments, problems, and resource needs for the next phases. These sessions are needed to keep up morale and renew enthusiasm. Each milestone meeting is discussed in the next section.

21.5   SPECIFIC MEETINGS HELD ON SPECIFIC OCCASIONS

Here are major events in a project which call for input from several minds. You could have a meeting dedicated to each event, or discuss several topics in one sitting.

The Go/No-go Decision Meeting

Anytime you are evaluating risks, call a meeting of those who have experience with similar projects (or experience with the client if that is where most of the risk appears to be). This meeting should be held before the proposal is written to decide whether or not to bother with the proposal and to ensure that all the risks have been evaluated and *priced into project.* The PM, PL, and outside experts attend.

The Project Kick-off Meeting

Not many people have this meeting. Just as the coach brings the team together before the game, the PM calls this meeting after the proposal is signed. Have a management session first, followed by a technical one. For the first session invite *everyone* who will be involved in the project (client, resource providers, steering committee, technical staff) to introduce all the players, set up the interfaces and explain general background and objectives. Use this session to establish the required enthusiasm. Have a second session for the technical people only. At this meeting you can establish the guidelines (design standards, programming standards,) procedures (reports, administration, hours of work, place of work) and so on. Find out exactly how much everyone knows and arrange for any necessary training.

The Project Planning (Estimating) Meeting

As we saw in Chapter 13, estimating is very productive when done in a small group of three or four people. This group can be used to produce the work breakdowns, determine the resources required, and put the tasks in order.

The Functional Specification Signoff (Milestone) Meeting

Hold a technical session first to go over the specific problems of the last phase, and to revise the estimates and schedule, especially if the requirements have changed. Then hold the management session with everyone as described earlier. Announce any change in plans, such as a slip in the delivery date or a rise in cost. Get commitment from those who will provide the design and programming resources.

The Top Level Design (TLD) Walk-Through

The PL chairs this meeting. There are at most five attendees consisting of other designers, outside experts or the senior programmers on the PT. The design author presents the alternative TLDs with the pros and cons of each one. Others suggest any missed pros and especially cons, and any other TLDs that they can think of. At the end the best TLD is chosen. This walk-through should take approximately 2 to 4 hours.

The Medium Level Design Walk-Through

For a large project, walk through each level of the design as it is completed. In all projects walk through the complete design when it is done. The purpose of the walk-through is to find all the problems in the design. The designers present their design; the PL moderates the meeting, notes any suggestions, and follows up later with the designers. Depending on the number of modules there may be several sessions, but use no more than five persons (other designers, outside experts, project team members,) and take no longer than 3 to 5 hours per session.

The End of System Design (Milestone) Meeting

The approach and objective is the same as for the FS signoff meeting. Revise the estimates again, and get commitment for items such as the delivery of the hardware, staff for programming, acceptance, user documentation and so on.

Module Design, Documentation and Test Plan Walk-Through

These three items can be walked through together. Only the PL, the responsible programmer, and perhaps one other programmer need to attend. The purpose of the meeting is to ensure that the best design approach is chosen and to find any problems. Consider walking through several modules at once. Take no more than 1 to 2 hours per module, and no more than 4 hours for the session. The author of the module presents, notes any suggestions, does not attempt to fix the problem there but later reports back to the PL on the progress of the solutions.

Code and User Documentation Walk-Through

All the comments made for the module walk-through above hold true here. These will be the most detailed walk-throughs in the project, so more people may attend.

Acceptance Test Completion (Milestone) Meeting

This is less of a milestone than some of the others (plus it probably comes soon on the heels of the system test milestone) so not that much fanfare is needed. Consider a meeting of the client and PM only.

Operation Completion (Milestone) Meeting

This session is informal (it is the biggest party) and everyone is invited. Use this session to let off steam and leave the business issues to the post-project review.

The Post Project Audit Meeting

This is a meeting most people would rather not have. I realize that most of the time you wish to forget all about the project but this is the most important review. There should be two sessions here: one with the client, and one without. In the first session, invite the client, the PT, and upper level management. Do not let this degenerate into a finger-pointing session. The objective is to analyze the problems that were under the control of the user (or the management if it was an internal project), and to avoid this type of problem in the future. If the user is unhappy, this meeting can be an opportunity to show him or her all the problems that were not under your control. If the user is happy, get a letter of recommendation.

The second session is attended by the PT and associated management. Make sure that this one is also a *constructive criticism* session. Hindsight is perfect or better. Analyze what went wrong, *determine how those problems can be avoided in the future* and write it all down. If there is any finger pointing necessary get it over and done with.

The post project report.   The result of the Post Project Audit meeting is a formal report by the PM. The report is a stand-alone document that will be circulated to many project as well as nonproject people. Here are the topics to include in the report:

- How the project got started, what the original objectives were, and the pro-posed solutions. This is included to make this report stand alone.
- The project method and organization, with recommendations on improve-ments, if any.
- Estimates compared to the actual results, with explanation of when and why the actuals crept away from the plan.

- Update of the estimating formulas and ratios.
- Successful aspects of the project.
- Problems that were encountered, with suggestions on how to avoid each one in the future. Update of the Risk Quiz.
- Reusable portions of the product.
- Recommendations that answer the questions, ''Should we stay in this application area?'' or ''Should we stay in the project business at all?''

'Major Problem Cropped Up' Meeting

There are times when the PM alone cannot solve a serious problem. The issue could be turnover, major resources not materializing, project wide burn-out or conflict, or user-PT communication breakdown. The PM should call a meeting of all those involved and those who could provide a solution. Usually higher levels of management in the user department or project department attend.

21.6 CONCLUSIONS

Reviews are absolutely necessary to ensure the quality of the product. Other meetings are held to provide project communication with the outside world. But let us not meet each other to death. A meeting should only be called if two-way communication is needed. High level managers in North America spend over 90% of their time at meetings and hate every minute. Use memos, phone calls, and electronic mail whenever possible before resorting to a meeting.

QUESTIONS

1. What types of meetings must a project have and why? Which of these happen at a set frequency? Which of these are event driven?
2. There may be three status meetings in a large project. What are they and why separate them?
3. Why have the status meeting at the end of the week?
4. What is the major problem with status reports? What is the solution?
5. What determines the frequency of the status report?
6. Group Exercise:

   Following is the plan for the installation of the hardware for the Bell Family Communications project:

   At the end of February you discover that TECH-2 will be away for the month of March. Write a status report (2 pages) for the project dated Feb. 28.

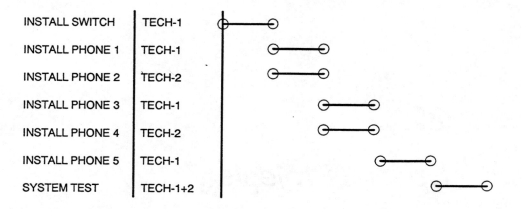

INSTALL SWITCH	TECH-1
INSTALL PHONE 1	TECH-1
INSTALL PHONE 2	TECH-2
INSTALL PHONE 3	TECH-1
INSTALL PHONE 4	TECH-2
INSTALL PHONE 5	TECH-1
SYSTEM TEST	TECH-1+2

7. List three planning activities that are necessary to run a good meeting.
8. Who should attend a module (code) walk-through?
9. Why have a steering committee?
10. Why hold milestone meetings?
11. Why hold a project kickoff meeting?
12. What comes out of a post project audit? What is the main purpose of this document?

22

Special Projects

Does the Method Still Apply?

22.1 INTRODUCTION

Certain types of projects require a unique approach. In this chapter we will discuss how the project management method needs to be changed *slightly* for real time projects, very small projects, conversions and maintenance projects.

22.2 REAL TIME PROJECTS

Let us see how the seven phases of project management must be applied to real time (RT) projects:

Requirements

The major difference in the requirements for a RT project and those of other projects is that in RT systems such as process control, response is dictated by something physical in the environment. For example, if the system is to insert control rods into a nuclear reactor to stop the reaction, the response is dictated by the speed of the nuclear reaction.

You start gathering RT requirements as you would gather non RT requirements, in that people are interviewed and existing systems and methods are investigated. However, in RT you must investigate and measure the physical systems that need to be controlled as well.

Sometimes the final requirements for a RT system cannot be determined until some tests are run using a working system. Take the case of a new communication network message routing system. The system design depends upon the types and frequency of the messages that are to be routed, but there may be no accurate data about the messages at first. The approach must be somewhat like prototyping—a model system must first be built based on assumed requirements. The seven phases in the development are still followed, but some phases are intentionally recycled as shown in Figure 22.1.

PHASE	ACTIVITIES
Definition	Define initial 'best guess' requirements.
Analysis	Specify building of model based on initial requirments.
Design	Design model.
Programming	Program model.
System Test	Test model.Determine changes required for final system.Cycle back to ANALYSIS, DESIGN, PROGAMMING, SYSTEM TEST for final system. Once is usually enough.
Acceptance	User accepts final system.
Operation	Final system implemented.

Figure 22.1   SDLC for real time system

An unusual fact of life has to be kept in mind when determining real time requirements: never believe the quoted time constraints. I have seen a requirement demanding that the system respond *in a few milliseconds* to a malfunctioning turbine by activating a control valve that took 20 seconds to close. (Sometimes the response is to warn a human operator who is probably asleep!) Obviously a slower response would be acceptable here. The slower the response time required of an RT system, the cheaper and easier it is to develop it!

Design

RT systems are usually designed bottom-up. Section 7.2 details such a design for an automobile engine monitoring and testing system. Another approach to designing RT systems is to break up the functions by the required response time. For example, there may be a set of functions requiring less than one second response, another set requiring one to five second response and so on; the last set may be the functions not requiring real time response at all. The next step would be to design modules to handle each response class. Figure 22.2 is another design for the automobile engine control and monitoring system that we saw in Section 7.2. Note that in this design the system is broken up into the following four modules:

The first module handles items that require less than one second response time. If heat, oil pressure, and engine speed are not reacted to this quickly, the engine will blow up. This module will probably be activated by a hardware interrupt.The second module handles items that require between one second and five seconds response time. Engine vibration, power, and operator commands may be in this class. This module will probably be activated by a timer, and will poll the appropriate devices to see if service is required. The third module handles items that require between five and twenty seconds response.

Warnings to the operator or response to operator inquiries are in this class. This module will probably run when nothing else requires CPU time. The last module runs items that need little or no response, such as reports generation. This can be serviced in non real time, such as background mode.

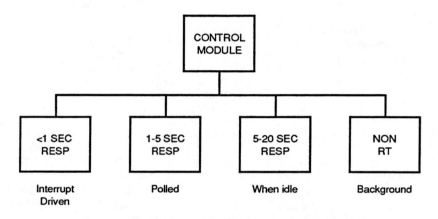

Figure 22.2   Real time module design by response time

You may be wondering what this has to do with the management of the project. Plenty, because a design such as this dictates that the project has to be developed in one of two ways: You either buy an operating system that supports priority levels or foreground/background processing so that these classes of responses can be handled. Or you buy two computers (or one with multiple processors,) one for the real time functions and one for the non real time. In both cases the cost of the project is affected.

Programming and System Test

Programming of a RT system is exactly the same as that of a non RT one. Lower level languages such as assembler, C or Fortran (more recently ADA) tend to be used because these languages have hardware control capabilities. Integration and test will be different because it will probably have to be done from the bottom up. Do the test in this order:

1. Start with the hardware: test the sensors, the interrupt rates, and the clocking of the system.
2. Test the system response to the different interrupt classes module by module. Use expected or normal data.
3. Test the control modules.
4. If there is a background set of tasks, test those independently first, then put the background and foreground tasks together.
5. Do not forget to test all the human interfaces.
6. Test the overload conditions: see how the system reacts to multiple (unexpected) inputs and rates that are greater than the requirements.

Testing an RT system is difficult because you may not want to try it in the real environment. Would you test an aircraft control system for the first time on a real airplane with real users? The environment usually has to be simulated. There may be simulator tools available or you may have to write software to provide the data. In the last case do not forget to include the simulator as part of the project.

Acceptance and Operation

Acceptance of an RT system has to be a trial run. Since the environment was only simulated at system test, there will be many problems found when the system is turned on for the first time. Operation is exactly as before—a warranty period, user training and hand-holding must be provided as necessary.

22.3 VERY SMALL PROJECTS

Why Tiny Projects Fail

A single person project that takes two months or less is considered a *tiny* project. These projects have a history of failure—they fail because they do not get the full formal project treatment. Let us say that most of your projects are one month (plan), but you deliver in two months (actual). One month of slip does not sound too bad until you consider that the project is 100% late. Will they choose you to build a one year project?

All seven phases must be done even for the smallest project. Keep in mind that *to the user there is no difference between a tiny and a large project.* He or she has a problem to solve, and whether the problem is solved by one report or a whole system the attitude is the same. Therefore the phases that involve interfacing to the user will take relatively longer to do than the corresponding phases of a large project.

Tiny projects are easy to start but unfortunately easiest to cancel as well. A small project does not have the same priority and visibility as a large one, so when resources run short the small project is the first to suffer. If all of your projects are little ones and others get the big ones you are the lowest man on the totem pole. Try to fit in some larger ones. Small projects can still be very successful if all seven phases are there with the following caveats:

Definition and Analysis

The requirements for a tiny project are usually determined informally. The user and the analyst sit down over coffee and discuss a report that the user requires. The format is drawn on a napkin and the analyst says, ''This will take a couple of weeks.'' The analyst means three or four weeks, the user interprets one or two. It will take even longer than four weeks. The analyst is ignoring that even one report will have to be formally documented, accepted, and the user will have to be trained.

A better way to do the analysis is a formal session (it may only take one hour) with a *written* FS of three or four pages—the format of the report, the acceptance method (ATP), and an outline of the documentation and training. The FS is signed off before development starts.

Design, Programming, Test

These phases may only take two weeks. Do not forget the programming documentation, especially if it is part of a larger system. Test the new program thoroughly.

Acceptance

The acceptance plan was written in the FS, and a full formal demonstration must be run for the user.

Operation

This phase will be relatively long. The user must be trained, questions must be answered, problems fixed, and warranty provided for the usual period of three to six months.

22.4 CONVERSIONS

A conversion may involve rewriting an application to run on new hardware, a new operating system (or new version), or a new language (or new version). The word 'conversion' brings fear to any experienced DP professional's heart. There are few of us who have not been burned by a conversion, yet hardware and software vendors constantly force conversions on us. Again, the key is to apply the seven phases of the project methodology. I once agreed to convert a COBOL system written in 1964 for an IBM 7040 (yes, I am that old) to a DEC VAX. Not only was there no documentation for the application, there was no documentation for the old COBOL compiler! I thought COBOL was COBOL, so I converted the programs (taking into account the obvious syntax differences), and tried to run the new system. Unfortunately, some of the old routines were written to get around some quirks in the old COBOL compiler. Additionally, the files did not contain what the user said they did. The conversion took 100% longer than I had anticipated.

Definition and Analysis

You must begin by becoming thoroughly familiar with the old and the new systems. The user will request that the converted system appear to the user exactly as the old one does. However, the new hardware or software may have features that enhance the old system. Use the opportunity to suggest new ways of doing business. Convince the user to change his requirements to make the most of the improvements that are available.

Design, Programming, Test

As for analysis, redesign for the new system. Test everything thoroughly. Draw up an acceptance test plan (ATP)—it should be as thorough as a plan for a new system. Relatively large amounts of machine time will be required for a conversion. Time will be needed for source conversion, file conversion, document reprocessing. New programs may have to be written and compiled as well. When converting old files never destroy the old copies—you may have to go back!

Operation

Cut over to the new system cleanly. Training will have to concentrate on the differences between the old and the new systems.

22.5 MAINTENANCE PROJECTS

The Seven Phases for a Maintenance Project

Eventually every system has to be maintained or changed. Consider even the smallest change as a tiny project:

Define why the old system needs changing and what the difference will be after the change. *Analyze* the appearance, performance or function that the change will accomplish and write it down. Get agreement from the potential users. Plan exactly what resources will be required—usually a few hours of your own time and a bit of machine time is all that is needed, but schedule the time.

Look at the present *design* of the system. The design of the change will have to fit cleanly into the system. Make sure that the appropriate function, design and maintenance documents are updated.

Program and *test* the change. If it is a production system you may have to do it after regular hours. When testing a modification, first run test data that exercise the change, then run real data to make sure nothing has been broken by the change. It is wise to define a thorough set of 'real-life' tests that can be reused with every change. Document the change in the User Guide, train the user, and provide the usual warranty.

An alternative approach, especially if changes are requested frequently, is to save up many changes and apply them at once. These would be new versions or releases of large systems such as operating systems. A new release is considered a full project, with its own budget and all the phases applied.

Doing Maintenance Along with Development

One of the most frustrating aspects of a developer's life is that as soon as you get deeply involved in the development of an exciting new system, the phone rings and someone is asking you to answer a question or fix a bug in some other program. It is very difficult, if not impossible, to get back to the point where you left off in the development.

You cannot do development and be expected to fight maintenance fires at the same time. One method that successfully avoids this problem is to appoint a fire chief to fight the fires. This person handles the phone calls, answers any questions and solves the problems if he or she can. Only if this person cannot solve the problem are the developers interrupted, but at an agreed upon time of the day—say after 4:00 pm. The problem is usually solved by the next day. Here are some additional thoughts on this:

- This fire chief position should be rotated every three to four months.
- The fire chief wears a pager so that he cannot escape.
- It is a good way to train juniors, or seniors who need experience with interfacing to users.
- It is amazing how many problems disappear if someone has to wait for the answer until the next day (usually they revert to reading the manuals).

22.6 CONCLUSION

Special projects may need special attention, but basically they all must follow the rule that we started out with—any software activity that results in a deliverable must be considered a project.

QUESTIONS

1. Compare the project development methodology of a RT project to that of a business application.
2. Is a small project more prone to failure than a large one? Is the failure of a small project less of a problem?
3. What is a conversion? What are the major causes of problems in a conversion and how would you plan to avoid them?
4. How do you handle simultaneous development and maintenance?

23

Conclusion

Is It All Worth It?

23.1 INTRODUCTION

Congratulations! You have made it to the end of the book. Before you put it down, I would like you to leave with some thoughts.

23.2 CAN YOU BE A GOOD PROJECT MANAGER?

In Chapter 19 we detailed the skills and talents of the PM, but here are several important questions to ask yourself that may tell you whether or not you have got what it takes.

1. ''Can I say 'NO'?''
    Saying no takes courage and wisdom. It is difficult to do but at times absolutely necessary for a successful Project Manager. Practice saying 'NO'. Every day when you wake up go to your mirror, smile, and say 'NO' a few times.
2. ''Can I attack problems as they arise?''
    If a problem crops up, you must get on the phone immediately, investigate it, fix it as quickly as possible or it will turn into a disaster. This is especially true for people problems.
3. ''Can I live unloved?''
    A PM is not a popular person at the best of times. Every failure is the PM's fault (every success is due to upper level managers). He or she has to make unpopular decisions, announce slips, say ''NO,'' crack the whip, discipline people—all of these things make the PM a pain in the neck, if not an outright ogre. But it is not the love of your people that you need, it is their loyalty and respect.

23.3 THE FUTURE OF PROJECT MANAGEMENT

Software Tools

Expect to see better automation. Project management is becoming more and more important, and software products that make our lives easier are appearing daily. I am especially excited about the emergence of artificial intelligence (AI) in some software products. AI will allow software to solve some of the complex scheduling problems that the PM is faced with, and to provide an English language (perhaps even voice!) interface to the program.

Visibility in the Organization

We have seen MBO (Management by Objectives), then MBE (Management by Excellence), MBWA (...by Walking Around), MB1M (...by One Minute), and many more. None of these methods have provided significant improvements in the business. A few years ago someone tried MBP&C (Management by Planning and Control—that is, Project Management) and lo and behold, profit and business improved.

Many companies have discovered the advantages of organizing by projects. It is common to see 'Project Manager' as job titles high up the organization chart. In fact, many companies have appointed a Vice President of Projects. The skills that you have learned from this book (I hope) will be more and more important for your company, and you should of course ask for a raise and promotion at once.

Personal Growth

If you think these methods and skills are only used on a software project, you are dead wrong: they can be applied to any project that you undertake. In fact, project management is a philosophy that can be applied to any activity in life. Everything has a good chance of success if it is planned and controlled, and you will become a better person if all of your endeavors are successful.

23.4 CONCLUSIONS TO THE CONCLUSIONS

Applying All of This

You are probably thinking, ''Boy, will I have to change a lot of things!'' But do not go to your boss and say, ''Here are the 500 things we need to change in the next six months.'' You cannot move a mountain, but you can whittle away at it. Pick a small (no more than three month) project, one that will get some management visibility, and use the proper methods to manage it. Advertise your sucess and soon you will get the commitment to do a larger project. Slowly but surely, you will turn the world around. GOOD LUCK!

QUESTION

1. Manage a major software application!

Appendix A

Case Study   (An Example of All Project Documents)

AMALGAMATED BASKETWEAVING COURSES SOFTWARE AND HARDWARE PROJECT

INTRODUCTION

[This project started with the following memo: All items in square brackets are comments by the Author.]

Amalgamated Basketweaving Courses Ltd. gives different types of weaving courses. They have classes in 10 major cities in North America, each one presented at least every three months. Students come from all over the country, but can register by phoning headquaters (collect) in Rattan.

MEMO
FROM: John Strawman, President
TO: Larry Loom, Technical Department
SUBJECT: Need for Automation

Larry, we have to do something about our registration and information system. When a student phones to register for one of our courses, Joan takes the information on a piece of paper, then transfers it to a course file (another piece of paper), which eventually gets collated (on paper).
Last month alone we lost 3 registrations, told 2 students to go to the wrong course, did not have enough material for 2 courses (twice as many people showed up as we anticipated, and we had no way of telling who was officially registered) and

---

we forgot to tell the instructor about one course. I also suspect we are not billing everyone—our revenues are down but the number of students seems to be up. I also suspect we should give courses in Montreal, and that we are giving the wrong courses for the time of the year.

Can a system be implemented to solve this?

John.

P.S. If we do not have our act together in six months we will be out of business.
P.P.S. We have $200,000 left in our bank account.

REQUIREMENTS DOCUMENT

REQUEST FOR PROPOSALS

Amalgamated Basketweaving Courses Ltd.
14 Weaver Rd., Rattan, On., K1M 1L5
Contact: Mr. Case Basket
Controller, ABC.

This document is prepared to provide vendors with information to quote a price on providing and installing software and hardware for the information system required for ABC. All bids must be received by date X. Terms and conditions for selection are outlined in Section 16 of this document.

1. INTRODUCTION:

ABC gives different types of weaving courses. They have classes in the following major cities in North America [list here].

Each course is presented at least 4 times per year per city. Students come from all over the country, but can register by phoning (collect) our main office in Rattan. We have no computer expertise. All expenditures must be approved by our fearless leader and CEO, Mr. Barry Strawman.

Major problem: General confusion in registration and course administration. Presently, when a student phones to register for one of our courses, the secretary writes the information on a piece of paper, then transfers it to a course file (another piece of paper), which eventually gets collated (on paper).

Last month alone we lost 3 registrations, told 2 students to go to the wrong course, did not have enough material for 2 courses (twice as many people showed up as we anticipated, and we had no way of telling who was officially registered) and we forgot to tell the instructor about one course. We also suspect we are not billing everyone—our revenues are down but the number of students seems to be up.

We also suspect that we should give courses in other cities, and that we are giving the courses at the wrong times of the year.

2. PROJECT GOALS:

Replace existing manual registration system at ABC with:

Registration that is fast (on phone), no losses, with timely notification to student, instructor and ABC of appropriate information.

Financial system to accurately produce billing, accounting, and course material information when needed.

Reporting to management, for better decisions about where and when to hold appropriate courses, available immediately on a terminal or to be printed on request.

Project should be done within 6 months of initiation, for under $200,000.

3. MAJOR FUNCTIONS:

Registration on-line by a phone operator, with information on all courses such as enrollments (list of students), cost, location visible. Automatic confirmation to student, and summary of enrollments to ABC. Two weeks before a course, enrollments go to instructor, ABC, and course material warehouse.

Course Administration on line. Add/remove courses from a schedule. Change pricing on a course. Close a course (tell system that a course ran and who attended.)

Financial system that invoices student within two weeks after attending course, keeps Accounts Receivables, roll up of revenues by course type, time period and geography monthly. Warning about students who owe us but want to enroll.

Warehouse system notifies warehouse clerk two weeks before course, of items required for the course, where the course is, location of items in warehouse. Enter/alter materials required for a course. Automatic inventory decrement and re-ordering as well.

Management Information Reporting system: Weekly report to CEO, or on request, of number of registrations, courses, revenues. On request, reports detailing courses, enrollments, and revenues by course type, geography, time of year.

Although not needed at this time, we are also thinking of producing mailing lists, instructor schedules, and location schedules in the future.

4. GENERAL OUTPUTS:

On line: if a student phones, answer questions such as:
"When are the next 3 XYZ courses, where, what price?"
"I am John Smith. Where am I registered? How many others are registered?
"What is the maximum enrollment?"
"Please register me for XYZ course."
"Please cancel me from course XYZ."

Confirmation: Printout of student confirmation mailed to student. (What course he enrolled in, when, payment information.)

Weekly print-out: all enrollments for the week by course and location, revenues associated with courses that ran.

Monthly print out: course sales for the month by type, location, time (for management). Accounts Receivables report with items invoiced and outstanding and paid to Accounting.

Two weeks before a course: print out of enrollments, location, course material (for instructor and warehouse). Revenue summary (for management). List of materials required and location of the course (to warehouse).

One day after a course: invoice (to student), a diploma (to student), update Accounts Receivables.

Reports on request: on-line reports of registrations, attendance, and/or revenues by course, by geography, by time of year.

5. GENERAL INFORMATION INPUTS REQUIRED:

[The *project team,* after further interviews with the user, fills in the following:]

Registration: Student name, address, course to register on, payment information, etc.
Financial: course cost, billing status by student, material cost, etc.
Warehouse: material required by course, minimum inventory, information on vendor of material, reorder quantity, etc.
And so forth.

6. PERFORMANCE:

Registration or general enquiry phone calls are expected approximately 2 per minute (maximum 5), registrations one per 20 minutes maximum 10 min; reports may be requested at most one per 10 minutes. Other reports and requests weekly, monthly or driven by occurrance of courses as detailed above.
There are at most 15 courses per month.

7. GROWTH:

ABC expects a general 30% growth per year. This system must perform for the next three years.

8. OPERATION AND ENVIRONMENT:

The computer will reside in room 105 at our Rattan office. Terminals must be available to our two registrars, one each in the offices of Mr. Case, Mr. Strawman, and Ms. Administrator, and 2 in the warehouse. Printout capability is required in the office area and in the warehouse. The warehouse is full of paper dust.

9. COMPATIBILITY, INTERFACES:

We are considering opening a branch office on the West coast. There we would do only local registration functions, with all other functions to be done in Rattan. We have a Brand X word processor presently. We wish all documents accessible or converted to the new system.

10. RELIABILITY, AVAILABILITY:

[Quote Mean Time Between Failures (MTBF) figures, Mean Time to Repair (MTTR) and percentage up time required. All manufacturers publish these figures for their hardware, except that they are never over 95%, so do not request anything greater than that.]
We wish the computer to be up 99% of the workday period, and we cannot lose any information.

11. HUMAN INTERFACE:

ABC has no computer experience. Mr. Strawman's son has this computer that has a 'mouse'. He wishes our new system to have menus driven by 'mouses' (meeces?). We wish detailed help at the push of a button.

12. ORGANIZATIONAL IMPACT:

[This paragraph will be filled in by the PT. The user may state items such as, "Due to a strong union in our shop, we cannot reduce the number of people on our staff."]

13. MAINTENANCE AND SUPPORT:

The vendor must fix any problems with the system for 6 months after delivery, within 24 hours of being notified.

14. DOCUMENTATION AND TRAINING:

Vendor must provide documents and training for all of the users. The documentation and the training will explain in detail each person's job on the computer. The vendor must also provide training for one computer operator.

15. ADVANTAGES [RFP ONLY]:

Vendors must supply: Names and phone numbers of 3 locations where they implemented successful sytems. A description of the project management method they use, including size and relevant experience of their project teams.

16. TERMS AND CONDITIONS (T'S & C'S) [RFP ONLY]:

ABC company has the right to select among vendors based on their own criteria. Any submitted documents will become the property of ABC. The winner will be announced no later than date X. ABC has the right to accept and/or reject any portion(s) of the proposed systems. Pricing for such will be renegotiated with the vendor.

ABC will own all softwares implemented, including the right to resell it. The vendor must guarantee the delivery of the software and hardware 6 months after signing a contract, or there will be a penalty of 10% of the project price per month of late delivery.

PRELIMINARY PROJECT PLAN ABC PROJECT

1. PROJECT TEAM

The Project Team will consist of the following 6 individuals:

PROJECT MANAGER: Jane Flynn
PROJECT LEADER: Jim Bean
PROGRAMMERS (4):   Not yet assigned. The levels required are:
   1 Level 1 (Senior)
    Level 2 (Intermediate)
   2 Level 3 (Junior)

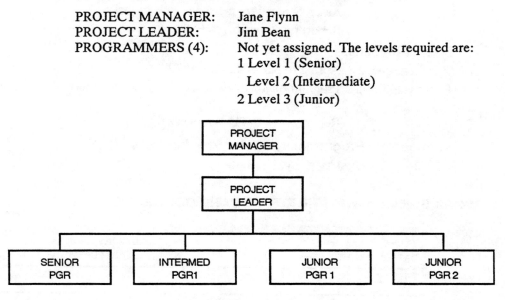

Figure A.1

Time Frames and Responsibilities

Project Manager

Time Required: January 1 to November 30, 1990

Responsibilities: Project team management; including input (at least) into salary reviews of team members.

All communication to and from ABC. All communication to and from upper levels of management.

Weekly status assessment, scheduling, and status reporting.

Chair all major review (management, milestone) meetings.

Obtain all resources from outside.

Handle any unforseen events.

Project Leader

Time required: January 1 to December 30, 1990

Responsibilities: Assist PM on technical aspects of planning, for example project network and schedule.

Do project analysis.

Lead the design team.

Do the ATP, system test, and spend three weeks at the user site for operation.

Supervise programmers: make programming assignments, and quality control.

Assist Senior Programmer on major tasks.

Report project status to PM.

Senior Programmer

Time required: April 1 to November 30, 1990

Responsibilities: Program major modules A and B, assist Junior programmers as necessary.

Report status to PL as requested.

Intermediate Programmer, Junior Programmers

[Supply detail as for Senior Programmer]

2. WORK BREAKDOWN STRUCTURES AND COST ESTIMATES

```
TASK ESTIMATE DETAIL FOR PROJECT:  ABC
ITEM:   Summary                           AUTHOR: Jim Bean
DATE:   Dec 1, 1990                        WBS REFERENCE: 0.0 ABC
```

TASK	DESCRIPTION	CMP LX	EST DYS	COMMENTS
1.0	Definition	H	38	Analyst (MR)
2.0	Analysis	H	40	Analyst (MR)
3.0	Design	H	40	Designer (BB)
4.0	Programming	M	80	Pgr's, Designer
5.0	System Test	H	15	All
6.0	Acceptance	M	8	
7.0	Operation	L	20	Incl. 10 day crs
8.0	Proj. Mgt. & Mtgs.	H	53	Proj. mtgs only
9.0	Contingency	H	30	Hardware delivery
TOTAL PROJECT			324	

Figure A.2

```
TASK ESTIMATE DETAIL FOR PROJECT:  ABC
ITEM:   Definition                        AUTHOR: Jim Bean
Date:   Dec 1, 1990                        WBS REFERENCE: 1.0
```

TASK	DESCRIPTION	CMP LX	EST DYS	COMMENTS
1.1	Requirements Document	H	10	
1.2	Go/Nogo Decision	H	10	
1.3	Proposal	H		
TOTAL FOR 1.0 Definition			38	

Figure A.3

```
TASK ESTIMATE DETAIL FOR PROJECT: ABC
ITEM:  Requirements Document          AUTHOR: Jim Bean
DATE:  Dec 1, 1990                    WBS REFERENCE:1.1
```

TASK	DESCRIPTION	CMP LX	EST DYS	COMMENTS
1.1.1	Meet with User	M	4	User Mgr. A, Sup.B
1.1.2	Assist in Preparation	M	4	User will do most
1.1.3	Negotiate	H	1	with User
1.1.4	Approvals	M	1	Director level
TOTAL FOR 1.1 Req.ts Doc.			10	

Figure A.4

```
TASK ESTIMATE  DETAIL FOR PROJECT: ABC
ITEM: Go/No-go                        AUTHOR: Jim Bean
Date: Dec 1, 1990                     WBS REFERENCE: 1.2
```

TASK	DESCRIPTION	CMP LX	EST DYS	COMMENT
1.2.1	Feasability Study	H	5	Eval build vs buy 2 pckgs
1.2.2	Write Report	M	2	
1.2.3	Risk Analysis	H	2	
1.2.4	Approvals	L	1	Director level
TOTAL FOR 1.2 Go/Nogo			10	

Figure A.5

```
TASK  ESTIMATE  DETAIL FOR  PROJECT: ABC
ITEM: Proposal                        AUTHOR: Jim Bean
DATE: Dec 1, 1990                     WBS REFERENCE: 1.3
```

TASK	DESCRIPTION	CMP LX	EST DYS	COMMENTS
1.3.1	Plan Proposal	H	1	JR
1.3.2	Do the Work	M	10	
1.3.3	Prepare Proposal Doc.	M	2	20-30 pgs
1.3.4	Internal Approvals	H	.5	VP level
1.3.5	Dry Run	L	.5	
1.3.6	Present to User	M	1	JR + MR for .5
1.3.7	Negotiate	M	1	
1.3.8	Technical Revision	M	1	
1.3.9	Approvals	L	1	
TOTAL FOR 1.3 Proposal			18	

Figure A.6

```
TASK ESTIMATE  DETAIL FOR  PROJECT: ABC
ITEM: Do the Work                    AUTHOR:  Jim Bean
DATE: Dec 1, 1990                    WBS REFERENCE: 1.3.2
```

TASK	DESCRIPTION	CMP LX	EST DYS	COMMENTS
1.3.2.1	Prelim. Proj. Plan	M	5	
1.3.2.2	Detail Scope	L	1	
1.3.2.3	Detail Financial	H	1	
1.3.2.4	Detail Dev't Plan	H	2	
1.3.2.5	Detail Support Plan	M	.5	6 mos warranty
1.3.2.6	Discuss T's & C's	H	.5	with User
TOTAL FOR 1.3.2 Prep. Proposal Doc.			10	

Figure A.7

```
TASK  ESTIMATE DETAIL  FOR PROJECT: ABC
ITEM: Analysis                       AUTHOR: Jim Bean
DATE: Dec 1, 1990                    WBS REFERENCE: 2.0
```

TASK	DESCRIPTION	CMP LX	EST DYS	COMMENTS
2.1	Interviews	M	10	
2.2	Analyze existing systems/document		10	
2.3	Synthesis	M	9	
2.4	Prepare Functional Spec Document		3	
2.5	Negotiate	H	4	of our time
2.6	Revise	M	3	
2.7	Approvals	H	1	VP
TOTAL FOR 2.0 Analysis			40	

Figure A.8

```
TASK ESTIMATE DETAIL FOR PROJECT: ABC
ITEM: Synthesis                      AUTHOR: Jim Bean
DATE: Dec 1, 1990                    WBS REFERENCE: 2.3
```

TASK	DESCRIPTION	CMP LX	EST DYS	COMMENTS
3.3.1	Reusability of old system	M	3	
2.3.2	Changes to old system	M	3	
2.3.3	New functions needed	M	3	
TOTAL FOR 2.3 Synthesis			9	

Figure A.9

```
Task Estimate Detail for Project: ABC
ITEM: Programming                    AUTHOR: Jim Bean
DATE: Dec 1, 1990                    WBS REFERENCE: 4.0
```

WBS	ACTIVITY	CMP LX	ESTIMATE DES	DOC	CODE	TEST	TOT	CMNTS
4.1	Driver module(A)	H					40	Menu
4.2	Module B	M					10	INQ
4.3	Module C	L					20	REP'S
4.4	Module D	L					10	UPD
TOTAL							80	

Figure A.10

```
TASK ESTIMATE DETAIL FOR PROJECT: ABC
ITEM:  Programming Driver Mod A    AUTHOR: Jim Bean
DATE:  Dec 1, 1990                 WBS REFERENCE: 4.1
```

WBS	ACTIVITY	CMP LX	ESTIMATE DES	DOC	CODE	TEST	TOT	CMNTS
4.1.1	Mainline A1	H	3	1	4	2	10	
4.1.2	Subroutine A2	M	2	1	1	1	5	MOUSE
4.1.3	Subroutine A3	L	.5	.5	.5	.5	2	GRAPH
4.1.4	Subroutine A4	L	1	1	1	1	4	ERROR
4.1.5	Subroutine A5	L	.5	1	1	.5	4	IFCE
4.1.6	Subroutine A6	L	1	1	3	1	5	I/O
4.1.7	Subroutine A7	L	2	1	1.5	2	5	ENT/EX
4.1.8	Integrating Driver	H				5	1	
TOTAL							40	

Figure A.11

```
COST CALCULATION (Example)
Programming Module A
```

RESOURCE	HRS	OVRTI	RATE	VAR CST	FIXED	TOT
Senior Pgr	160	0	40.00	6400.00	0	0
Junior Pgr	60	0	25.00	1500.00	0	0
Comp. time	40	0	100.00	4000.00	0	0
Buy Word Proc.			0.00		5000	5000

[A chart like this should appear for all of the estimated tasks.]

Rates: Rates quoted include all overhead, plus a profit factor of 33% for staff and 15% for fixed price items.

Risk: A risk factor of 0% to 33% has been added to individual tasks in the estimates. For further detail see Jane.

3. PROJECT SCHEDULE

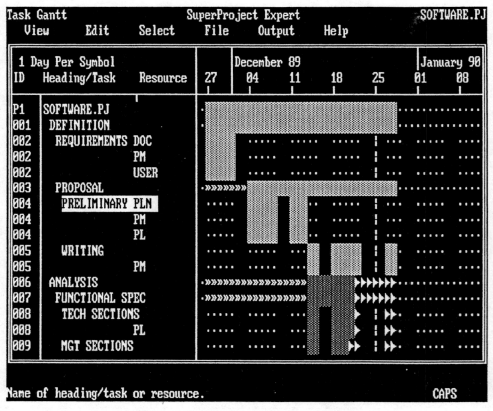

Figure A.12   Superproject project schedule

4. REVIEWS AND MEETINGS

Steering Committee Reviews (every three months, or as needed).

March 3, June 9, September 8, December 12, 1991 .

Attendees: PM; Functional Managers A, B, C; Department Directors X, Y, Z; Client project representative; Account Manager A.

Milestone Reviews: Functional Spec sign off: February 14; Design finalized: April 12; Mid programming Review: July 4; Final programming and ATP review: September 15; System test: November 18; Post project review: January 1, 1990.

Attendees: All of steering committee plus appropriate personnel from hardware manufacturer or technical staff, depending on the previous and next phases.

Technical Meetings

A status meeting will be held every Friday afternoon from 1:00 to 3:00 with all of the project team. The PM and PL will optionally meet alone Fridays from 3:00 to 4:00.

There will be a medium level design walkthrough held March 12, and final design walkthrough held April 1.

Attendees: PL, Designers A and B.

5. REPORTS

A Status Report will be published by the PM every Monday.

The contents include progress past period, problems encountered, plan for next period and progress against plan. A schedule produced by SUPERPROJECT will be included to show actuals versus plans for every task.

The recipients will be: project team, steering committee, clients A, B, C (this may be an edited version); resource providers D, E, F; troublemakers [you may choose a different word] G, H, I. If any recipient notices a problem he must report it to the PM within one week of receiving the report.

6. DOCUMENTATION

User Documents

DOCUMENT	RESPONSIBLE PERSON
User Guide	Junior Programmer 1
Operator Guide	Junior Programmer 2
Maintenance Guide	Senior Programmer
User Training Manual	Intermediate Programmer

Project Documents

Requirements Doc	Client, Project Leader assists
Functional Spec	Project Leader
Design	Project Leader, Senior Programmer
Program in-line Doc	Programmers
ATP	Senior Programmer
System Test Plan	Project Leader

Word Processing

Secretary M. Blink will be available during the months of February through October. The Secretary will word process all of the user documents, as well as the FS and the ATP.

7. CHANGE CONTROL

Since this is a fixed price project, any client requested change will be submitted to the PM on change request form A-3. It will be assessed by the PL, and the client must agree to pay extra for any change as per terms and conditions in the contract. Project team requested changes will also be submitted on change request form A-3 to the PL, who will deal with each one.

8. ASSUMPTIONS

a. The personnel mentioned in Section 1 of this document will be available full time for the required periods.

b. Hardware, operating system, and DBMS will be delivered on date X as promised.

c. All of the volume, performance, and throughput maxima detailed in the Requirements Document are correct.

PROPOSAL

1. COVER LETTER

> September 1, 1989
>
> Mr. J. Strawman
> President
> Amalgamated Basketweaving Courses Ltd.
> Rattan, Ontario
>
> Dear Mr. Strawman,
>
> Thank you for giving XYZ Software Co. the opportunity to discuss with you the needs for a new registration system at ABC. As a result of these discussions, included please find a Proposal to implement this system for you.
>
> XYZ proposes to implement computer hardware, purchased software and custom written software to solve your present problems with registration, course administration, management information and warehousing. The system should meet your needs for the next 3 years.
>
> The cost of the hardware will be $100,000, the purchased software $20,000 and the software custom written by XYZ is estimated to be $80,000. The system can be implemented in six months if we are given a timely go-ahead.
>
> If we are given a go-ahead by October 1, 1990, we can start your project January 1, and deliver by July 1, 1991. This price quotation is good for 30 days. Hardware vendor is raising his prices by 10% on September 30th., so a quick decision on your part will save both time and money.
>
> Hoping to blah .. blah ..
>
> > Signed by,
> > Project Manager
> > (optionally)
> > Account Representative

2. TITLE PAGE

''Proposal,'' the title of the system, author, date, revision number, company logo, and so forth.

3. TABLE OF CONTENTS

PROPOSAL FOR AMALGAMATED
BASKETWEAVING COURSES LTD.

1. SCOPE

The purpose of this proposal is to prove how XYZ Software Co. can solve ABC's problems with registration, course administration, management decision making, and warehousing. [The general items that will go in here are:]

Background. [Summarize the problem statement, and how the previous interviews and/or assistance given to the user in writing the RD gave XYZ a thorough understanding of ABC.]

Solution. [Summarize the hardware/software that you are recommending, and show why it is the best choice. Show proven track record, etc.

Summarize [one or two sentences per department where the new computer system and terminals will be located, the departments that will use them and how. For example, ''The registrar will have a terminal and will be able to answer students' queries by phone as well as register them on-line.'' Emphasize the improvements that will be noticed by each department.]

Future growth. [State the growth that will be anticipated as well as future improvements that can easily be added on (you are already selling your next project!]

Limits. [This is not a specific section, but ensure that the user does not read into this proposal major items that you do not intend to provide.]

2. ADVANTAGES

XYZ has been in the software business for over seven years. We are experts at training-oriented software. We implemented three such systems in the past, including Maintenance Courses Ltd.

The Brand X hardware and purchased software that we are recommending has been available for the past five years, and has proven to be one of the most reliable in the industry. Brand X is the world's nth largest computer manufacturer and has an excellent reputation for reliability and service. XYZ has extensive experience on this recommended hardware and software. We used it successfully on products for the past four years.

XYZ has an excellent reputation for quality and we stand behind every product that we develop.

3. FINANCIAL

```
Delivery Date( given go-ahead by July 1): Dec 30,1988
Costing Breakdown
     Hardware
        Brand X model 123 CPU......nn
        Memory
        Disks
        Terminals
        etc. [include manufactorer's quotes]
                    TOTAL HARDWARE        100,000
     Software
        Purchased DBMS                     10,000
        VSM Operating System               10,000
        XYZ provided custom software       80,000
                    TOTAL SOFTWARE        100,000
                    GRAND TOTAL          $200,000
```

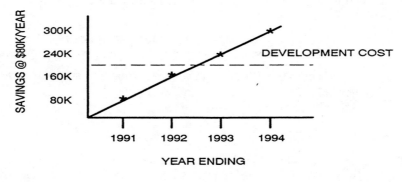

Figure A.13

The system will pay for itself in two and one half years, by the middle of 1992.

Other benefits: Reduction of Registrar turnover due to job satisfaction, savings in warehouse due to fewer losses, better customer relations, and unquantifiable benefit because you will be able to make better management decisions.

4. PLAN

The following will be the seven major activties involved in your project:

Analysis. In thorough interviews with yourself and all the users of the proposed system, we will determine and agree upon exactly how the system will behave.

Design. Our best designers will determine how we will build the system. [A few words on PROGRAMMING and SYSTEM TEST]

Acceptance. We will demonstrate the system to you before delivery to prove that it works as we promised.

Operation. We will turn the new system on at your site, train your users, and provide someone at your site for three weeks to handle any problems.

[Describe the project team and the project organization, as in the Preliminary Project Plan, but include only the items that will be visible to the user.]

We use the following seven phased, step-by-step project management method that insures thorough planning and control of your project. [List here the seven phases, and where the user approval/sign off will appear.]

In each phase there will be milestones that you will be able to review and see project progress.

In addition, you will have the opportunity to be part of a steering committee...and you will attend milestone review meetings...and you will receive a Status Report weekly...etc.

You will have to provide for our use a project representative: someone who will be available to answer business questions regarding your present operation and the proposed system. This person must have the authority to make decisions about what the new system will provide. You will also have to provide sample data and files that you presently use. ABC will receive certain documents for sign off from XYZ. These documents must be approved and returned within five working days of receipt.

5. DELIVERABLES

XYZ will deliver the following:

Brand X Hardware, VSM Operating System, DBMS softwares listed above. These items are available now with a delivery time of three months.

Custom written software listed above, to be produced in six months.

Warranties. Brand X warrant their hardware and software for one year after the date of delivery. Subsequent warranty can be purchased for...[detail]. XYZ warrant their software unconditionally for six months after the date of delivery. There will be one person at your site for one month after delivery to solve any problems. For two months after this, a person will be available to solve any problems by phone. He/she will attempt to solve the problem first on the phone, otherwise by beginning work immediately on your problem. For three more months after this period, a person is guaranteed to begin working on a phoned in problem within four hours of the call. Subsequent warranty can be purchased for...[detail].

Documents. The following manuals will be delivered:

Brand X complete VSM documentation [detail it all].

XYZ will produce: User Guide: tells each of your users how to use the system specifically for their job. Operator Guide: tells how to bring the system up, shut it down, backup/restore and handle errors.

Training. We recommend Brand X 'VSM Concepts and Utilities' and 'VSM System Management' courses for one person.

XYZ will provide. User Course: teaches each of your users how to use the system specifically for their job.

Operator Course. Teaches how to bring the system up, shut it down, backup/restore and handle errors.

Method of delivery. The hardware and software will be delivered and installed at the user's appropriate locations. One copy of the documentation will be delivered with the system. Training will be delivered at the user's site, on his computer.

6. ACCEPTANCE

Acceptance will involve a thorough, step by step demonstration of all the system functions to the user before the actual delivery of the system. If ABC agrees that all the functions work, they will pay XYZ all funds still owing less $10,000, which will be paid upon successful delivery of the computer system.

7. ALTERNATIVES

An alternative solution would be to use Brand Y with the IDOT data base. We have not chosen this one for the following reasons:...[detail]

8. TERMS, CONDITIONS AND ASSUMPTIONS

- Amounts quoted here are good for 30 days after receipt of this letter.
- XYZ reserves the right to all source code and documentations produced.
- XYZ is not liable for any losses due to our software.
- This document is copyrighted.
- XYZ is not responsible for any problems with Brand X hardware or software, or for the delivery dates promised by Brand X.
- It is assumed that the user responsibilities will be fulfilled as detailed in Section 7 of this document.
- It is assumed that all information in terms of volumes, throughput, number of users, and response requirements are as written down in the Requirements Document Version 2.1 dated August 30, 1990.

9. TERMINOLOGY

[Glossary of all computer terms used.]

FUNCTIONAL SPECIFICATION

1. TITLE PAGE

FUNCTIONAL SPECIFICATIONS

FOR AMALGAMATED BASKETWEAVING COURSES

BY

XYZ SOFTWARE COMPANY

AUTHOR: GEORGE SMITH

JULY 8, 1990

VERSION 3.0

2. TABLE OF CONTENTS

[Section names with page numbers.]

3. SYSTEM OVERVIEW

Amalgamated Basketweaving Courses Ltd. gives different types of weaving courses. They have classes in 10 major cities in North America. Each course is presented at least every three months. Students come from all over the country, but can register by phoning headquarters (collect) in Rattan.

Presently, there are major problems in registration, course administration and warehousing, and useful data to make management and marketing decisions is not available.

To solve this problem, XYZ Software Company will implement a system consisting of hardware and custom software as shown in Figure A.14.

The system consists of 4 major components:

1. An INQUIRY component that handles questions regarding students and courses, such as "When is a course running?", "How much is it?" "Who is in it?" and so forth. This component also gives management information for marketing decisions.

2. An UPDATE component that allows changes of any information regarding students or courses, for example change of course location or status, or change of student address.

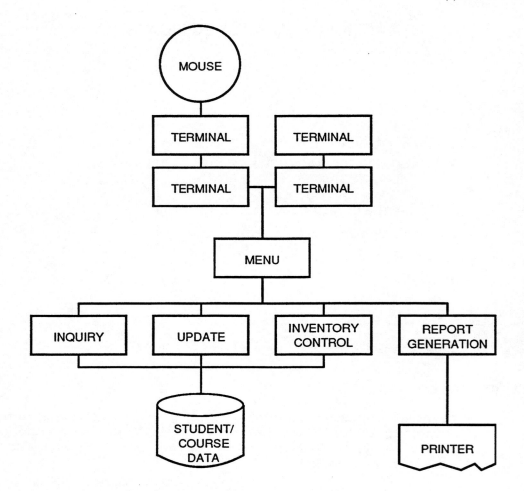

Figure A.14 Major functions of the system

3. A INVENTORY CONTROL component that handles the instructions to the warehouse for shipment of material, reordering of material if a minimum is reached and keeping the appropriate financial data for material.

4. A REPORT GENERATION component that handles all requests for printout. Reports such as class enrollments, confirmation, attendees by course, by geography, and so forth are handled here.

5. To make all this easy to use, all conversation with the user is via MENUS, and choices on these menus is by use of a mouse.

All of the student and course information will be kept on a disk.

4. MAJOR OBJECTIVES

INQUIRY will allow *immediate* response to questions on the phone such as "How many students enrolled in a course." It will also allow fast management decisions to be made since inquiries such as, "How many students attended course X in the past year?" can be answered immediately.

UPDATE[... detail]

REPORT GENERATION will allow immediate written confirmation to be sent to the student, a report on attendees to be printed for the instructor...

[General description of how each component solves specific problems.]

The new system will improve [do not use 'affect'] the work of the following people:

Mr. Strawman will have a terminal and a printer in his office. He will be able to access all course data, student data, enrollment data, and revenue/expense data. He will not be able to change student or course data though. He will automatically get a report after each course on ... a report weekly on ... [and so forth,]

Ms. Accountant will have a terminal in her office. She will be able to .... She will therefore no longer need the Klunker adding machine in her office. She will be able to ask for financial information on line ...She will be able to ask for financial reports ... which will be printed on the printer in the main office area.

Mr. Warehouse Supervisor will be able to.... This means that only two people will be needed to staff the warehouse.

[List all the people that will be involved.]

5. SPECIAL SYSTEM REQUIREMENTS

Although no electronic communication is required, Brand X hardware and VSM operating system can easily be updated with CEDNET computer-to-computer communication. This would allow another computer in another location of the country to store local information and communicate it to Rattan.

The present GONG word processor files will be converted to Brand X word processing format by XYZ.

Performance

Although the ABC Requirements Document asks that "The system respond to every input in 5 seconds," XYZ cannot guarantee this. Even the fastest computer ever manufactured will under certain circumstances take longer than 5 seconds to respond to certain requests. The new system will respond to 95% of the requests within 5 seconds in a 24 hour period, and the main design objectives will be user friendliness and system response. As per the requirement that the ABC system suffice for the next three years: The ABC system will be able to handle up to 25 on-line inquiries per minute. The system will keep history on up to 10000 students, 100 courses and keep track of 200 registrations at any time. This would more than handle the present requirement of 10 on-line questions, 2000 students and 100 registrations. The anticipated growth of 20% per year for the next three years will also be handled. Although only 10 simultaneous users are anticipated, the system will handle up to 16.

6. COMPONENT DESCRIPTIONS

Menu System

When the computer is turned on, the ABC system automatically starts up and the following 'MAIN MENU' appears:

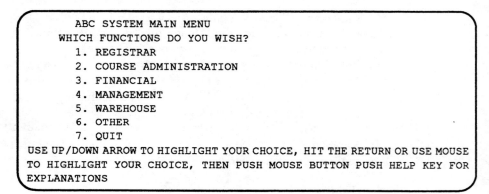

```
        ABC SYSTEM MAIN MENU
    WHICH FUNCTIONS DO YOU WISH?
        1. REGISTRAR
        2. COURSE ADMINISTRATION
        3. FINANCIAL
        4. MANAGEMENT
        5. WAREHOUSE
        6. OTHER
        7. QUIT
USE UP/DOWN ARROW TO HIGHLIGHT YOUR CHOICE, HIT THE RETURN OR USE MOUSE
TO HIGHLIGHT YOUR CHOICE, THEN PUSH MOUSE BUTTON PUSH HELP KEY FOR
EXPLANATIONS
```

Figure A.15 System main menu

The error messages are:

```
YOU HAVE MOVED OUT OF RANGE if user tries to move too low or too high.
INVALID INPUT if a key other than RETURN is pressed [and so forth for
all messages that you can foresee].
```

The HELP messages that will appear when the HELP key is pushed are:

```
HIGHLIGHTED        HELP MESSAGE
NUMBER

1.        Do Registrar's functions
2.        ... etc.
```

Action taken when '1' REGISTRAR functions are chosen:
Registrar Main Menu Appears

```
REGISTRAR FUNCTIONS
            1. INQUIRE ON A COURSE
            2. INQUIRE/CHANGE STUDENT INFORMATION
            3. ENROLL/CANCEL A STUDENT
            4. QUIT
USE EITHER UP/DOWN ARROW TO HIGHLIGHT CHOICE  THEN RETURN, OR MOVE
MOUSE TO HIGHLIGHT, THEN PUSH BUTTON ON MOUSE  PRESS HELP KEY TO
GET HELP ON HIGHLIGHT ITEM
```

Figure A.16 Registrar main menu

Functions allowed when student phones registrar:

Data. Verbal over phone, or mailed in Inquiries handled:

Location, dates of courses, number enrolled/maximums, cost, skills taught, Instructor name, Previous knowledge required.

Responses given. Course locations, dates (next 6 months), number enrolled (next 6 months), maximum allowed, cost, volume discounts, skills taught list (max. 25 lines), instructor name (next 6 months), Previous knowledge required (max. 25 lines) status (running or cancelled)(next 6 months).

Changes. Update name, address, payment information of student, cancel a student from a course.

Register a student. Obtain and enter name, address, course (by number), payment information.

Performance. Must handle up to 3 calls per minute.

When '1' 'Inquire on a Course' is pressed on Registrar Main Menu, the INQUIRE ON COURSE menu appears:

```
INQUIRE ON A COURSE
ENTER AS MUCH OF THE FOLLOWING INFORMATION AS
POSSIBLE. USE UP OR DOWN ARROW TO GO TO A FIELD
THEN RETURN,
OR MOUSE TO GO TO A FIELD THEN PRESS BUTTON
WHEN FORM IS ALL DONE.


COURSE NUMBER
COURSE TITLE
COURSE LOCATION
COURSE DATE (OR RANGE)
```

Figure A.17 Inquire on course menu

[Thus all of the possible system interfaces for the Registrar function are addressed.]

Action Taken When '5' WAREHOUSE functions are chosen:
Warehouse Main Menu Appears

```
WAREHOUSE FUNCTIONS
        1. INQUIRE ON INVENTORY/COURSE MATERIAL
        2. CHANGE INVENTORY/COURSE MATERIAL INFORMATION
        3. ISSUE MATERIAL FOR A COURSE
        4. QUIT

USE EITHER UP/DOWN ARROW TO HIGHLIGHT CHOICE THEN  RETURN, OR MOVE
MOUSE TO HIGHLIGHT, THEN PUSH BUTTON ON MOUSE PRESS HELP KEY TO GET
HELP ON HIGHLIGHTED ITEM
```

Figure A.18 Warehouse main menu

Item X will be reordered at the beginning of each month if amount on hand is lower than the number specified in '2' CHANGE INVENTORY/COURSE MATERIAL INFORMATION on this menu. [Detail all the user menus, commands, messages, inquiries, and reports.]

Data Kept by the System

Course Data.   Course title, date, number enrolled, material required, location, instructor, status (running or cancelled).

Student Data.   Name, address, phone, SIN, course number of course(s) enrolled in, course number of past course(s) enrolled in, payment method flag, bill to address, amount owed to us.

Materal Data.   [Detail all data items kept.]

7. OTHER DELIVERABLES

Documentation

User's guide.   Shows all the appropriate users how to sign into the system, use their menus, do their work, respond to error situation, and sign off the system. It is divided into sections, one for the Registrar, one for the Administrator...

The User's Guide will be useful for two areas: First, as a learning tool since all the commands will be presented in the order that the user will see them in his/her work situation. Second as a reference since at the end of the guide all the commands and messages will be presented alphabetically. Following is the table of contents (not final):

Training

Registrar's Course.   This will be a five day course, teaching three registrars how to get on the system, use all their commands, handle any problem situation, and sign off the system.

Modules (not final)

Warehouse Course.   This will be a two day course for two warehouse personnel...etc.

8. SPECIFICATION CHANGES

Since changes that are requested after the Analysis Phase can be costly and can cause delivery delays we propose the following change control procedure:

We will form a "change control committee," consisting of at least one person from ABC (can be the project coordinator), the XYZ Project Manager. All changes must come to the PT through the user change person . Each week, the committee meets and all changes are presented to the PM. XYZ should prioritize the changes from a rating of "critical" to "desirable." The PM then takes the changes to the technical members of the PT, who classify the changes as "easy" or "hard." The PT will usually implement as many of the easy changes as possible.

A hard change usually involves a large cost—in dollars of effort and/or project delay. The PT will calculate this cost and will present it to ABC, usually at the next meeting, perhaps sooner if it is a "critical" change. ABC must give written go-ahead to any change, accepting the impact such as a price raise or delivery date slip.

9. ACCEPTANCE

Acceptance will be done as follows: A set of tests, and the expected results of these tests will be written up. These tests will be designed to demonstrate step by step all the functions that the system is supposed to do. These tests, called the ATP (Acceptance Test Plan) will be approved by ABC before acceptance. As each test is run, ABC will sign off all successful tests. Only failed tests are repeated. If all the tests work, the system will be accepted and payments by ABC to XYZ will be made as agreed.

10. USER AND PROJECT TEAM INTERFACES

ABC and the Project Team must communicate at both technical and management levels. At a technical level the PT needs fast and accurate answers to technical questions. These questions do not stop at the Analysis Phase, they in fact get more and more complex as the project proceeds. ABC should appoint at least one person to be available to answer questions. This person must know the user's business well, and have authority to make decisions for every department that the proposed system will affect. We suggest Ms. Jones as the ABC project coordinator, to be in constant contact with XYZ's Jim Flynn.

ABC and XYZ must communicate at management level as well. This will be done by at least the ABC project coordinator and the XYZ project manager. They will discuss issues such as budgets, schedules, major changes or people problems. We suggest ABC's Mr. Administrator to be in contact with XYZ's Project Manager.

11. USER'S RESPONSIBILITIES

ABC	must provide test data with which to test the system by September 1, 1991.
ABC	will write chapter 3 of the User's Guide by October 12, 1991.
ABC	will return within one week (if approved) the following documents (Dates tentative)

| ATP | October 1, 1991 |
| User's Guide | October 30, 1991 |

This Functional Spec must be returned within two weeks.

12. TERMS, CONDITIONS AND ASSUMPTIONS

[Can be duplicated from the proposal]

DESIGN SPECIFICATION

1. TITLE PAGE, TABLE OF CONTENTS

DESIGN SPECIFICATION
FOR AMALGAMATED BASKETWEAVING COURSES
BY
XYZ SOFTWARE COMPANY
AUTHOR: GEORGE SMITH
JULY 28, 1990
VERSION 4.0
[On next page, Table of Contents,
section names with page numbers.]

2. SYSTEM OVERVIEW

Amalgamated Basketweaving Courses Ltd. gives different types of weaving courses. They have classes in 10 major cities in North America, each course is presented at least every three months. Students come from all over the country, but can register by phoning headquarters (collect) in Rattan.

Presently, there are major problems in registration, course administration and warehousing, and useful data to make management and marketing decisions is not available.

To solve this problem, XYZ Software Company will implement a system consisting of hardware and custom software that will do the following:

Allow online response to questions from students, registrars, managers, financial people, etc. regarding students and courses.

Allow online course registration.

Automatic notification of students, instructors, and appropriate ABC personnel when a course runs, and after a course runs.

Automatic invoicing of students, and accounts receivables/payables.

Automatic notification of warehouse to ship materials for a course, as well as inventory control with automated material reordering.

Allow on-line or on printer management report generation regarding course attendance by date and geography.

3. HARDWARE/SOFTWARE

CPU Brand X WAX Model 800
4 megabyte RAM
2 RD50 (75 megabyte) fixed disk drives
1 TX51 streaming tape drive

1 MN terminal controller

2 LP300 Printers

10 TV440 Terminals with appropriate cabling

VSM Version 5.0

Datatrees data base management system

PASCAL V3.0

SETDEC development environment (CMS, MMS, DTM, SCA, with PAS-
CAL LSE)

4. DESIGN PRIORITIES

User friendliness, response, cost, time.

5. DESIGN DIAGRAMS AND MODULE DICTIONARY CONVENTIONS

The design method used is the hierarchical breakout method. In the top level (see
Section 11) each box represents a major component. Each major component is numbered N.0 where N is an integer. The medium levels of design (see Section 12) break
out each top level module into functional components. In the first level of MLD the
boxes are numbered N.1, N.2, where N was the number on the appropriate box of the
TLD.

On the design diagrams, a solid line will (usually) represent control flow (procedure call). The dotted arrows represent data flow; the direction of the arrow is the
direction of the parameters passed. The arrows are labeled with the parameters to be
passed.

Please follow this convention as you break down further in module design.

6. MODULE NAMING CONVENTIONS

Modules are named as follows. Every module begins with the letter 'A' for the ABC
system. The next character represents the TLD module name: 'M' for MENU, 'I' for
INQUIRY, 'U' for UPDATE, 'W' for WAREHOUSE, 'R' for REPORT. The next two
characters represent the second level breakout module name, followed by 4 characters
for the general function. For example, the module name 'AMSTMVCR' is constructed
as follows:

A	-	ABC system
M	-	MENU component
ST	-	start function at second level
MVCR	-	move cursor

At higher levels, fill the module name with '0's.

7. PARAMETER PASSING AND DATA DICTIONARIES

All parameters are passed via procedure calls. They must be passed in the order that the subroutine will use them. All parameters are variables (no indirect or address references please). If a parameter need not be passed in a particular call that would normally take the parameter, use ',' as place holder. All parameters used must appear in the Data Dictionary (Section 12).

8. ERROR HANDLING

Module AME0000 is a system wide error handler. If an error is detected anywhere in the system, exit from your module with global variables ERR1 through ERR5 signaling context to AME0000. For example:

```
PROCEDURE ERROR;                {error trap}
  BEGIN
    ERR  1: = 'AMXYABCD';       {name of my routine}
    ERR  2: = '2';              {severity code}
    ERR  3: = 'R';              {wish return}
    ERR  4: = 'RESUME';         {label to return to}
    ERR  5: = -1;               {return with code}
  END;
```

9. STRUCTURED PROGRAMMING STANDARDS

Break down your module until there are approximately 50 to 100 executable statements per submodule.

Attempt to use the structured constructs IF, FOR, CASE, WHILE, UNTIL, or named Procedure. Avoid GO TO, except for an unconditional exit.

Entry must be at the called statement. Exit must be using a single procedure named 'RETURN.'

Comment lines for routine description, author name and so forth are available in a 'template' program in account [SYSTEM] file TEMP.PAS. You must start with this and fill in the appropriate code.

10. PROGRAMMING TOOLS

PASCAL V3.0 is available, with all the appropriate tools, to code the project.

The PASCAL Language Sensitive Editor is available. Call it by... Using this LSE will make coding easier and standard in format. For information on how to use this tool see Document...

An automated testing tool that allows you to predefine a set of inputs to your program as well as the expected outputs is available. DTM will allow you to repeat standard tests, especially in batch mode. For information on how to use this tool see Document...

All sources should be kept in the CMS library [CMS]your name.SRC. CMS will keep your sources, track the changes, and prevent in advertent erasure. For information on how to use this tool see Document...

There is a wealth of source subroutines for parameter handling, I/O, and so forth in [PAST]LIB.PAS. Look to see if any of these will do some/all your job and use them if at all possible.

11. TOP LEVEL DESIGN

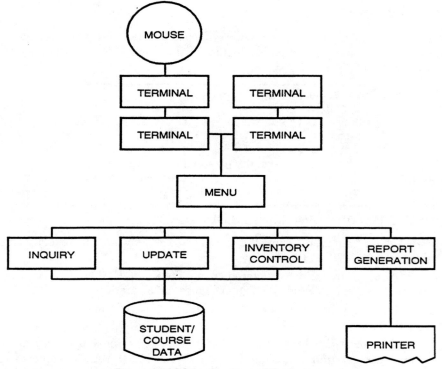

Figure A.19 Major functions of the system

The general functions to be performed by the five major components are:

Menu

Automatically called when the system is started. It handles all mouse input, and behaves as the overall system control module, receiving control when nothing else is active. It handles all the errors throughout the system, on-line help when the HELP key is pressed, and activates the general INQUIRY, UPDATE and REPORT GENERATION programs. It also shuts the system down.

Inquiry

[Fill in the detail.]

12. MEDIUM LEVEL DESIGN

MENU Component

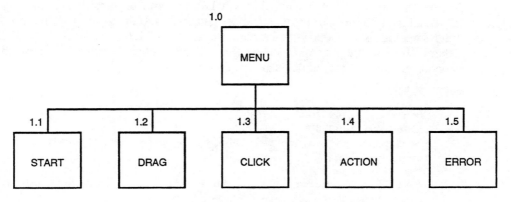

Figure A.20 Menu second level of breakout

You may consider breaking it down further. Example of third level breakdown is found in Figure A.21.

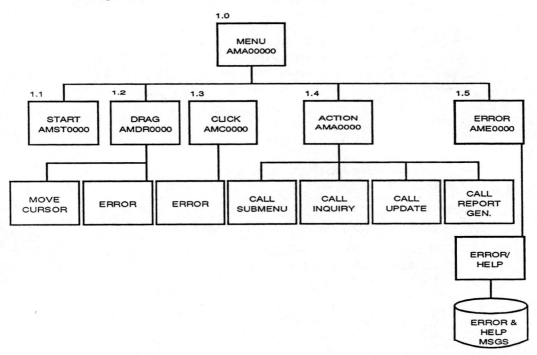

Figure A.21

Module AM000000 gets control when the operator types ABC at command level. (May be automatically started by a LOGIN file.) It first calls AMST000 to open all system files and do some initializing. When control is returned AM000000 displays the main menu, then waits for an asynchronous interrupt from the mouse or the keyboard. On mouse interrupt, control is passed to AMDR000 with the position of the mouse. AMDR000 highlights the appropriate entry and returns. If the mouse button is pressed, control goes to AMC00000 with the status of the menu (highlighted item). AMC00000 either calls a sub-menu or takes some other indicated action. [And so forth until all the general functions of the modules are detailed.]

MODULES:

```
Module name: AMST000
Called by: AM000000
Subroutines called: to be filled in by programmer Input parame-
ters: none
Displays: none
Returned parameters:  if no errors exit code 0 if error, exit code
is error number
External variables used: (list)
Files used: STUDENT.DAT (open), COURSE.DAT (open),MATERIAL.DAT
(open), SYSTEM.DAT (open)
Functions: Open the files STUDENT.DAT, COURSE.DAT,
       MATERIAL.DAT, SYSTEM.DAT. If error, exit with code...
       Initialize variables...
       Check for abnormal shutdown by checking Record 1 of
          SYSTEM.DAT file. Byte 1 = -1 means propershutdown
          (See module AM SHUT00). If not -1, do following ...
          On error exit with error code ...
Ensure correct status of
       Mouse by checking...
          On error exit with error code ...
       Screen by ...
          On error exit with error code ...
       Network by ...
          On error exit with error code ...
Normal exit error code 0
```

Figure A.22

[The following sections were filled in by the programmer.]

Dictionary 1. Entries added:

```
1.1.1  AMSTSHCK Handle warm/cold start
1.1.2  AMSTHWCK Check hardware status
1.1.3  AMSTOPFI Open files
1.1.4  AMSTINVA Initialize variables
1.1.5  AMSTMENU Present main menu
1.1.6  AMSTERR0 Handle error return
```

Second level module breakouts:

```
1.1.1.1   AMSTSHOP Open SYSTEM.DAT file and check record 1
1.1.1.2   AMSTSHWM System warm start handler
1.1.1.3   AMSTSHER System cold start handler
1.1.1.4   AMSTSHCK error trapping and return

1.1.2     AMSTHWCK ... [etc. for all the 1.1.n modules.]
```
[End of information inserted by programmer.]
```
Module name: AMDR000
Called by: AM000000
Subroutines called: to be filled in by programmer Input parameters:
mouse position, integer 0-9 Displays: turn appropriate line to inverse
video
Returned parameters:     if no errors exit code 0
                         if error, exit code is error
                         number...
External variables used: (list)
Files used: none
Functions:
     Calculate bit map position of menu  entry
        If invalid position exit with error code ...
Turn entry to inverse video
     On error exit with error code ...
Normal exit error code 0
```
[And so forth until all the medium level modules are detailed.]

Figure A .23

13. MODULE DICTIONARIES

As you progress through the design, build the following three dictionaries:

Dictionary 1. Numerically ordered by component number, gives the routine name and a short description for every module. For example:

```
0.0     A0000000        Amalgamated Basketweaving System
1.0     AM000000        Menu system
1.1     AMST0000        Start and display 1st menu
1.2.1   AMDRMVCR        Move cursor depending on mouse move
1.5     AME00000        System wide error and help message
```

Dictionary 2. Alphabetically ordered by component name, gives the routine number and a short description for every module. For example:

```
A0000000    0.0     Amalgamated  Basketweaving  System
AM000000    1.0     Menu system
AMST0000    1.1     Start and display 1st menu
AMDRMVCR    1.2.1   Move cursor depending on mouse move
AME00000    1.5     System wide error  and help message
```

This can easily be created from Dictionary 1 using a sort program.

Dictionary 3. Alphabetically ordered by short description, gives component number and the routine name. For example:

```
Amalgamated Basketweaving System    0.0        A0000000
Menu system                         1.0        AM000000
Start and display 1st menu          1.1        AMST0000
Move cursor dep. on mouse move      1.2.1      AMDRMVCR
System wide error and help message  1.5        AME00000
```

This can also be created from Dictionary 1 using a sort program.

You can use these dictionaries during design, programming, or subsequent testing and maintenance—anytime you need to find a module, its calls or its parameters.

The (common) data dictionary (CDD). The VSM CDD will be used to store all data information. Enter into it all new parameters that you define. All the parameters that are shown on the data flow arrows are already entered. For each data item (parameter, file element) enter into the CDD the name, type, length, restrictions, and the modules that use it.

14. FILES AND TABLES

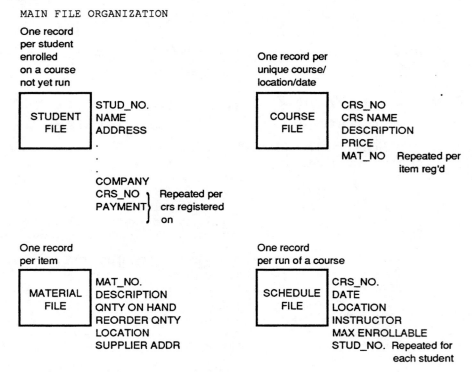

```
MAIN FILE ORGANIZATION
```

One record
per student
enrolled
on a course
not yet run

One record per
unique course/
location/date

```
┌──────────┐   STUD_NO.
│ STUDENT  │   NAME
│  FILE    │   ADDRESS
└──────────┘   .
               .
               .
               COMPANY
               CRS_NO   ⎫ Repeated per
               PAYMENT  ⎬ crs registered
                        ⎭ on
```

```
┌──────────┐   CRS_NO
│ COURSE   │   CRS NAME
│  FILE    │   DESCRIPTION
└──────────┘   PRICE
               MAT_NO   Repeated per
                        item req'd
```

One record
per item

One record
per run of a course

```
┌──────────┐   MAT_NO.
│ MATERIAL │   DESCRIPTION
│  FILE    │   QNTY ON HAND
└──────────┘   REORDER QNTY
               LOCATION
               SUPPLIER ADDR
```

```
┌──────────┐   CRS_NO.
│ SCHEDULE │   DATE
│  FILE    │   LOCATION
└──────────┘   INSTRUCTOR
               MAX ENROLLABLE
               STUD_NO. Repeated for
                        each student
```

Figure A.24

```
COURSE.DAT (RMS file, location ... Primary Key ...
    Secondary Key(s) ...
Use: [all modules that use a field from this file]
FIELD  NAME     TYPE SIZE DESCRIPTION/COMMENTS
NO.
01  CRS_NO    A 7        Course no (Primary Key)
02  CRS_NAME  A 30       Course name (Secondary key 1)
 .
 .
 .

STUDENT.DAT

 .
 .
 .

Special Comments: Each course will be assigned a unique course number,
placed in the COURSE_NO field in the COURSES.DAT file record. If a
student registers on a specific course, the field COURSE_NO in the
record for that student in the STUDENTS.DAT file will contain this
course number. The system uses these fields to correlate the STUDENTS
and COURSES files.
[detail as above.]
MATERIALS.DAT
HISTORY.DAT
```

[and so on for every file.]

If you must define a new file (discouraged!) or table, show Organization (e.g. RMS), attributes, record length, keys, and what modules in the system use the file.

Include a record map that details each field name, length, restrictions, and so forth. Indicate if a field has a specific system purpose.

ACCEPTANCE TEST PLAN

1. TITLE PAGE

As usual

2. TABLE OF CONTENTS

As usual

3. INTRODUCTION

The following tests are designed to demonstrate to ABC that the computer system provided by XYZ functions fully as promised in the Functional Specifications. If all of these tests function successfully, ABC accepts the system.

4. TEST SETS

The tests are organized into the following sets:

> MENU tests
> INQUIRY tests
> UPDATE tests
> WAREHOUSE tests
> REPORTS tests

These sets will test the ABC system in the same order as described in the FS, Sections 6.1 through to 6.5.

The tests are organized into groups. These groups facilitate setup of the testing: a single setup should suffice for all the tests in the group.

Certain items are listed as tested by 'Inspection.' These are the file sizes, certain error messages, and all of the documentation. Tests indicated as 'Analysis' are calculations done to check formulas. This will be done by ABC together with XYZ with each appropriate test.

5. MENU TESTS

5.1 Main Menu

Purpose:	to demonstrate ABC System Main Menu
FS Reference:	Sec. 2.1, par. 3
Setup:	CPU with ABC software installed, 2 terminals on-line
Action:	Power up the computer
Result:	(Within 120 seconds) 2 terminals display MAIN MENU of format FS Sec. 6.1

Action:	UP/DOWN arrow keys move highlight of items 1 to 17 up and down...
	Going up beyond item 1 and down beyond item 7 produces error message...
	Pressing HELP key on item 1 produces HELP message ... Pressing HELP at other items produces messages as per FS Sec. 10.1...
Action:	...etc.moving mouse up and down...

Successful Completion Date:
Client Signature:
Comments:

5.2 Registrar Menu

Purpose:	to demonstarate ABC System Registrar Menu
FS Reference:	Sec. 3.1, par. 3
Setup:	10 test students on history file, 5 test courses on course file, each course with 3 test students registered on it.
Action:	on MAIN MENU select '1. REGISTRAR'
Result:	REGISTRAR MENU of format FS sec. 6.2 appears
Action:	UP/DOWN arrow keys move hilite of items 1 to 4 up and down.
	Going up beyond item 1 and down beyond item 4 produce error message...
	Pressing HELP key on item 1 produces HELP message ... Pressing HELP at other items produces messages as per FS Sec.10.5 ...
Action:	moving mouse up and down ... etc.

Successful Completion Date:
Client Signature:
Comments:

5.3 Similar explanation of each Menu Test.

6. INQUIRY TESTS

[Detail as required.]

7. UPDATE TESTS

7.1 Enroll/Cancel a Student

Purpose:	to demonstarate ABC System capability to register and cancel a student.
FS Reference:	Sec. 3.1, par. 3
Setup:	test course with title 'BASKETS' number B-123-5 is on the COURSE FILE
Action:	on REGISTRAR MENU select '3. ENROLL/ CANCEL A STUDENT'
Result:	FORM of format FS Sec. 6.6 appears....etc.

Successful Completion Date:
Client Signature:
Comments:

8. OPERATION TESTS

8.1 System Backup and Restore

[Detail as required.]

9. MANAGEMENT TESTS

9.1 Set-up of Files and Accounts

10. CLIENT ACCEPTANCE

ABC and XYZ agree that the tests that were run in the ATP detailed here were successfully completed and verified by both parties:

ABC SIGNATURE:	DATE:
XYZ SIGNATURE:	DATE:
WITNESS SIGNATURE:	DATE:

References

SECTION 1   BOOKS AND ARTICLES

1. GOLUB, H., 1967. *Laws and Lore of Computerdom According to Golub*. McKinsey & Company: London.

2. GILDERSLEEVE, T. R. 1974. *Data Processing Project Management*. New York: Van Nostrand Reinhold.

3. BROOKS, F.T. 1975. *The Mythical Man-month: Essays on Software Engineering*. Reading, Mass.: Addison-Wesley.

4. PETERS, T., & WATERMAN, R. 1982. *In Search of Excellence*. New York: Harper & Row.

5. METZGER, P. 1973. *Managing a Programming Project*. Englewood Cliffs, N.J.: Prentice Hall.

6. WARNIER, J.D. 1981. *Logical Construction of Programs*. New York: Van Nostrand Reinhold.

7. ORR, K.T. 1977. *Structured System Development*. New York: Yourdon Press.

8. Booch, G. 1986. Object Oriented Design. *IEEE Trans. on Software Engineering* SE-12, (February) No. 2.

9. NASSI, I., & SHNEIDERMAN, B. 1973. Flowchart Techniques for Structured Programming. *ACM SIGPLAN Notices* 8, 8, (August) 12-26.

10. YAU, S., & TSAI, J. 1986. A Survey of Software Design Techniques. *IEEE Trans. on Software Engineering* SE-12,, June, No. 2 .

11. YOURDON, E., & CONSTANTINE, L.L. 1979. *Structured Design*. Englewood Cliffs, N.J.: Prentice Hall .

12. BERGLAND, G.D. 1981. A Guided Tour of Program Design Methodologies. *Computer*, October.

13. JENSEN, R.W. 1981. Structured Programming. *Computer*, March.

14. WEINBERG, G.M. 1971. *The Psychology of Computer Programming*. New York: Van Nostrand Reinhold.

15. BOEHM, B.W. 1981. *Software Engineering Economics*. Englewood Cliffs, N.J.: Prentice Hall.

16. ROETZHEIM, W. 1986. *Proposal Writing for Data Processing Professionals*. Englewood Cliffs, N.J.: Prentice Hall.

17. INTERNATIONAL BUSINESS MACHINES. 1967. *Management Planning Guide for a Manual of Data Processing Standards*, White Plains, NY

18. GENERAL ELECTRIC Co. 1986. *Software Engineering Handbook*. McGraw-Hill.

19. GOLSTEIN, R. C. 1985. *Database Technology and Management*, John Wiley & Sons.

20. STEVENS, W. P., Myers, G.J., & Constantine, L.L. 1974. Structured Design. *IBM Systems Journal*, 13:2, 115-139.

21. BLANCHARD, K.H., & JOHNSON, S. 1982. *The One Minute Manager*. New York: Morrow.

22. KIDDER, T. 1981. *The Soul of a New Machine:* New York, Avon.

23. MARTIN, J. 1977. *Computer Data Base Organization*, 2nd ed. Englewood Cliffs, N.J.: Prentice Hall.

SECTION 2   COMPANY NAMES AND ADDRESSES

2.1. DIGITAL EQUIPMENT CORP. Maynard, Mass. (or any office) VMS Product Codes: CMS, QX007. MMS, QX500. SCA, QXZB2. PCA, QX119. DTM, QX927 DECSPM, QLA82A9. LSE, QX057. DECDESIGN, QAYFDAAHS

2.2. EXCELERATOR, INDEX TECHNOLOGY CORP. One Main St., Cambridge, Ma.

2.3. FOCUS, INFORMATION BUILDERS INC., 1250 Broadway, New York.

2.4. POWERHOUSE, COGNOS INC., 3755 Riverside Dr., Ottawa, Canada, or 2 Corporate Place, Peabody, Ma.

2.5. Gordon Group, 1425 Koll Circle, Suite 102, San Jose, CA. 95112

2.6. Oraqcle Corp., 20 Davis Dr., Belmont CA 94002.

SECTION 3   EVALUATIONS OF SOFTWARE PACKAGES

3.1. Soft Decisions, Mill Valley, Ca.

3.2. John J. Rakos & Assoc. Consultants Ltd., Ottawa, Ontario, Canada.

3.3. Francis M. Webster, *Survey of Project Management Software Packages*. Project Management Institute, Drexel Hill, PA. (published yearly)

Index